T0290722

DOPERS IN UNIFORM

Also by John Hoberman

Age of Globalization (2014)
*Black and Blue: The Origins and Consequences
    of Medical Racism* (2012)
*Testosterone Dreams: Rejuvenation, Aphrodisia,
    Doping* (2005)
Doping and Public Policy, coeditor (2004)
*Darwin's Athletes: How Sport Has Damaged Black
    America and Preserved the Myth of Race* (1997)
*Mortal Engines: The Science of Performance and
    Dehumanization of Sport* (1992)
*The Olympic Crisis: Sport, Politics, and the Moral
    Order* (1986)
Sport and Political Ideology (1984)

TERRY AND JAN TODD SERIES ON
PHYSICAL CULTURE AND SPORTS

Also in the Todd Series

*Mr. America: The Tragic History of a Bodybuilding
    Icon* by John D. Fair (2015)
*Drug Games: The International Olympic Committee
    and the Politics of Doping, 1960–2008* by Thomas
    Hunt (2011)

DOPERS IN UNIFORM

THE HIDDEN WORLD OF POLICE ON STEROIDS

—

JOHN HOBERMAN

UNIVERSITY OF TEXAS PRESS, AUSTIN

Requests for permission to reproduce material
from this work should be sent to:
    Permissions
    University of Texas Press
    P.O. Box 7819
    Austin, TX 78713-7819
    utpress.utexas.edu/rp-form

The paper used in this book meets the minimum
requirements of ANSI/NISO Z39.48-1992 (R1997)
(Permanence of Paper). ∞

Library of Congress Cataloging Data
Names: Hoberman, John M. (John Milton), 1944- author.
Title: Dopers in uniform : the hidden world of police on
    steroids / John Hoberman.
Description: First edition. | Austin : University of Texas
    Press, 2017. | Includes bibliographical references and
    index.
Identifiers: LCCN 2016058736
    ISBN 978-0-292-75948-0 (cloth : alk. paper)
    ISBN 978-1-4773-1397-8 (library e-book)
    ISBN 978-1-4773-1398-5 (non-library e-book)
Subjects: LCSH: Police—Drug use—United States. |
    Police—Drug testing—United States. | Steroid abuse.
Classification: LCC HV7936.D78 H63 2017 | DDC
    362.29/9—dc23
LC record available at https://lccn.loc.gov/2016058736

doi:10.7560/759480

We cannot have a grown-up conversation about race in America until we acknowledge the violent conditions engendered by government policy and police practice.

—REVEREND DR. WILLIAM BARBER II,
president of the North Carolina NAACP

The physical dangers of police work are grossly overrated but the emotional dangers make it the most hazardous job on earth.

—JOSEPH WAMBAUGH,
The Choirboys

CONTENTS

PREFACE

Dopers in Uniform is the first comprehensive account of the police steroid culture in the United States. Most people are surprised to learn that many police officers use anabolic steroids, given the notoriety of these drugs and their widespread illegal use. But we should not be surprised. Most police officers come from a young male population in which anabolic steroid use has been expanding for decades. Many police officers lift weights to build muscle, and steroids can promote dramatic muscle growth. Some police departments have sponsored bodybuilding contests. What is more, some cops believe that conspicuous muscularity gives them a tactical advantage in confrontations with physically powerful criminals, especially ones who have built rippling torsos by lifting weights in prison. One big-city police chief told me that he wants to put "smart" officers on the street, and that muscle mass counts for very little. Suffice it to say that many cops do not share this view.

    Dopers in Uniform cannot be a definitive account of cops on steroids for two reasons. First, an illicit drug culture is an underground culture whose members do not welcome inquiries or respond to questionnaires. "Very little is known about the prevalence of drug use among police officers," one expert wrote in 2015.[1] Furthermore, the code of silence that imposes an iron discipline within police ranks precludes one cop's exposing the steroid use of another cop. In ten years of research, I have not come across a single case of a police officer turning in a fellow officer for using steroids. Second, most police executives want to know as little as possible about steroid use in their ranks. Police departments refuse to do credible drug testing—and would not release the test results even if they did. They never produce data that might allow us to estimate how many police officers use steroids. Given the choice between publishing with incomplete data and not publishing at all, I believe the public's right to know comes first.

Only a handful of police executives have made a point of condemning steroid use. Most either seem unconcerned about the risks of side effects or do not want to antagonize police unions. Charles Ramsey, one of the most prominent police executives in the country and the former police commissioner of Philadelphia, said in 2012 that steroids were a problem because they exacerbate the problem of domestic violence committed by police officers, whose family violence rate is reported to be four times higher than that of the general population. That ostensibly compelling argument has found no public support from his high-ranking colleagues.

Exposing the police steroid culture to public scrutiny is important because these drugs can produce emotional instability in armed men who are in a position to act out their drug-fueled anger, irritation, and aggressive urges on civilians. Anabolic steroids appeal most to men who join police forces in order to achieve dominance over others. Toleration of this type of drug use by cops encourages a "steroidal" policing style that results in the kinds of behaviors and hulking physiques that alienate many citizens. The more important reason to expose how police departments deal with steroid use is that their de facto policy is to overlook many police officers' violations of the law. Police chiefs are effectively immunizing illicit police steroid use from indictment and prosecution. Police officers commit a felony under the Anabolic Steroids Control Act by possessing anabolic steroids without a valid prescription; granting these officers immunity from this felony charge has become a convention.

Covering up the police steroid culture is another characteristic of an institutional leadership that feels entitled to operate beyond the law. Police chiefs' tolerance of steroid use signals a willingness to turn a blind eye to other forms of professional misconduct.

This steroid policy needs to be understood by the public because it is not the only way, and not the most destructive way, that major urban police departments routinely operate outside the law. Policemen who are domestic abusers are often shielded by highly selective investigation and prosecution practices that are never formally acknowledged but nonetheless widely understood.[2] But the most damaging extralegal convention is police officers' near-total immunity to discipline or prosecution in the many thousands of excessive-violence cases that have occurred in major urban jurisdictions.

The current bargain between the police and civil society says that none of this matters enough to change the status quo. A Chicago police commander tortured black suspects for twenty years on city property, yet this atrocity has played no detectable role in the current debate about police brutality at the expense of blacks. So the prime victims of the deal we have made with the police are African Americans. That is the most important reason to expose the police steroid culture—as further evidence that the police command structure can simply refuse to enforce the law against their lawbreaking colleagues.

DOPERS IN UNIFORM

INTRODUCTION

Thirty years ago, the *Miami Herald* published a dramatic report titled "Steroid-Using Police Causing Brutality Fears." This story described the criminal exploits of a gang of rogue policemen involved in the *Miami Vice*–style world of drug trafficking in southern Florida. This investigation may have been the first time that anabolic steroids were publicly linked with violent criminal behavior by police officers. The sensational revelations about the "Miami River Cops" prompted a former Miami police chief named Ken Harms to make the following comment: "It's probably time that the department makes a conscious decision about whether it's acceptable for officers to take steroids."[1]

This book demonstrates that no such "conscious decision" has ever been made. While police departments across the country have often declared that steroid use is unacceptable, the political will to eliminate steroid use from the profession is lacking. The police establishment has reacted to the steroid culture by equivocating: announcing zero-tolerance policies while doing the absolute minimum to detect and control steroid use. What is more, this policy conforms to police departments' inconsistent or even delinquent record on disciplining and prosecuting serious employee misconduct, including drunk driving, domestic violence, and the violent mistreatment of suspects.

This policy of disengagement raises questions about the goals and limits of command authority. What does tolerating steroid use portend for commanders' ability to maintain discipline within the force? Allowing steroid use signals a lack of command resolve to enforce regulations. This in turn can result in a loss of credibility at the top. The combination of command uninterest and police unions' resistance to steroid testing has made it impossible to control the use of steroids by rank-and-file officers. Middle-aged police executives' use of medically prescribed testosterone for "antiaging" purposes may be another obstacle to implementing effective testing.

This accommodating policy is in part a concession to the tidal wave of synthetic testosterone that has flowed into the adult male population over the past two decades. At the same time, bodybuilding has become a common preoccupation among young males, including many police officers. An instructive example of police involvement in this subculture comes from Newtown, Connecticut, where in August 2016 a former police sergeant named Steven Santucci was sentenced to sixteen months in prison for manufacturing and distributing anabolic steroids. His criminal activities as an importer, manufacturer, and drug dealer grew out of his devotion to extreme muscularity. A court document explained that "he has always been a fitness guy and he wanted to be a weight lifter." This decorated police officer—who eventually spent more than $300,000 on first-class trips around the world, including a safari—became involved in the steroid trade "in part because of the level of acceptance of steroid use in the body-building community." He was sentenced to a relatively short prison term due to "his exemplary life and a career characterized by a high degree of public service."[2] The jarring contrast between "exemplary" public service and steroid-related criminal behavior is one that appears more than once in this book.

The research reported in this book suggests that a significant minority of police officers—perhaps amounting to tens of thousands of law enforcement personnel—use anabolic steroids. The size of that minority varies with the environment being patrolled. Anecdotal evidence suggests that police officers who patrol in hazardous urban areas consume more steroids than those who serve in rural or small-town departments. Higher levels of consumption appear to correlate with the risks of the job, since some officers argue that bulking up promotes their safety on the streets. The potential costs and benefits of steroid use by cops have never been studied systematically or quantitatively. *Dopers in Uniform* was written to describe this steroid underworld as thoroughly as it can be described in the absence of officially generated data, which police agencies have no intention of collecting—or of providing to the public if they did collect it.

STRESS AND COPING IN POLICE CULTURE

The stressors that affect the lives of police officers are among the least-reported aspects of policing. As we will see, the threat of gunfire is vastly overpublicized, while the routine emotional stress of policing is rarely presented to the public realistically. Few outsiders are likely to understand how hard it is to manage the emotional consequences of the social isolation, the on-the-job frustrations, and the anxieties that come with being in regular contact with a public that may express as much resentment as appreciation for what cops do.

Unsurprisingly, police officers use a variety of coping drugs, because policing in the United States is an unusually stressful and often dangerous occupation. A 2012 symposium involving police chiefs and other senior personnel confirmed that alcohol abuse is by far the most serious drug problem in policing.[3] "For as long as there have been police officers, alcohol has been a problem in policing," Milwaukee's police chief said in 2012. "We have a lot of officers who are arrested for DWI, and a lot of officers involved in other alcohol-related problems off-duty."[4] Police suicides are often connected with alcohol abuse. Estimates have put the rate of alcohol abuse at a quarter of all officers, or about twice the rate of the general population. Forty percent of police officers' families experience domestic violence—a rate far higher than that found in the general population—and this is due in part to the abuse of alcohol.[5] Police officers' injuries can lead to the abuse of prescription painkillers such as Oxycontin. *Police* magazine reported in 2013 that "20% to 25% of working police officers are chemically dependent on either alcohol or drugs."[6] Within this potentially dangerous medical context, steroid abuse is ignored in a way that alcohol abuse is not, and there is little public awareness of the drug problems that affect police culture.

The ethos of toughness within police culture limits the interest of officers with drug problems in the therapeutic options available to them. At the 2012 symposium, the San Diego police chief, Bill Lansdowne, acknowledged this problem. His department had created a Wellness Unit to treat officers who had committed offenses such as drunk driving, domestic violence, and sexual assault. "We found," he said, "that officers know when they're in trouble, and they want help—whether for prescription drug abuse, alcohol abuse, steroid use, or domestic violence."[7] The problem is that most police officers are not inclined to seek out therapeutic solutions to these problems.

My ten years of research on cops and steroids supports this perspective. I have never come across even one report of an officer seeking help or treatment for steroid abuse. The same resistance to therapy was noted by a professional counselor who worked with police officers: "Paradoxically, despite the significantly high risk for alcoholism and other related problems, law enforcement remains one of the most difficult groups to reach with intervention and prevention services, due largely to the insular, clannish nature of police culture." At the same time, "police officers face heavy pressure to drink, to where non-drinking officers are often viewed as suspicious or anti-social by their colleagues."[8] Unlike beer and liquor, anabolic steroids are not coping drugs; their effects on mood are both different and less predictable. In addition, the police steroid culture is smaller and more secretive than the more conspicuous alcohol culture, which does so much tangible harm. At least in the first stages of use, steroid-injecting officers see their drugs not as a problem but as a solution. Most police steroid use is driven by an interest in muscularity for its own sake, and some officers see hypermuscularity as a way to intimidate potential adversaries on the streets. This "functional" argument for police steroid use is examined later in the book. What alcohol and steroids have in common is the police authorities' lack of interest in taking preventive action against either substance. Police managers who might dare to implement an antialcohol campaign would encounter fierce resistance from rank and filers and their unions. The same managers appear to have decided that an antisteroid initiative would meet a similar fate.

KEEPING POLICE STEROID USE OUT OF THE MEDIA

Given the well-known association of anabolic steroids with violent behavior, why do the unending reports of police killings of unarmed black men never mention the possible role of anabolic steroid abuse? Keeping the police steroid culture out of the public eye conforms to the media's unwritten but strictly enforced policy of preserving a positive image of the police. Journalists' unwillingness to associate police killings with documented evidence of the police steroid culture has meant that police steroid use has never become a part of the national conversation about policing.

It should be noted that today's major-media blackout regarding the police steroid culture coincides with the steady expansion of steroid use by the adolescent and adult US population that provides recruits for local police forces. The scant coverage of cops on steroids is, therefore, wholly illogical, since expanded use of the drugs has coincided with minimal exposure of those who use them. When policemen's use of steroids was in its early phase, local media coverage of the Miami River Cops in 1987 did not treat steroid use as hypothetical. One southern Florida police chief told his investigators to be on the lookout for police officers who looked like "small mountains," since his most bulked-up officers were drawing the greatest number of complaints from civilians.[9]

What might compel a police chief to attempt to purge his force of these drugs? It seems that even years of public speculation about the role of steroids in a police department's conspicuous descent into lawless violence are not enough. The troubling story of the Albuquerque Police Department (APD) shows how a police executive made his steroid problem go away after years of "investigations" that went nowhere.

The fatal shooting of James Boyd by Albuquerque police officers was an extreme event even by the standards that can apply when law enforcement personnel respond to the eccentric behaviors of mentally disturbed people in public places. Boyd had been diagnosed as paranoid schizophrenic and was known to have once physically assaulted a female officer. On March 16, 2014, police officers approached the homeless man on a boulder-strewn slope to charge him with illegally camping in the foothills of the Sandia Mountains. He was holding two knives and standing about twenty feet from the officers, a distance that precluded him from posing any physical threat to them. The video taken by a camera on an officer's helmet shows Boyd standing and shouting that he is "no murderer." At this point, he is attacked by a police dog, turns away from the officers, and is immediately hit in the back by six gunshots fired from two weapons. As Boyd lies prostrate on the ground facing away from the police, he is attacked once again by the police dog and hit by two beanbag shots, by which time he was already dying.[10]

In September 2016, the two officers who fired the fatal shots, Dominique Perez and Keith Sandy, were on trial on charges of second-degree murder.[11] The trial ended in a hung jury, and the judge scheduled a retrial, tentatively set for July 2017, for both defendants. At the trial, Randi McGinn, the special prosecutor, described defendant Sandy as "somebody who was out there with something to prove, whether it was to regain his reputation, whether it was to show how tough he was, whether it was something darker, I'll let you be the judge of what was happening there."[12] What she did not mention was the possibility that anabolic steroids might have played a role in the officers' conduct.

For reasons that will soon become clear, it is surprising that the role of anabolic steroids in the culture of the APD did not come up either before or during a trial that involved yet another controversial killing of a homeless man by APD officers.[13] In fact, less than a month after the killing of James Boyd, the US Department of Justice issued a report stating that the APD had "engaged in a widespread pattern of excessive and deadly force during encounters with civilians who posed little if any threat."[14] We may assume that the City of Albuquerque paid the parents of James Boyd $5 million because his death at the hands of the APD fit this pattern.

The omission of steroids from the public discussion of this police killing is striking, since concerns about steroid use by APD officers had been circulating for years, even before they went on a killing spree that attracted nationwide attention. Between 2010 and 2014, APD officers shot thirty-eight people, killing nineteen of them. Most of these people were mentally ill. The rate of fatal shootings by APD officers during this period was eight times that of their New York City counterparts.[15]

Years before these serial killings, the *Albuquerque Journal* reported in 2007 that the APD was "concerned that steroid use can trigger outbursts of rage and unpredictable behavior," and that it would soon start testing some of its officers for anabolic steroids. According to the APD, only new officers, before being hired, underwent this kind of testing. A new procedure approved by city leaders and police administrators authorized the testing of any employee who showed signs of using steroids. "Under this new procedure, we need some sort of reasonable suspicion in order to test," Police Chief Ray Schultz said. "Change of behavior, their physical appearance or reliable information they are users would be good enough for us to order the employee to take a test. It's important we do this because we are finding more and more that the use of anabolic steroids can result in rage or unpredictable behavior." But after declaring that steroid use by cops could be dangerous, the chief proceeded to demonstrate a curious lack of urgency about the whole matter. The department's random drug testing would not include steroids, he said, because doing so would require negotiating with the police union.[16] A week later, however, Ron Olivas of the Albuquerque Police Officers' Association said the police union had no objection to steroid testing if it were carried out for "some sort of just cause"—another way to describe the "reasonable suspicion" criterion that police chiefs frequently invoke but seldom act on.[17]

Five years later, in November 2012, the US Department of Justice announced an investigation of the APD after its officers were involved in a long series of police-initiated fatal shootings and cases of abuse that appeared to involve the use of excessive and deadly force. The investigation was to see whether the APD harbored a police "culture" that encouraged the use of unconstitutional excessive force. At a press conference, Chief Ray Schultz said that while detectives had been investigating possible steroid use by APD officers, he did not know how many were under scrutiny or who they were. Schultz raised doubts about the utility of steroid testing "because someone using steroids will only test positive during an 'active cycle,'" and because the APD would have to have "specific probable cause to do testing" in order to meet the requirements of the employment contract the department had signed with the police union.[18] Like most police chiefs, Schultz emphasized the obstacles to testing and expressed little or no interest in taking proactive steps that might identify steroid-using cops.

When the Department of Justice began its inquiry, which the FBI monitored, no APD officers had been tested for steroids, despite the chief's promise five years earlier. "We never got to the point to where we could do a probable cause drug test on officers," Schultz said in late 2012.[19] Federal prosecutors, one report said, were trying "to establish connections between potential use of anabolic steroids and violence."[20] Three years later, the Justice Department required the APD to add more than fifty types of steroids to its drug-testing panel.[21] How diligently, or even whether, this testing has been done is anyone's guess. In fact, it is more than likely that no testing at all has been done.

The federal investigation of the APD for steroid use among its officers was, as the *Albuquerque Journal* put it, "only the latest instance of an allegation that has persisted for years." Inquiries were carried out via litigation: "At least one local civil rights attorney has sought information about officers using steroids for 20-plus years through lawsuits, but to no avail." The civil rights attorney, Brad Hall, had been requesting information since the early 1990s about both steroid use by APD officers and testing for the drugs. "Over the years," he said in 2013, "the rumor of steroid use at APD would come up. So we would ask about it from time to time, when we felt we had a good-faith basis to do so. . . . We never got the question officially answered. Cases would settle, or the steroid issue would get swallowed up by the facts of the individual cases."[22] As of October 2016, this attorney's questions about APD steroid use remained unanswered.[23]

This book demonstrates that thousands—and probably tens of thousands—of police officers in the United States use anabolic steroids. (In doing so, the great majority commit a felony for which they are almost never indicted.) There are cops on steroids in every metropolitan police force in the United States. But measuring the effects of this steroid use is impossible because police departments don't want to know its extent. The chief of the APD, for example, asserted that he was unable to confirm whether any of his officers were on steroids. This reluctance of a police chief to find steroid use in his ranks is standard operating procedure in police departments across the country.

The James Boyd killing presented Chief Schultz with two signs of possible steroid use. The first is that one of the shooters, Keith Sandy, had been fired from the New Mexico State Police for his involvement in a time-fraud scandal. Steroid-using officers frequently demonstrate a willingness to break the law, apart from the steroid-possession offense. More importantly, Sandy was a member of the Repeat Offenders Project (ROP), an elite and controversial special-action unit that was disbanded shortly after the James Boyd killing, in conformity with the city's agreement with the Justice Department.[24] At one point the ROP logo was a hangman's noose.[25] Elite SWAT-style units attract especially ambitious and aggressive officers, who are more likely than others to pursue what they see as a steroid advantage.[26] What is more, the James Boyd killing was that rare case that resulted in second-degree murder charges being brought against two officers. A police executive who was really motivated to uncover steroid use in his force would look for a cluster of steroid users within the special-action units and look into officers' weightlifting habits and the gyms where cops meet steroid dealers (who include some cops) and buy drugs.

STEROID USE AND POPULAR IMAGES OF THE POLICE

The failure to convict the APD officers who killed James Boyd points once again to the visceral benefit of the doubt juries give to police officers, including those involved in controversial killings. Such confidence in the dependability and truthfulness of police officers was confirmed by "The Public Image of the Police," a 2001 study commissioned by the International Association of Chiefs of Police (IACP).[27] This long report found that most Americans have a generally positive view of the police. At the same time, public attitudes oscillate between approval and gratitude, on the one hand, and, on the other, periodic concern about abuses of power such as police brutality inflicted on suspects. The traditional view in white America puts the emphasis on the indispensable role of the police in protecting citizens; they are the "thin blue line" that preserves civil order and prevents chaos. Public tributes to the police emphasize qualities such as courage and selflessness while excluding unpleasant topics like episodes of online racism and homophobia (like the recent examples in New York and San Francisco) and the many cases of excessive police violence that have occurred over the years in cities across the country. The iconic image of the police is the result of a selective process that eulogizes alleged virtues while excluding misconduct, including serious misbehaviors brought to public attention by the media. Police officials and politicians regularly invoke the iconic image of the police to counteract the negative publicity that arises when police brutality cases create uneasiness about police officers' personalities and motivations.

Fictionalized accounts of police exploits have been a staple of the entertainment industry for a century. Films and television programs are major sources of popular images of the police, and they contribute significantly to public feelings about police work in general. Television networks and film studios have produced hundreds of police dramas, including cinematic films, television series, and "reality TV" shows such as *Cops*, which has been on the air since 1989. Virtually all this programming endorses the legitimacy of police officers' powers and the necessity of preserving their authority to guarantee law and order.

Entertainment about police forces, as opposed to shows about private detectives, can be divided into two genres. A reality-TV show like *Cops* seems to convey a raw authenticity that fictional shows cannot. As of 2013, *Cops* had broadcast more than 900 episodes, set in 140 cities, to a weekly audience that eventually reached more than three million viewers, far larger than the viewership of cable-news channels. In these dramas, a hand-held camera is in constant and often frenetic motion, zooming in on and away from handcuffs, packets of white powder, and wrestling matches pitting police officers, male and female, against suspects of both sexes who appear to be the dregs of society. Big, brawny cops, calm and rubber-gloved against the threat of infection presented by their unkempt adversaries, demonstrate a self-control that is all the more impressive in the face of the often profane and deeply disordered people they deal with. At the same time, *Cops* is a racial spectacle. One African American critic objected in 2012 that *Cops* had "turned the criminalization of black folks and other communities of color into entertainment for millions."[28] While some of these policemen are big enough to look like stereotypical steroid users, *Cops* never raises the possibility that any of these men might be bulking up on synthetic male hormones. "Reality television," a journalist pointed out in 2016, "offered beleaguered police departments a way to reassert their dominance. . . . Police departments could simply show camera operators only what they wanted audiences to witness."[29]

A conventional television police show such as *Blue Bloods*, which has broadcast more than a hundred episodes since 2010, is a far more polished production. Its continuing story lines enable the audience to build relationships with an ensemble cast of appealing characters. *Blue Bloods* is a paean to the long Irish Catholic tradition within the New York Police Department (NYPD). Henry Reagan is a crusty former police commissioner (PC) who reminisces nostalgically about the rough policing methods of his era. His son, the paterfamilias, Frank, who has taken over the PC role from his father, is endowed with an iconic toughness and quiet nobility. Frank's elder son, Danny, is a hot-tempered detective whose traumatic experience in the Iraq War may account for his physical abuse of the suspects he interrogates (without incurring legal consequences). The younger son, Jamie, has a degree from Harvard Law School but has chosen to be a cop. Frank's daughter, Erin, is a beautiful, honest, and tenacious district attorney who periodically attempts to check Danny's impulses to bend the law. The Reagan household, where regular family dinners begin with the saying of grace, is a wholesome, harmonious, and intact world unto itself, inhabited by three generations of "New York's finest," who symbolize the NYPD itself, its traditions, its devotion to service, its noble essence.

Beyond the walls of the stately Reagan manse, situated in a leafy suburb, this law enforcement family lives out the standard cop-show "action" themes: SWAT team raids, breathless chase scenes, wild shooting in the streets. Lost in all the mayhem are the daily realities of police work: the boredom of unending paperwork, directing traffic, standing guard at construction sites, and uneventful street patrols. Also lost is the fact that in 2014, the 35,000 officers of the NYPD discharged their weapons in the line of duty a total of seventy-nine times. That is, only 1 out of 450 officers fired his or her gun in the course of a year. Only 1 in 900 officers fired an intentional shot in a conflict with a suspect. Eighteen of the seventy-nine shots were fired to kill animals.[30] These numbers make it clear that melodramatic rhetoric about the endangered police officer, whether it comes from entertainment or police officials, exaggerates the threat that gunfire poses to police officers and serves to legitimize police violence.

Steroids are mentioned in an episode ("Growing Boys") of *Blue Bloods* that was broadcast in November 2013. Danny gets a call from a former girlfriend who asks him to help her cope with a violent boyfriend she suspects of steroid use, so the police investigate the gym where he trains. The fact that actual steroid-using NYPD personnel train at gyms is a disturbing reality that the writers of *Blue Bloods* are unwilling to confront. A precedent for such daring is the 1994 film *Cries Unheard: The Donna Yaklich Story*, in which a woman finds herself in a marriage with an unstable police officer named Dennis. He is one of the many male obsessives who combine weightlifting and steroid use. Dennis goes into violent rages during which he rapes Donna and beats her with a belt.[31] Here, too, the *Blue Bloods* writers missed an opportunity to portray the concealed dysfunction of police life, since cops engage in much more domestic violence than the general male population.

American audiences have long been conditioned to accept police culture on its own terms, which have included a great deal of secrecy about police operations and types of misconduct that include the use of illicit drugs. The crucial difference between managing the image of the police before and after the Second World War has been television. *Dragnet*, which went on the air in 1951, was the first of hundreds of police shows to follow. Since then, police departments have wielded tremendous power over how televised police dramas depict them on the job. With some exceptions, the dysfunctional private lives of cops have been often exempted from coverage; portraying them would violate the censored version that police officials want to preserve.[32] One notes that the 2001 IACP report, which argues that "the entertainment media present an extremely distorted view of the nature of police work," confines its criticism to the melodramatizing of policing and does not address officers' personal problems. The entertainment media, the authors say, errs by overemphasizing "crime fighting, police violence, and individualism (as exemplified by Dirty Harry)." The authors do not, however, object to withholding from the public what is known about the dysfunctional aspects of police officers' lives that can affect their public duties.

STEROIDS FOR "ACTION-ORIENTED" POLICEMEN

A fundamental argument of this book is that police officers in the United States belong to a global fraternity of "action-oriented" males who are attracted to anabolic steroids for their muscle-building and mood-enhancing effects. Police personnel occupy a uniquely conflicted position within this fraternity: they are the only members of the tribe who are ordered to arrest the producers and dealers of muscle-building drugs they may be using themselves. More importantly, police officers interact with other members of the action-oriented fraternity in other venues. Police culture's affinity with weightlifting can include departmental sponsorship of weightlifting and arm-wrestling contests, and even bodybuilding competitions, such as the 2015 World Police and Fire Bodybuilding and Figure event. Officers who train at gyms outside the department will encounter (and might buy drugs from) devotees of the muscle-building cult. The world of mercenaries, now known as "private security contractors," recruits former police and military personnel and includes a paramilitary steroid culture (described later in this book). Police officers who moonlight as bouncers at nightclubs often work in chaotic venues staffed by steroid users. A growing number of police officers have joined police motorcycle clubs that allow cops to experience a legal version of the freewheeling outlaw lifestyle. This emulation of the biker gang ethos can produce a split identity—"biker by night and cop by day"—making it difficult to determine where the lawman ends and the outlaw begins. Entertainment such as action films and mixed martial arts (MMA) cage-fighting matches popularizes the steroid-boosted male torso as an iconic version of masculine identity. Police officers participate in the steroid culture in all these social venues. And all these scenarios create tension between professional self-discipline and an appetite for "action" that subverts policing standards.

CHAPTER ONE

WHAT WE KNOW ABOUT COPS ON STEROIDS

Major urban police departments in the United States are out of control in two ways. The more notorious form of lawlessness is the use of unjustified deadly violence against suspects or bystanders, which is tolerated by police commanders and almost never results in disciplinary action. The second, virtually unpublicized form of lawlessness is felony anabolic steroid use, which is tolerated by police commanders and almost never prosecuted. Cops on steroids, like the great majority of hyperviolent cops, are above the law. American law enforcement has accepted the police steroid culture as a fact of life that it will not oppose in any effective way.

Police officers who use excessive violence are almost never disciplined or prosecuted. The Chicago Police Department (CPD), for example, has abused thousands of citizens with virtual impunity over many years. Between 1972 and 1991, Jon Burge, a Chicago police commander, operated a torture chamber to extract confessions from black suspects. While his immediate superiors celebrated his effectiveness, Burge extracted confessions by applying electric shocks and suffocating his victims with plastic bags. Years later Burge was sent to prison, finally, for perjury.

In 2007, the chance of a Chicago police officer receiving "any meaningful discipline as a result of being charged with abusing a civilian" was 0.2 percent.[1] The heralded CPD reforms of that year accomplished nothing. By 2015, citizens had filed charges of abuse against thousands of Chicago police officers; in more than 99 percent of these cases, there was no discipline. The *New York Times* spoke of "the cloistered world of internal police discipline."[2] By December 2015, following the release of a video of a police officer firing sixteen bullets into the body of an unarmed seventeen-year-old black boy, the beleaguered mayor, Rahm Emanuel, announced "nothing less than complete and total reform of the [police] system and the culture that it breeds."[3] In January 2016, he vowed "to root out the cancer of police abuse."[4] This empty promise signaled the political desperation of a mayor who was acknowledging that his city's police department had long been out of control.

In other American cities, abusive officers enjoy the same degree of immunity to investigation and discipline. Broward County, Florida, which includes Miami, has produced its own series of police steroid scandals. From 1980 to 2015, not one officer was charged in any of the 168 fatal shootings during that period.[5] Between 2005 and 2015, Houston Police Department (HPD) officers shot 268 people, 111 of them fatally. None of these shootings resulted in either criminal prosecution or meaningful discipline by the department.[6] Over the period 2008–2012, the department's Internal Affairs Division ruled all but 1 of 636 shootings of all types, including accidental firearm discharges, to have been justified.[7] From 2007 to 2013, the division dismissed all but 4 of the 588 police brutality ("use of force") claims filed by civilians. During the same period, HPD officers filed 118 reports of unjustified violence against citizens perpetrated by fellow officers. Internal Affairs dismissed all but 11 of them.[8] Houston's Independent Police Oversight Board, despite its dignified title, has no power to regulate police conduct.[9]

The disciplinary void in American policing includes police authorities' refusal to investigate or prosecute police officers' illegal use of anabolic steroids. Police chiefs and commissioners have been unwilling to stop the increase in steroid use in their ranks. Police departments and police unions have made sure that effective steroid testing does not happen. It is all but impossible to identify *any* departments that are testing. In recent years, only a handful of police departments have announced they were testing for steroids. Yet even here the facts are elusive. When asked in 2015 how many police departments across the country were testing their officers for steroids, the director of legislative policy for the 325,000-member Fraternal Order of Police replied: "I have no idea."[10]

Police officers who are caught using anabolic steroids are almost never prosecuted for felony drug possession. They are allowed instead to resign or to keep their jobs. Rank-and-file cops are protected by informal arrangements within law enforcement and prosecutors' offices that minimize the significance of steroid use by police. The lack of interest shown by police chiefs and local district attorneys has triggered investigations by national agencies such as the Federal Bureau of Investigation (FBI) and the Food and Drug Administration (FDA) into steroid use by local cops. Nor do police departments employ effective "early warning" procedures. Police departments announce but do not implement the "reasonable suspicion" procedures that are supposed to detect steroid use by potential troublemakers. The result is a hidden police steroid culture that will inevitably contribute to "excessive violence" incidents and unjustified police killings of citizens.

In 2005, Larry K. Gaines, chairman of the Criminal Justice Department at California State University at San Bernardino, commented as follows regarding the lack of information about police officers' use of anabolic steroids: "Steroids should be a part of the drug policy and be included as a topic of discussion. It's too quiet right now. Things happen here and there around the country, but no one has been smart enough to connect the dots."[11]

Dopers in Uniform is an attempt to "connect the dots" in a way that makes sense of the widespread use of anabolic steroids by police officers in the United States. At the same time, the book tries to explain why steroid use by police is tolerated by police departments, and why steroid-using cops enjoy virtual immunity from legal prosecution. Possession of an anabolic steroid in the United States without a valid prescription is a felony. Yet after ten years of research, I have found only a single case of an officer being arrested for simple possession of the drug. This giant of a policeman had made himself locally prominent as a "drug free" powerlifting hero in a town in New Jersey—until his steroid use was exposed. His indictment for possession may well have been vindictive payback for having served as a false role model to his young admirers. The standard scenario, however, proceeds entirely differently. Hundreds of cops have been caught using and possessing anabolic steroids, but they are prosecuted on drug charges only if they have committed other steroid-related crimes, such as importing and dealing the drugs. The standard protocol allows steroid-using policemen to stay in their jobs or to resign without charges being filed. Professional courtesy shields them from prosecution on the kinds of drug charges that other citizens would face in these circumstances.

Police doping has never been a topic of national discussion. In a society where steroid-using athletes are periodically subjected to prolonged public vilification, steroid use by police officers has been treated as local news since the 1980s. The *New York Times*, our de facto newspaper of record, has covered the cops-on-steroids issue only episodically and only as local news. The *Times* provides extensive coverage of sports doping scandals, but neither its editors nor its editorialists have found cops' use of doping drugs to be worth anything more than perfunctory coverage. Similarly, a 2004 *Wall Street Journal* story headlined "Elite Users of Steroids Rarely Face Criminal Prosecution" identifies "elite users" exclusively as athletes; police evasion of criminal prosecution for use of the same drugs is never mentioned.[12] Only one investigative series on the use of steroids by police officers has appeared in an American publication, and it won a national journalism award.[13] Local news sources, including television stations, are an essential source of information about the police steroid culture. The great majority of such stories are reported in smaller urban newspapers.[14] Online chat rooms can also be useful, although the anonymity of commentators requires a researcher to take special caution in evaluating what is found there. One source of information about cops and steroids in Britain is bodybuilding message boards, where bodybuilders who are thinking about joining a police force send out inquiries about whether they will be drug-tested.[15] Some policemen are bodybuilders, and the gyms where law enforcement personnel do their weightlifting are prime venues for mixing and mingling with drug dealers and other criminals.

Whereas most people are taught to respect police officers, others take a cynical view and see their steroid use as more evidence of their capacity for lawlessness and degenerate behavior. Police officers with bull necks, bulging muscles, bald crania, and bad attitudes have become a part of our civic life as well as a staple of the flourishing steroid folklore. "Steroid rage," often known as "roid rage," serves as a popular myth about the drug-induced violent behavior of aggressive males, whose ranks include policemen.

One consequence of the secrecy surrounding police steroid use is that is impossible to know, and difficult to estimate, how many police officers in the United States use steroids. Whenever possible, departments treat steroid use in-house and out of view of the public and the press. In the absence of survey data, the researcher must depend on as much anecdotal evidence as can be collected, as well as on the testimony of police officers who have used the drugs and are willing to talk about it. In 2007, for example, a Phoenix police officer named Albert Smith, having been suspended for his use of illegal steroids, offered an estimate of how many first responders were using these drugs: "There's tons of guys out there, tons of guys, on the fire department, on the police department, that are using," he said. "My honest opinion? I don't believe they should be illegal. I think it's a personal decision. I'm not hurting anybody."[16] Despite the fact that possession of anabolic steroids without a valid prescription is a felony, Smith was allowed to remain a police officer.

Many people are surprised to learn that police officers use anabolic steroids. Having absorbed the moral lessons of the "war on drugs," most citizens do not expect law enforcement personnel to break drug laws that they have sworn to uphold. This public unawareness of the steroid epidemic in law enforcement is not surprising, for two reasons. First, knowledge of steroid use within police agencies has been limited by the news media's curiously selective interest in steroid abuse. The coverage of high-profile athletes who use doping drugs has been thorough unto obsessive, while the covert and illegal use of the same drugs by armed police officers remains uncontroversial, apart from the transient scandals that flared up and then quickly faded away in Boston, New York, Phoenix, Albuquerque, Dallas, and some other major cities. This book explains why the problem of cops on steroids has never become a nationally prominent issue.

Second, what we can know about steroid use among law enforcement personnel is limited by the secrecy that surrounds many police procedures and behaviors. It was reported in 2015, for example, that the Chicago Police Department has not disciplined *even one* of the thousands of Chicago police officers against whom citizens have filed complaints. As mentioned, a Chicago police captain operated a torture chamber where he abused black men for twenty years (1972–1991) without interference from his superiors. The curtain of secrecy thus conceals both police brutality and the police steroid culture. This police culture of secrecy is the product of an informal collaboration between rank-and-file officers and the police commanders who direct them.

The code of silence among police officers—the legendary "blue wall of silence"—has made it difficult to investigate, let alone eliminate, either police brutality or steroid use by cops. In the case of drug abuse, steroid-using police officers and the law enforcement agencies that employ them have worked out a tacit and effective arrangement that minimizes public awareness of the problem. Many police commanders do not know—and do not want to know—about their officers' illicit drug use. At the same time, police administrators do little to resist, much less reverse, the trend of expanding steroid use. Police officers have, in fact, proved to be almost immune to prosecution for the illegal possession and use of anabolic steroids. This immunity is consistent with the fact that police officers are rarely indicted for committing *any* kind of crime, including, prominently, cases of police brutality. Prosecutors' unwillingness to indict police officers is almost total. In this sense, the legal immunity of steroid-abusing police officers is just a symptom of a police culture that has shown itself to be almost impervious to reform—and of an institutional intransigence that is inherent in the system.

Public unawareness of the police steroid culture is one aspect of a broader unfamiliarity with police officers' lives. Few people outside the ranks have a real sense of how police officers think and feel as they deal with constant exposure to stressful situations, both dramatic and mundane, and how they treat opportunities to exploit their power to question, arrest, subdue, and kill. Officers' real lives are unfamiliar to us because we take their services for granted and see them only in their functional roles. News media accounts and the endless series of police shows on television distort the reality of police work by featuring constant gunplay and SWAT raids, thereby reducing real people to one-dimensional action heroes or the occasional rogue cop. Missing from these melodramas are the police unions and their power, officers' drinking and drug habits, their problematic part-time employment, their racial attitudes, and the blue wall of silence, which mandates that cops give false testimony both inside and outside the courtroom when police credibility is on the line. The emotional stress of police work drives rates of alcoholism, divorce, and domestic violence that are well above national norms.

Nor are many people aware of some of the activities that police officers engage in when they are not on duty. Some work as bouncers in nightclubs. Some are bodybuilders who compete at the annual World Police and Fire Games. Many officers belong to police motorcycle clubs that operate all over the United States. Very large numbers of officers are engaged in weightlifting at gyms that serve the general public. All these activities are likely to bring law enforcement personnel into contact with users and dealers of anabolic steroids. This book offers detailed accounts of the sorts of extracurricular activities that bring police officers in contact with the underground steroid culture, which has expanded its influence throughout modern societies.

Dramatic evidence demonstrating the dimensions of the police steroid culture has been accumulating over the past decade. In 2005, I noticed a sudden increase in published reports that law enforcement personnel had been caught using anabolic steroids, and the number of these reports has continued to go up. Growing use of these drugs by police has coincided with a surge in legal testosterone use, which is promoted on television by the "antiaging" industry and pharmaceutical manufacturers. It should come as no surprise that police officers are among the customers who drive this market, often with the help of unethical doctors who write prescriptions for anyone who pays them.

A massive scheme involving one of these unscrupulous doctors, along with many of his police and firefighter "clients," was uncovered in New Jersey in 2010. Dr. Joseph Colao, an antiaging doctor and bodybuilder who dropped dead of a heart attack at age forty-five, prescribed illegal anabolic steroids and human growth hormone (HGH) for thousands of clients. His patients included 248 law enforcement officers and firefighters from fifty-three agencies in New Jersey, all of whom acquired their hormones at taxpayer expense. Even after their names were published in the *Newark Star-Ledger*, and New Jersey's top public officials expressed outrage at this misconduct, only a fraction of these men were disciplined.

The failure of police executive leadership during the brief uproar that accompanied the New Jersey scandal amounted to a coordinated cover-up. Indeed, as demonstrated later in this book, every public authority figure in the state of New Jersey chose not to confront the implications of massive steroid use among first responders, and chose not to impose penalties on men who had broken the law and defrauded the state. Such reluctance to face down the police steroid culture is the norm among US police officials. One of the few exceptions is the former police commissioner of Philadelphia, Charles Ramsey. In 2012, while still in office, he stated: "Not only are steroids illegal, but they also have some serious negative side effects. Some of the worst domestic violence by officers that we have seen involved 'roid rage.' The whole personality changes, and they are more aggressive when interacting with citizens."[17] A year later a steroids-and-domestic-abuse scenario that came up during a courtroom proceeding demonstrated the breakdown of discipline within the Pittsburgh Police Department. The public learned that a detective who had hit his wife and choked his son in 2007 had been ordered to undergo steroid testing and serve a suspension of one day. Physical assaults on other people finally led to his firing in 2010.[18] The police chief's initial unwillingness to fire him, despite the assault on his family, points to how difficult it is to dismiss police officers in almost any circumstance. An imbalance of power often undercuts the authority of police managers, who face fierce opposition from police unions and from arbitrators who sympathize with the accused officers. So it is not surprising that few police administrators are willing to expend their limited supply of political capital on vocal opposition to the police steroid culture.

To get a sense of how anabolic steroid use has infiltrated many police departments across the United States, consider a news report that came out of Phoenix in July 2015. In 2006, the Phoenix Police Department had initiated the country's first random drug-testing program for anabolic steroid use by police officers. Revelations about steroid use by cops in other cities had not prompted police administrators to embark on testing regimens. The difference in Phoenix was the police commander, Kim Humphrey, one of only a handful of leaders in law enforcement who has made a point of warning the public that anabolic steroid abuse presents a clear and present danger to American policing.

This form of surveillance seemed prescient, since only a year later twelve Phoenix officers and twelve firefighters were implicated in a US Drug Enforcement Administration (DEA) investigation into doctors who provided fraudulent prescriptions for steroids to clients masquerading as patients. As this book shows, many police officers have engaged in this type of medical fraud with pliant or unethical doctors who, for a fee, will write prescriptions for testosterone or other anabolic steroids.

Those familiar with the story of Phoenix's pioneering 2006 initiative may have been surprised to learn that in 2014 this steroid-testing program was quietly dismantled. Department administrators and an official of the Phoenix police union explained that the sheer expense of the steroid screening, up to $200 per test, had made the program unaffordable. It is hardly surprising that the union portrayed this as an intolerable cost; police unions have routinely fought steroid testing as a violation of officers' right to privacy. But there was another problem with steroid testing, one to which the union may not have wanted to call attention. So many tests were turning up steroid traces left by legal supplements and doctor-prescribed testosterone that it had become all but impossible to distinguish between legal and illicit androgenic drug use among Phoenix police officers. The rising tide of testosterone drugs ingested by cops had created a reason, or a pretext, for simply giving up on trying to prevent the spread of anabolic steroid use among the rank and file. "We're in a different time," the union man said. "Testosterone therapy is extremely prevalent." This point was reiterated by Dr. Harrison G. Pope, director of the Biological Psychiatry Laboratory at the Harvard-affiliated McLean Hospital. "There's no real way to stem the tide, so to speak, as far as access to steroids" is concerned, he said, "and there's no prospect in the near future that use of them is going to decline. We are going to continue to see its use with law-enforcement officers."[19]

A 2013 investigation into steroid use among police officers and firefighters in the state of Georgia indicated that the practice had spread to other departments across the country, and that its prevalence was widely underestimated. Here we meet a few of the characters who will become familiar throughout this book: the first responder who did not see this type of drug use as a problem but rather as a way to boost "sexual performance." A firefighter who said he decided "to take some steroids to get in better shape." A third who told investigators he didn't know that having a prescription meant he had to buy the drug from a pharmacy. One police officer stated, "Given our profession, some guys . . . use those types of substances that maintain a level of fitness or . . . ability to do your job."[20]

These first responders alleged that the use of anabolic drugs in the ranks is common. The firefighter who sold the steroids said, "There's more people than you would think that are taking it." "I think it's all over the nation actually [in] public service," one of the firefighters who bought them said. When asked, "How widespread with the fire department and the police department do you think this is?" another answered, "If you . . . went through everyone's personnel files and found out who is on testosterone, I would guess that 90 percent of them are abusing." Every officer involved in this steroid scandal "made it clear," two investigators said, "that illegal steroid use is rampant in Public Safety throughout Georgia." The extent of this steroid use had critical implications: "If any of these individuals is taken to trial for their crimes, it will draw in and expose corruption throughout public safety in the State of Georgia to the point that it would be decimated and therefore crippled. For this reason, and to maintain the image of local public safety, the authors believe that there is no incentive to bring any of these individuals to justice."[21]

The first and still the only national publicity devoted to police steroid use was a segment of the CBS-TV program *60 Minutes* broadcast on November 5, 1989. "Beefing Up the Force" presented interviews with three officers whose use of steroids had apparently caused the hyperaggressiveness that had gotten them into serious trouble. The worst case involved what one psychiatrist called "a real Jekyll and Hyde change" in the personality of a prison security guard in Oregon who kidnapped and shot a woman who had made a casual remark he didn't like. He got twenty years in prison, and she was paralyzed for life. The personality he presented during his prison interview made it seem utterly improbable that he would have been capable of such an act. But his testosterone level when he committed the crime was fifty times the normal level. This story conveyed the message that steroid problems were lurking in many police departments and prison systems across the country, and that supervisors were turning a blind eye to a significant threat to public safety.

The *60 Minutes* segment paid special attention to a "hard-core group" of steroid users on the Miami police force. As mentioned in the introduction, the *Miami Herald* had run a long article on steroid-using police officers two years earlier. The seven notorious Miami River Cops, who in 1987 were on trial for alleged crimes including cocaine trafficking and conspiracy to commit murder, included Armando "Scarface" Garcia, a weightlifter who had publicly admitted to taking steroids. "There's a great potential for an officer abusing steroids to physically mistreat people," said the police chief of nearby Hollywood, Florida, who had told his investigators to be on the lookout for officers who looked like "small mountains."[22] The *Miami Herald* article may have been the first of the few analytical treatments of this subject that have appeared in American newspapers since the 1980s.

WARNINGS ABOUT POLICE STEROID USE

Warnings about police officers' use of steroids have appeared over the past two decades. According to a 1991 article in the *FBI Law Enforcement Bulletin*: "Anabolic steroid abuse by police officers is a serious problem that merits greater awareness by departments across the country."[23] In 2003, one of the authors offered a similar assessment. Larry Gaines, a former executive director of the Kentucky Chiefs of Police Association, stated: "I think it's a larger problem than people think."[24] In *Steroid Abuse by Law Enforcement Personnel* (2004), the DEA reported: "Anabolic steroid abuse, once viewed as a problem strictly associated with body builders, fitness 'buffs,' and professional athletes, has entered into the law enforcement community. Law enforcement personnel have used steroids for both physical and psychological reasons."[25] In 2008, *Police Chief Magazine* issued a long position paper advising against the use of anabolic-androgenic steroids by police officers and recommending that law enforcement agencies "proactively address this issue": "Rather than look back on what could be an embarrassing 'steroid era' of law enforcement—one in which the profession might be riddled with lawsuits, corruption, and claims of heavy-handedness—it is critical to address the current and future impact of this issue head-on."[26] In fact, by 2008 the steroid era of law enforcement had long been under way. Many reports since the 1990s confirm this assessment. Looking back over the past two decades, it is clear that steroid use in fields such as law enforcement and professional sports has been routinely underestimated. Boston police commissioner Edward F. Davis took this line in 2009 when he was forced to deal with a steroid scandal in his ranks: "There's an emerging trend in law enforcement regarding the use of steroids," he said after a three-year internal investigation. "Unfortunately, we were on the leading edge of this. Luckily, it's not very widespread."[27] Nor is the tendency to underestimate steroid use inside and outside police ranks confined to the United States. In 2005, the Australian Bureau of Criminal Intelligence prepared a secret report on the use of performance- and image-enhancing drugs (PIEDs). In response to the report, the federal Department of Health and Ageing stated: "There is widespread agreement that the extent of use of PIED's is underreported, so the information is likely to significantly underestimate the size of the problem." The report identified police officers among the ten subgroups, not including athletes, of regular PIED users.[28]

A POLICE CHIEF ASKS WHETHER COPS SHOULD USE STEROIDS

The idea that steroids might play a functional (and, therefore, socially legitimate) role in enabling police officers to do their jobs more safely was not beyond the pale in 1987. That year the notorious Miami River Cops were on trial for alleged crimes including cocaine trafficking and conspiracy to commit murder. Among those rogue officers was Armando "Scarface" Garcia, a weightlifter who had publicly admitted to taking steroids.[29] The scandal appears to have been the first public airing of police use of anabolic steroids.

The *Miami Herald's* exposé of an entire gang of rogue policemen prompted a former Miami police chief, Ken Harms, to make the comment that begins this book: "It's probably time that the department makes a conscious decision about whether it's acceptable for officers to take steroids."[30] At the time, the association of these drugs with physical strength was well established. Arnold Schwarzenegger's film *Pumping Iron* (1977) had made an enormous impact on popular culture by promoting the mainstreaming of the hypermuscled male torso, which has expanded its influence ever since. While the American public knew little of anabolic steroid use in American professional football, it was easier to see that bodybuilders were using androgenic drugs and getting spectacular results. It was thus easy to imagine that steroids could create stronger and faster police officers. The sheer political incorrectness of Chief Harms's musings about enhanced police officers, when judged by today's standards, speaks volumes about how the social status of these drugs has changed in the interim. Although Harms did not parse the pros and cons of steroid-boosting by police officers, it is not difficult to imagine how he could have framed the debate. This book explores this ongoing debate by examining the functional argument for steroid use, along with the opposing argument, which emphasizes the dysfunctional effects of these drugs on policing.

Police officers' use of male hormone drugs for functional purposes is analogous to steroid use by other action-oriented male groups, and both can be understood as "workplace doping." Large numbers of men around the world consume steroids because their professions or criminal activities require physical self-assertion and self-confidence. A 1996 report from Scotland, for example, identifies policemen, firefighters, military personnel, and private security guards as steroid users.[31] In Australia, the list includes prison guards and a group of elite troops that in 1998 were discovered to be "using steroids to bulk up, boost stamina and self-esteem and to recover more quickly from injuries they have sustained."[32] In

Britain, Australia, and some European countries, nightclub bouncers use the drugs to produce the "frilled neck lizard response" that intimidates unruly customers.[33]

"The thinking is that big is better than small, tough is better than weak," a former police officer and longtime police psychologist, Gene Sanders, said in 2005. "There is a sort of underground, unspoken tradition among several departments that I've worked with that if you really want to bulk up, this is the best way to do it."[34] A website maintained by the DEA reports the same attitude toward functional steroid use: "Law enforcement personnel have used steroids for both physical and psychological reasons. The idea of enhanced physical strength and endurance provides one with 'the invincible mentality' when performing law enforcement duties."[35] "Most of the police officers I've known who have used these drugs consider them a tool of the trade," the epidemiologist and steroid expert Charles Yesalis said in 2005.[36] As a result of this steroid use, the widespread visibility of bulked-up officers has created a new and menacing image of the street cop.

THE EMERGENCE OF "COLOSSAL COPS"

How many Americans have noticed a gradual and unsettling physical transformation of some of the police officers who serve them? Here is John M. Wills, a former Chicago police officer and retired FBI agent: "Have you ever seen one of your colleagues, or an officer from another department, who was larger than life? I am not speaking in figurative terms about how he influences his environment. I am referring literally to his physical size. The guy whose biceps are bulging out of his shirt sleeves, with 'Popeye' size forearms, veins as big as snakes crisscrossing his skin, seemingly alive. I have seen them; these guys are an awesome sight to behold, almost a caricature of what police officers look like."[37]

This police professional's incredulous and disapproving response to the physical appearance of some officers closely resembles the appalled responses of civilians who have reacted with unease and astonishment at the unnaturally swollen appearance of many policemen. "I see quite a few cops," the Texas law enforcement blogger Scott Henson wrote in 2005, "especially in the larger Texas cities, bulked up to near inhuman proportions, frequently with Barry-Bonds-style forehead bulges. (Austin and Houston both have more than their share matching that description.) I've always wondered if steroid use was the probable explanation." From this example, it seems likely. As a Montana blogger put it in 2008: "I'm sure the surge of steroid use in the police gyms, used by and peddled by cops has nothing to do with [domestic violence] at all. On the other hand you've surely noticed the super-buff cops on your local police force who have pipes like they should be playing in the NFL and [have] a temper to match."[38]

News coverage in December 2010 of a steroid scandal in New Jersey that involved hundreds of police officers and firefighters produced similar online observations about their appearance: "For the past 15 years or so," one reader in New Jersey asked, "hasn't anyone noticed the increase in officers and firefighters who resemble the incredible Hulk? In the small town I live in there are quite a few. One thing they all appear to have in common is a lack of a sense of humor. This phenomenon has been prevalent amongst the NJSP [New Jersey State Police] for 25 years or more." "Exactly!" another reader chimed in. "The average person noticed how they went from bellies hanging over their belts to looking like the Hulk overnight. . . . Those at the top turned their heads while these men and women took what some view as the easy route to getting fit."[39] The *Newark Star-Ledger* editorialized that taxpayers "shouldn't have to pay for synthetically engineered Colossal Cops."[40] In 2011, a California law professor pointed to the emergence of a "positive status in having a sort of 'big department muscle' in smaller departments."[41] Police departments that sponsor weightlifting and bodybuilding competitions for officers recognize the appeal that sheer muscle has for many officers.

A recurring theme of online critical remarks about police officers' appearance is the hairlessness of the massive cops. A Reddit poster observed in 2013: "One aspect of this epidemic substance abuse is so blatantly visible, so 'right out there in plain sight', that I reckon most people don't even notice it any more. It's the Police Hairline. Look at the photos and videos in the news every day and check out the hair (or lack of it) of the police officers. Is there something about the law enforcement profession that causes hair loss? They all look like a bunch of skinheads." The commenter linked steroid abuse with the widespread recruitment of military personnel into police departments: "[Soldiers] had to wear thickly insulated steel helmets in desert heat and dealt with it by buzz-cutting their hair. So right there are THREE things that the latest generation of cops has brought back with them from their army days. A knee jerk 'shoot first, talk later' mindset; extreme hair cuts; and a taste for the 'roids."[42]

"If you watch 'Cops', it's remarkable how many police officers there are with a bald/shaved head, bulging neck muscles, reddish skin and moonface," stated another participant in the same discussion.[43] "Too many RAMBO's in the Police State. Is that why they all have no hair?" asks a citizen of New Jersey in another online chat room. In 2005, a reader of a steroid-promoting website sent me another observation about the television show *Cops*: "Just wanted to contribute that there's a certain episode of C*O*P*S that features the special detachment of troopers who patrol the NY-Miami interstate through South Carolina (whatever number that is—95?) and it shows them pulling over and commando-styling a few busts. All of those guys were HUGE, as in D-Bol [Dianabol] plus suspension plus anadrol huge, and as you know there's no mistaking the look of steroidal muscle on some guys."

STEROIDS AND POLICE SECRECY

Powerful institutions such as major urban police departments enforce secrecy in two ways: by concealing information and failing to carry out investigations that might threaten the authority or prestige of those in power. Police departments have used both methods to minimize public knowledge of police steroid use, and they have been aided and abetted by the lack of media interest in this topic. "It is important to understand," two experts on the topic note, "that not every law enforcement scandal is made public, and not every public scandal is covered by the press. More importantly, not all of them are fully investigated or even acknowledged by the agencies involved."[44]

Steroid-using police officers and the law enforcement agencies that employ them have worked out a de facto arrangement that minimizes public knowledge of steroid use in the ranks. Police responses to evidence of steroid use take on the quality of a ritual in which each participant plays an assigned role. Both those who are using and the officers whom the users work with keep quiet about steroid use; known complaints about dopers from fellow officers to police authorities are few and far between. Police commanders who become aware of steroid use prefer to handle the matter in-house and avoid publicity. Police chiefs who read about the drug problems of their officers in the newspapers issue appropriate statements about the department's zero-tolerance policy for any kind of illicit drug use on the force. Some police chiefs might point to random drug-testing programs run by their departments, whose operations are impenetrable to the public and are ignored by the news media. And as previously discussed, such testing regimens are all but useless: police officers consume so much legal testosterone and so many androgen-enhancing supplements that it may no longer be possible to distinguish between legal and illegal use. The authors of *Anabolic Steroid Abuse in Public Safety Personnel: A Forensic Manual* (2015) add that police supervisors "hope that the FBI and DEA don't take an active interest" in departmental investigations, and that "the public forgets" what all the fuss was about.[45]

Illicit drug use within a police department occurs behind a double layer of secrecy. Although the administrators of police departments are likely to disapprove of or feel ambivalent about such drug use, they are powerfully motivated to keep illegal drug use out of the public eye and to handle the problem themselves. The second layer of secrecy is inherent in the nature of an illicit drug culture. To an even greater degree than most societal institutions, an underground drug culture is a universe unto itself. Obtaining survey data from such a milieu is virtually impossible.

Secrecy about androgenic drug use is strengthened by police officers' relationships with steroid-prescribing physicians, because of laws governing doctor-patient confidentiality. While medical privacy is a fundamental right, in these cases hormone-prescribing doctors and their clients are pursuing nontherapeutic goals such as building muscle. The following report comes from Broward County, Florida, which has seen a series of police-steroid scandals over decades: "Steroid abuse by police officers is obviously an ongoing problem in Broward County, but information is almost impossible to come by. Both Plantation [Police Department] and [the Broward Sheriff's Office] are hiding behind medical privacy laws to keep the identities of steroid-using cops secret. And they are hiding from public view investigations that exonerated officers who obtained steroids from fly-by-night, largely unregulated clinics that have since been shut down."[46] Other departments conceal steroid-abusing officers' identities with impunity. For example, two men who were beaten by sheriff's deputies in Merced County, California, filed suit against the deputies and the county. The official response to the litigation: "The Sheriff's Department acknowledged that at least four deputies used mood-altering steroids. They were disciplined in-house and their names never released."[47]

THE NECESSARY ROLE OF ANECDOTAL EVIDENCE

The familiar dismissal of anecdotal evidence is grounded in a justified preference for systematic analysis of large amounts of information, rather than reliance on fewer, sporadic accounts, which offer a less reliable foundation for reaching conclusions about how the world works. Anecdotal evidence can consist of a relatively small number of reports that are presumed to be a sampling of a much greater number of phenomena that have gone unreported. Such evidence acquires credibility and a cumulative power by providing consistent accounts of the phenomena being studied. The reader of this book will find that the large number of anecdotal testimonies assembled here meet this test of consistency and provide an accurate description of the police steroid culture in the United States.

Many of the anecdotal accounts presented here concern groups of officers engaged together in steroid use. In some cases, one officer is selling drugs to the others. A group of similar anecdotal accounts indicate a pattern of behavior across departments rather than merely idiosyncratic, isolated behaviors. Sometimes there is a revelatory event involving so many steroid-abusing personnel that it is not an anecdote at all but rather a mass of information that stands in for survey data. The 248 police officers and firefighters in New Jersey who were exposed as abusers of anabolic steroids and HGH drugs in 2010 fall into this category. The corrupt doctor who served all of them may be an anecdotal figure, but his clients constitute a drug-abusing cohort that implicates entire subpopulations of first responders in illicit drug use.

THE NECESSARY ROLE OF "INTRUSIVE" INVESTIGATION

Investigators from federal or state agencies can pursue evidence of steroid use by a local police force. Outside agents can sometimes penetrate the police culture of secrecy. The blue wall of silence, which makes possible systemic police brutality, provides cover for any form of misbehavior or criminal activity encouraged or tolerated by an aberrant but influential minority of officers and the police union. Systemic police abuse of black males is the most notorious form of criminality that can take root inside the culture of an urban police department.

Interventions by US government agencies have made it possible to pursue police steroid abuse cases that local officials could not be expected to deal with themselves. In 2003, for example, in Walker County, Alabama, Sheriff John Mark Tirey told the press he had suspended four deputies without pay for using steroids. By possessing anabolic steroids illegally, these deputies had committed a felony for which cops are rarely arrested. The sheriff left it to the FBI to consider filing criminal charges against the suspended officers.[48]

When in 2005 federal agents were called in to review the customer records of PowerMedica, a Deerfield Beach, Florida, pharmacy that supplied anabolic steroids to a large customer base, they found so many boxes of documents that they had to summon reinforcements from the Broward County Sheriff's Office, an agency that has had steroid abuse problems of its own. Food and Drug Administration (FDA) investigators found many customers who identified themselves as police officers and firefighters.[49] It is possible that some of the assisting sheriff's deputies came across their own customer records or those of fellow deputies who had opted for covert male hormone supplementation.

In 2006, Steven C. Ward, a former police officer in West Valley, Utah, was cleared in the fatal shooting of an unarmed man. At the same time, Ward was indicted for importing anabolic steroids into the United States. Addressing the conjunction of the shooting and the former officer's use of steroids, a spokesman for the police department insisted that Ward was not experiencing roid rage when he shot and killed fifty-nine-year-old Bounmy Ousa outside his home. Federal intervention occurred when the DEA subpoenaed the local police department's internal affairs investigation.[50]

In Boston, a federal investigation initiated in 2006 led to (conspicuously lenient) penalties in 2009 for police officers caught using illegal steroids.[51] In 2008 the DEA investigated steroid use by police and firefighters in Phoenix, Arizona.[52] In 2013, the FBI and a state agency, the Texas Rangers, investigated a steroid ring operating inside the police department of Arlington, Texas.[53] In 2014, the Georgia Bureau of Investigation investigated possible steroid use by deputies in the Richmond County Sheriff's Office.

The outsourcing of steroid investigations to federal or state agencies points to the degree to which police forces are closed, tightly knit communities that cannot reasonably be expected to investigate themselves. Police departments have internal affairs (IA) units that are charged with investigating misconduct by police colleagues. But it is very difficult for a handful of officers to detect and expose fellow officers, in part because those who serve in IA units are vulnerable to being vilified as informers and rats. When Lieutenant Frank

Mancini, a detective in the Boston Police Department, served in the department's anticorruption unit, "he was careful to handpick officers who he thought would be up to the task of handcuffing friends or even relatives on the force." He tried to appeal to the professional self-respect of Boston's cops. "If we aren't able to watch our own shop and take down our own dirty cops," he said, "the federal government is going to come in and do it for us. It happened in Cincinnati. It happened in Pittsburgh. It happened in New Orleans. It happened in Detroit. It happened in Los Angeles. It happened with the New Jersey State Police. I don't want the feds coming in and watching over the Boston police. We have to take care of our own house, and we have to show everybody we can do it properly."[54]

The Georgia Bureau of Investigation (GBI) investigation of Augusta police officers in 2014 illustrates the kind of police culture that contributes to the general lack of interest in eliminating steroid use from police departments. The information about the officers alleged to be using steroids came not from the IA unit, but from a drug dealer who was arrested by the sheriff's narcotic investigators. When a polygraph administered by the state agency supported some of the dealer's claims, the GBI took over the investigation. The sheriff's reaction to the GBI probe, and to the speculations about who might be on the list of steroid users, was revealing. The opportunity to find out which of his officers were on steroids appeared to be the last thing on the sheriff's mind. His concern was focused instead on the possible consequences for those implicated. Speculations coursing through social media "affect this office because no one knows who is potentially affected," Sheriff Richard Roundtree said. "Everyone realizes it could be someone they know and no one wants to see any harm come to a friend of theirs. There's a lot of anxiety in not knowing." The threat came not from within, but from an external agency bent on finding misconduct within the departmental community. The possible ramifications of illegal steroid use by police officers were of no concern to this guardian of the law.[55]

HOW MANY COPS USE STEROIDS?

Estimates of anabolic-androgenic steroid use by police officers cannot be precise, because these steroid users constitute "a secretive subculture within a secretive subculture." "I've heard many, many accounts of police officers taking steroids," the Harvard psychiatrist and steroid expert Harrison Pope has commented. "But it's impossible to put a number on it."[56]

In 2008, Larry K. Gaines, former executive director of the Kentucky Chiefs of Police Association, said: "You cannot get [statistics] because police departments that find the problem usually take care of it in-house, without any publicity."[57] In 2005, a police psychologist in Washington State, Gene Sanders, said: "If I were going to be conservative, I'd say that probably five percent of everyone who walks in my door either is using or has used steroids. This is getting to be a major problem."[58] (This estimate suggests there are at least 25,000 steroid-consuming police officers in the United States.) In 2007, Sanders estimated that "up to 25 percent of all police officers in urban settings with gangs and high crime use steroids—many of them defensively."[59] In 2010, the DEA reported that police officers belong to one of the four professional groups that consume the most illegal anabolic steroids.[60]

Uncertainty and secrecy about the numbers of police officers on steroids have served as an excuse to ignore or minimize the problem. The almost total absence of departmental steroid testing, the lack of transparency about what little testing is done, and departments' unwillingness to take action on the basis of "reasonable suspicion" of officers' steroid use all guarantee that reports of steroid use will never rise above the threshold of concern that might catalyze official interest in regulating the use of androgenic drugs in police culture. The tiny number of reported positive tests grossly underestimates prevalence. Habitual underestimation of steroid use among elite athletes was likewise once the norm. In neither of these social worlds does an absence or paucity of findings signify the absence or rarity of steroid use.

Some of the material used in this book came from media reports about police steroid use from thirty-six states.[61] The absence of information from the fourteen other states does not indicate the absence of steroid use by law enforcement personnel there. On the contrary, the absence of reports from unpopulous states such as Idaho, Maine, Delaware, Vermont, Rhode Island, North Dakota, South Dakota, and Iowa is due both to the limited media coverage of this issue across the country and to the absence of major urban areas in these states. By contrast, the states from which we have reports are home to every major American city. The higher levels of street violence in urban environments drive steroid use by the police who patrol them.

Estimates of steroid use from high-level police administrators differ. A former Boston police commissioner and the current police chief of Oklahoma City have minimized steroid use. On the other hand, Kim Humphrey, a former Phoenix police commander, told a conference of high-ranking law enforcement officials in 2008 that steroid use is "going on everywhere" and that the drug-testing of officers is "an issue that needs to gain momentum."[62] The same year, a prominent Florida police official, Dr. James Sewell, commented: "I think. . . there is a professional concern in all agencies right now about the use of steroids and the impact of those steroids and its use on the way they do business."[63] Low public estimates by police officials should be received skeptically, since "very few in the criminal justice system want to admit that there is an anabolic steroid abuse problem, even when the physical and behavioral manifestations of steroid addiction are front and center."[64]

Anecdotal reports suggest that steroid use in some police departments is more than a minor issue. In 2008, a Canadian journalist reported on steroid use by an Ontario police officer who stated that the use of performance-enhancing drugs was openly discussed in the station house. This testimony constituted "a rare glimpse into a burgeoning subculture in the policing community throughout North America."[65] In the same article, Gene Sanders, a police psychologist and former police officer in Spokane, Washington, estimated the prevalence of steroid use in US police forces: "One in four officers working in high-crime cities are juicing, while the influence of weight-room culture is obvious even to the casual observer. Out are the moustaches and mirrored shades of old-time cop chic. In are bull necks, shaved heads and thighs that wouldn't look out of place on an Olympic powerlifter."[66]

In 2010 a former Immigration and Customs Enforcement special agent in Washington State who was caught importing steroids from China stated: "Steroid use was very common within my own police department, as well as neighboring agencies, so I again mistakenly felt it was 'no big deal' to use them."

The authors of *Anabolic Steroid Abuse in Public Safety Personnel* report anecdotal evidence from the state of Georgia. When asked in 2013 to estimate steroid use in the local police and fire departments, a firefighter replied: "If you . . . went through everyone's personnel files and found out who is on testosterone, I would guess that 90 percent of them are abusing." The authors point out that every officer involved in the steroid scandal then under investigation "made it clear that illegal steroid use is rampant in Public Safety throughout Georgia," an assertion "confirmed by [the testosterone dealer]." Despite the nearly unanimous agreement about the scope of the problem, "none [of the users] have been charged with any crime"; in fact, as far the authors could tell, "no investigation has taken place; certainly, no one has been arrested."[67] From this affair, the authors draw a sobering conclusion:

> If any of these individuals is taken to trial for their crimes, it will draw in and expose corruption throughout public safety in the State of Georgia to the point that it would be decimated and therefore crippled. For this reason, and to maintain the image of local public safety, the authors believe that there is no incentive to bring any of these individuals to justice. This also means that there is no incentive to identify others in public safety as criminal participants. As such, there appears no remedy in the criminal justice system for these crimes, and others are likely to suffer harm because of them.[68]

According to these criminologists, an accurate estimate of how many police officers in Georgia were using steroids would have brought down state law enforcement.

Low estimates of the extent of police misconduct, as we have already seen, are promoted by police departments' traditional claim that deviant policemen are "bad apples," unrepresentative of most officers. Media sources can share this view. "The majority of law enforcement officers do tough and valuable work. A few abuse their authority," the *Los Angeles Times* said in 1992.[69] The service of the great majority of good officers, a Dallas cleric wrote in 2014, "is dishonored by rogue officers whose bullying and violent behavior promote distrust, resentment and even hatred of the police."[70] The same year, the New York City police commissioner, William Bratton, declared that only 1 percent of NYPD officers were "poisoning the well." "We will," he said, "aggressively seek to get those out of the department who should not be here . . . The brutal, the corrupt, the racist, the incompetent."[71] A secret unit within the Los Angeles Police Department is tasked with, in the words of a member of the unit, "weeding out the bad police officers," specifically, "bad apples . . . that tarnish the badge."[72]

One version of the "bad apples" theory claims that steroid use among police is a rarity. In 2013, for example, a chief constable in Staffordshire, England, said: "In most forces there will be a police officer who will be into bodybuilding and the gym and would abuse steroids."[73] Boston's police commissioner, Edward Davis, responded to a highly publicized steroid scandal in 2009 by assuring the public there were very few police officers on steroids. He labeled the problem "an emerging trend" of which Boston, to his regret, found itself "on the leading edge," claims that showed only how out of touch he was with the reality of steroids in police culture.[74] The "emerging trend" had been under way for many years, so Boston was nowhere near the "leading edge" of it. His estimate of how many policemen use steroids was offered without any apparent foundation in fact. His entire response was an exercise in wishful thinking put out for public consumption rather than a thoughtful or empirical assessment of steroid use in the ranks.

The "bad apples" theory of police steroid use is misleading on several counts. A small-town police force might include a single officer who trains at a gym, but in urban departments in Britain or the United States the number of officers going to gyms to lift weights is far greater than that. (It is worth noting here that weight-lifting has become an obsession for many men serving in the British Army—the same cohort from which many police officers come.) A British steroid expert adds:

> Here in the UK ordinary police officers who walk, cycle or drive around do not carry guns and are rarely involved in anything physically demanding. From my own observations, very few of these [officers] use steroids or work out. However, other departments (who carry guns) deal with more serious crimes and these are more likely to work out (a lot) and perhaps use steroids. . . . When I was living in Liverpool I visited a number of gyms in the small towns surrounding Liverpool, each with their own gym. Here police officers from Liverpool would come to train and in many cases these gyms were very "steroid friendly," e.g. having safe disposals bins for needles and syringes hanging in the locker room.[75]

JUDGING AND PUNISHING COPS ON STEROIDS

How severely should the steroid-using officer be judged and punished? The special stigma of illicit drug use can put police executives who judge and impose penalties on these officers in a difficult position. Those at the top are torn between their appreciation of the services rendered by the officer and their responsibility to crack down on drug users in the ranks. This predicament is created by the police hero who compromises his position by using illicit drugs. An English judge stated in 2011: "When a police sergeant purchases class C drugs from one office and [intends to] supply them to another, right minded members of society will be truly shocked." Sentenced to three years and nine months in prison, the officer in question said he found his life "in ruins." During his twenty-five years of police service, "he had saved a boy's life, been attacked by a criminal wielding a samurai sword, served on United Nations peacekeeping missions in Bosnia and Sarajevo, and [been] ranked as the highest performing sergeant in the war against crime in St Helens."[76] Later on we will see that this fallen exemplar has a number of American counterparts. One of them is Tramell Taylor, who resigned from the Spokane Police Department in 2014 after the DEA reported that a shipment of steroids had arrived at his home. In twenty-seven years on the force, Taylor had been awarded the Washington State Medal of Honor, the Spokane Police Department Silver Star, the Distinguished Service Medal, and a Life-Saving Award.[77]

Police heroes who lose their careers as a result of anabolic steroid use confront us with fundamental questions about professional standards, institutional policies, and the meaning of "illicit" drug use in today's heavily medicated society. The massive New Jersey steroid scandal of 2010–2011, involving 248 police officers and firefighters, demonstrated that illegal hormone use does not carry the automatic penalty of dismissal from the force, since none of these men lost their positions as first responders. In fact, as this book shows, police commanders have generally followed lenient policies that avoid effective investigation of steroid use and that shield steroid users from the statutory legal penalties for drug use of this kind. This leniency is reinforced by the reluctance of local prosecutors to charge police officers, whose cooperation is essential to getting indictments and convictions. In summary, the pro forma condemnations of steroid use that police administrators offer to the public are not matched by their actions toward officers who are caught using illicit drugs.

The passivity of the police establishment toward anabolic steroid use by officers leaves the general public in the dark. Assertive questions are seldom asked of police administrators. An exception to this rule was a *Boston Globe* editorial titled "Too easy on rogue cops," which excoriated Commissioner Ed Davis's flaccid response when it came time to penalize eleven officers "who were involved in steroid use or who had frequented an afterhours club in Hyde

Park where drugs, alcohol, and prostitutes were present." For these offenses, Davis handed out penalties that ranged from written reprimands to a forty-five-day unpaid suspension. While acknowledging the inadequacy of these punishments, he claimed that his hands were tied by an aggressive union, contract provisions that minimized sanctions for first-time drug violations, and labor arbitrators who overturned harsher penalties. The *Globe* editors argued that Davis should have sailed straight into the wind, terminated the most compromised officers, and challenged the police union to stop defending dirty cops. In fact, Davis's passive reaction to the blatant antisocial conduct of the officers exemplifies a lack of political will that has manifested itself over and over again as police executives repeatedly forfeit opportunities to take strong positions against steroid use by their own officers.

These passive responses from police chiefs mean that action against steroid use in the force will have to come from outsiders. But this is a difficult assignment precisely because public discussion of police misconduct, whether involving drug use or "excessive violence," is paralyzed by the struggle between two primal narratives: the dangers of policing versus the damage done by police brutality and corruption. Both of these emotionally fraught topics must be dealt with at the same time to produce useful exchanges between police and the civilian population.

The core problem is that these primal narratives are incompatible on an instinctive level. An emotional commitment to one invalidates the other. Thus, invoking one of these primal narratives in isolation from the other is an instant conversation stopper. In this way, the police heroism narrative functions as a kind of emotional blackmail: its solemnity and drama demand from us a sympathy that rules out anything other than shared mourning and an unqualified devotion to the disgraced officer. Many will regard any dissent from such a commitment as a kind of sacrilege.

The dissenters from this unconditional loyalty to police officers, who are under siege from both emotional stress and physical danger, harbor traumas and resentments that rule out a devotional attachment to the police. Black citizens' attitudes toward police have been conditioned by decades of physical and psychological abuse at officers' hands. In the absence of a concerted and coordinated effort to break this deadlock, police authorities have little incentive to develop the political will to embark upon real reform, whether it involves racial tensions or the war on drugs, which has been waged just about everywhere except inside police culture.

THE DYSFUNCTIONAL STEROID-SEEKING POLICEMAN

Steroid use by policemen is often a marker of a disordered and trouble-prone personality. Only a small fraction of these users are engaging in testosterone replacement therapy, which is undertaken for medical purposes. Most police officers are too young and healthy to suffer from the "low testosterone" levels prominently featured in pharmaceutical company advertising aimed at the adult male population. We can define medically legitimate therapy as a clinical scenario that involves an informed patient in medical need, an ethical physician, and a legal therapeutic goal. This scenario does not lead to socially deviant or criminal behaviors.

Most steroid-seeking cops are interested in bulking up to achieve the cosmetic benefit of big muscles and a "ripped" torso resembling that of a bodybuilder. Some members of this group believe that a hypermuscular torso offers the practical benefit of intimidating potential adversaries. This nonclinical medical scenario involves a "patient" seeking a nonmedical benefit, possibly by attempting to deceive the doctor. Some doctors are willing to make a medically dubious diagnosis of "low testosterone," and some pharmacies will honor such doctors' fraudulent prescriptions. The inherent dishonesty of the nonclinical medical transaction, or the overt criminality of acquiring steroids on the black market, may be taken as predictors of deviant character traits in those involved in these transactions.

Thus, it not surprising that steroid offenses are often committed along with other crimes or eccentric behaviors. We know this from media coverage of officers caught using steroids; police-generated data on steroid-using officers, as we have noted, do not exist.

For example, in 2003 James Batsel IV bulked up on steroids and then joined a gang of police officers who specialized in burglarizing stores and nightclubs in the Atlanta area. During one burglary, Batsel shot and killed a nightclub owner. Regarding Batsel's steroid use, his father said: "The police force that he was on was rampant with it."[78]

In 2008 in Peel, Ontario, Constable Roger Yeo, a physically massive man known among his police colleagues as a "juice monkey," acknowledged using steroids in conjunction with his weight-training regimen. Among other crimes, he was charged with violating the Police Services Act by stalking schoolgirls in 2005.[79]

In 2010, a correctional officer at Concord State Prison in New Hampshire, Kevin Valenti, was indicted for possession of clomiphene, a prescription drug for stimulating ovulation, and testosterone. (Anabolic steroids shut down the natural production of testosterone, so steroid users take clomiphene to restart the process.) A year earlier, he had been ordered to pay a former prisoner $40,000 after a federal jury determined that Valenti and another officer had violated his Eighth Amendment right against cruel and unusual punishment.[80]

In August 2005, Officer Chad Michael Goulding resigned from the Phoenix Police Department following a positive steroid test that was administered after his girlfriend, a fellow officer, reported she feared he might "cause her harm." A year later, Goulding pulled off a series of bank robberies. It took four years for the FBI to catch him. In 2012 he was found guilty on multiple counts of armed robbery, theft, and kidnapping.[81]

In 2011 a Pennsylvania police officer, David Busemeyer, told detectives he had been addicted to steroids for several years. He was suspended after being accused of disclosing the identity of an informant to a suspected drug dealer, and he was indicted for attempting to tamper with evidence, obstructing official business, and obstructing justice. In addition, his superiors had confronted him over a report that he had harassed a woman he was dating.[82]

In 2014 in Washington State, Darrion Holiwell, a King County sheriff's deputy, chief firearms instructor, SWAT officer, and steroid

user, was sentenced to seventeen months in prison for prostituting his wife, theft, and violations of the Uniformed Controlled
Substances Act. Holiwell may have sold steroids to, among others,
members of Tac-30, the department's elite SWAT unit.[83] A photo of
Holiwell at a firing range shows his arms wrapped in the "sleeve"
tattoos that some police departments have banned.

In the absence of survey data about the prevalence of steroid
use among police officers, it is impossible to determine with confidence the significance of the association between steroid use and
these policemen's criminal acts or socially deviant behaviors. We do
know that nearly all the steroid-consuming police personnel who
come to public attention did not follow the clinical procedure. They
demonstrated a willingness to break the letter or the spirit of the law
by obtaining black-market steroids or by colluding in pseudothera-
peutic hormone therapies with unethical doctors. There is also the
possibility that steroid use is a kind of initiation into social deviance
as a way of life. "One wonders if," a journalist commented in 2005,
"for some cops, steroids are a sort of gateway drug: whether, having corrupted their code—and having gotten away with it—they
become more receptive to doing other illegal things."[84]

This reasonable hypothesis can coexist with another one, namely,
that police officers with certain personality traits are attracted
to steroid use because of their intense self-assertiveness and the
"body dysmorphia" that motivates some men to pursue extreme
muscularity. Some young officers join police forces because they
want to exercise physical authority over people; these ambitions
can generate "excessive force" accusations after confrontations
with citizens. In this sense, steroid use may serve as a "marker" of
trouble-prone personalities that do not belong on a police force.
The six steroid-using officers described above—Batsel, Yeo, Valenti,
Goulding, Busemeyer, and Holiwell—collectively engaged in drug
dealing, burglary, murder, stalking, sexual harassment, promoting
prostitution, and assault. The association between steroid use and a
wide range of serious crimes prompts us to ask: can we confirm that
steroid use is a predictor of criminal tendencies?

Researchers have observed an affinity between anabolic steroid use and antisocial behavior. A 2006 Swedish study published in the *Archives of General Psychiatry* points out that "a history of drug abuse is associated with a high risk for criminality."[85] Steroid use by policemen nearly always qualifies as drug abuse because it is either illegal or enabled by an unethical doctor, who may also be incompetent. An incompetent doping doctor will occasionally kill a patient through malfeasance—one more reason why police unions should discourage rather than defend nonclinical hormone therapies for cops.[86]

The Swedish study confirms the association between steroids and some (but not all) types of crime; interestingly, these particular findings do not support the roid rage hypothesis as an explanation for users' criminal acts. While convictions for weapons offenses occur twice as often among steroid users as among nonusers, suggesting a propensity for violent action in the former, this fact is not evidence of spontaneous violent behavior. An unplanned brutal outburst is the signature event of "steroid rage," but these authors found that criminals use steroids calculatingly. While steroids may well "trigger uncontrolled, violent rage . . . certain groups of criminals may use AAS [anabolic-androgenic steroids] with the intention of being capable of committing crime more efficiently." Bank robbers' use of steroids, for example, points to a type of "planned, premeditated violence among criminals." The practical approach to steroid use is evident when "criminals involved in heavy types of crime, such as armed robbery or collection of crime-related debts, derive an advantage from being muscular and/or having a heavy build." Finally, the authors found that steroids are "associated not only with impulsive antisocial behavior but also with an antisocial lifestyle involving various types of criminality." This "antisocial lifestyle" is adopted by some of the steroid-using "trouble-prone" personalities who manage to become police officers.[87]

Does anabolic steroid use make police officers dangerous? The conventional response to this question conjures up the by-now-familiar specter of steroid rage—a hormonal storm that supposedly takes possession of an intemperate steroid abuser, causing him to unleash a violent assault upon the victim of his fury. As we shall see later in this book, roid rage is a simplistic and misleading diagnosis of most steroid abusers' violent behaviors. While it is likely that such events occur, they are infrequent. In fact, the roid rage stereotype distracts attention from the forms of criminality that often accompany steroid use by policemen. To get a sense of the more dangerous consequences of police steroid use, let us examine the official accounts of how three men who were connected with cops and steroids killed themselves in 2008.

On the evening of January 28, 2008, John Rossi, the fifty-six-year-old co-owner of Lowen's Compounding Pharmacy in Bay Ridge, New York, was found dead, either facedown in a pool of blood on the floor of an upstairs office or, according to another account, "slumped over" a desk. On the desk were a bottle of Jack Daniel's and an open bottle of unidentified pills. Rossi's .380 semiautomatic Beretta was found near his body. His co-owner was a film producer and registered pharmacist named Julian Nasso, identified in a 2002 federal indictment as an associate of the Gambino organized crime family. At the time of Rossi's death, what had once been a small neighborhood pharmacy was being investigated as a center for the illegal distribution of anabolic steroids and human growth hormone (HGH) to police officers, firefighters, and thousands of other customers throughout the country.[88] Among the customers in law enforcement were New York Police Department officers and more than forty from Jersey City, New Jersey.

John Rossi died from what the *New York Times* called "two apparently self-inflicted gunshot wounds." The city medical examiner ruled Rossi's death a suicide. Why the two shots? "He wanted to make sure," a police source said.[89] The *Times* reported that Rossi "was being sought to testify in the steroid inquiry, and people who have doubts about the official story say he had a lot to live for, and a lot of information that could have hurt others."[90] "Rossi had information that could take down a lot of people," another law enforcement source said.[91]

The investigators who had expected Rossi to be a cooperating witness were surprised by the two-shot conjecture. Only 2 percent of all firearm suicides involve multiple shots. According to the police, Rossi fired the first bullet into his chest at an angle that sent the slug through his pectoral muscle and out his armpit. At that point he was ostensibly able to fire a second bullet into his head. On the desk he had left a note to his wife: "Dear Justine: I love you. Please forgive me." The note included an oddly formal touch: he had signed it with both his first and last names. The investigators compared the note with another handwriting sample and concluded that they matched.[92] Unanswered was the question of why a pharmacist with access to a vast array of medications would use a gun rather than pills to kill himself.

Investigation of the forty cops from Jersey City who were Lowen's customers was assigned to fifty-one-year-old Edward Shinnick. He had been promoted to captain in 2007 and put in charge of the Jersey City Police Department's Internal Affairs Bureau. Shinnick had received a number of awards for service and bravery, and the Jersey City police chief, Thomas J. Comey, said Shinnick had never spoken to him about personal problems. One of Shinnick's jobs was to supervise the drug testing of officers under suspicion for steroid use and to take away their badges and guns until drug tests showed they were clean. But six months into the Internal Affairs assignment, Shinnick "filed for retirement, telling his wife that the stress was too much." On May 28, 2008, he had lunch with a friend and then drove to a hotel—in Pennsylvania's Pocono Mountains. According to the police report, Shinnick checked into a room and then shot himself twice: one bullet went into his chest, the other into his head. A note was found with the body. A reporter's request to the Pennsylvania State Police (PSP) for its report and the contents of the note was denied.[93] On September 1, 2010, the PSP submitted a notarized affidavit confirming that all physical evidence had been "destroyed in accordance with [PSP] regulations, including any notes or letters." This evidence was by then irrelevant, according to the PSP, because the result of the investigation was already known.[94]

On June 5, 2008, a week after the death of Edward Shinnick, police in Plano, Texas, went to a house where they found the body of a well-known steroid dealer, David Jacobs, age thirty-five, and that of his "on-again, off-again" girlfriend, Amanda Earhart-Savell, thirty, a fitness model. Both had been shot multiple times by a .40-caliber semiautomatic handgun. Jacobs had been hit in the abdomen and head, and Earhart-Savell died from a gunshot wound in the back of her head, another in her right upper back, and five in her chest. Law enforcement officials at first saw the deaths as a double homicide, but the Dallas County medical examiner released a preliminary finding of suicide due to "self-inflicted" gunshot wounds.[95] "Our investigation is consistent with murder-suicide," said Andrae Smith, a public information officer for the Plano police.[96] There was no explanation of how a man suffering from the agony of a stomach wound had managed to shoot himself in the head after gunning down his girlfriend.

At the time of his death, Jacobs was under indictment on federal steroid-distribution charges. He was reported to be talking with National Football League officials about players to whom he had sold drugs. According to the *New York Times*, in May 2008 Jacobs had "provided the N.F.L. with documentary evidence and testimony that tied several players to performance-enhancing drugs."[97] He also claimed to have sold steroids to police officers in five cities in the region: Garland, Richardson, Dallas, Arlington, and Plano. "The kinds of people I know about could put a bullet in the back of my head," Jacobs told a sportswriter.[98] On May 27, the Texas police blogger Scott Henson wrote: "David Jacobs says he's ready to name names of police officers who got steroids from his network."[99] A week later, Jacobs was dead. According to an autopsy conducted by the Collin County medical examiner's office, Jacobs's testosterone level was five times the limit allowed by sports antidoping rules.[100]

One might speculate whether that much testosterone could have driven him to empty a gun into his female companion and then take his own life.

The violent death of this loudmouthed bodybuilding steroid dealer left a toxic cloud of doubt and suspicion in its wake. "After the bodies were found," the *Dallas Morning News* reported, "Plano police wearing masks over their faces were seen entering the house and taking evidence away, some in boxes. Police say they were undercover officers who needed to protect their identities because of other work."[101] "After Jacobs' death," Scott Henson noted, "no law enforcement agency disciplined any of his alleged police officer clients; of the five [police forces implicated by Jacobs], only Dallas PD implemented steroid testing going forward. Otherwise, the officers Jacobs sold to have never been identified or disciplined, and are likely still on the force using illicit steroids."[102] In other words, a police department that Jacobs had accused of harboring steroid dopers was conducting the investigation into how he died.

In fact, Jacobs's claim that he had sold steroids to police officers throughout the Dallas–Fort Worth Metroplex was entirely plausible, then and today. Five years after Jacobs's death, the Arlington Police Department experienced a multiofficer steroid scandal that drove one cop, David Vo, to commit suicide.[103] In 2014, the Dallas Independent School District (DISD) investigated and found illegal steroid use by members of its police department.[104] In short, there is no reason to believe that police steroid use in the Dallas area is confined to the departments in which it has been exposed, and the same principle applies to departments in any major urban area across the country.

It is hard to contemplate the deaths of John Rossi, Edward Shinnick, and David Jacobs and not see what makes them eerily similar. Although all three men were under pressure, none had exhibited depressive or suicidal symptoms. Police authorities and medical examiners presented all three as having committed suicide by means of a technique employed by every fiftieth victim of that way of killing. Most importantly, however, all of them knew or claimed to know the names of police officers who were using illicit anabolic steroids.

Police officers' power to detain, interrogate, arrest, and inflict both legal and illegal violence on ordinary citizens inevitably produces ambivalent attitudes toward the police in a civilian population. At the extreme ends of the spectrum, police are regarded either as heroes and guardians or as an invasive and abusive threat to the community. These two groups have radically different attitudes toward police officers' use of violence in the course of performing their duties. Socially advantaged admirers of the police are often willing to accept that police use rough tactics that target the lower social classes.[105] It is worth asking whether this endorsement of the extralegal use of force by police might also include tolerance for steroid use by the enforcers of the law. Indeed, influential elites' reliance on police power may help account for police departments' lack of interest in eliminating steroid use from their ranks. There may well be a tacit understanding that police officers are entitled to use anabolic steroids because they are seen as functional drugs.

Police use of excessive violence, often referred to in the media as "police brutality," can be portrayed as criminal deviance, as systemic behavior within a police force, or as both. Police department assessments of excessive violence by officers invariably depict these events as highly unusual misbehaviors. As an NYPD assistant chief once put it: "We don't want a few bad apples or a few rogue cops damaging" the reputation of the entire force.[106] One critical response to this official claim was a demand that a police chief go "beyond the 'few bad apples' basket of bromides" when an unusually large number of officers are involved in scandals and a department seems to be out of control. This was the scenario that New York City police commissioner Ray Kelly faced in the fall of 2011, with "allegations, some already proven, of drug-planting, ticket-fixing, Muslim-spying, gunrunning, pepper-spraying, and 'frying another n****r.'"[107]

People whose contacts with police result in having force used or threatened against them—a very small fraction (1.4 percent) of total police-civilian contacts—nearly always feel that the officer used excessive force or otherwise acted improperly. Many of these people report that they argued with, verbally abused, disobeyed, or interfered with the actions of the officer.[108] They may well believe they were victimized by "rogue" behavior on the part of a police officer.

The archetypal "rogue cop" is a deranged loner who explodes into deadly and ultimately self-destructive violence that originates in his own psychopathology. A well-known example of the deranged rogue cop was Christopher Dorner, a Los Angeles police officer who in 2013 killed four people—including a police officer—and wounded three others, five years after being dismissed from the force. Dorner claimed he was dismissed because he had reported excessive use of force by another officer. The police manhunt for Dorner continued for a week before he was finally cornered, at a cabin in the San Bernardino Mountains near Los Angeles, where he committed suicide. As a cop killer, Dorner had taken rogue-cop status as far as it could go. The rogue cop is, therefore, an outlier who makes every other cop look normal by comparison. The spectacle of his deviance seems to confirm the mental stability of the great majority of cops.

In fact, the great majority of "rogue cops" operate in groups that can morph into criminal gangs and occasionally achieve public notoriety. The violent, murderous Miami River Cops were convicted in 1987 of preying on drug smugglers. At a time when concerns about police officers' use of steroids were appearing in the Miami media, the *Miami Herald* described the gang members as "young, muscular officers" who lifted weights together while off duty.[109] Eventually, no fewer than eighty police officers were arrested, convicted, or disciplined. At least 10 percent of the Miami force was judged to be corrupt.[110] Several years later in New York, the so-called Dirty Thirty cops were convicted of drug-related crimes while operating out of Manhattan's 30th Precinct. This cop-generated crime wave was serious enough to prompt an investigation by the Mollen Commission, which issued a report calling for reforms in 1993.[111] These and other cases from around the country confirm that loner rogue cops make up a very small fraction of police officers who engage in criminal behavior.

There is no formal definition of what constitutes rogue behavior in a police department. The NYPD officer Justin Volpe's notorious sodomizing of the Haitian immigrant Abner Louima with a broom handle in 1997 was rogue behavior at its worst, committed by a reputed steroid user. At the same time, not one of the twenty officers in Volpe's station house reported anything about this terrible crime to their superiors. How should we categorize this perverse fidelity to the blue wall of silence? It is well known that absolute adherence to this code of silence is the rule, not the exception: "A Department of Justice study revealed that a whopping 84 percent of police officers report that they've seen colleagues use excessive force on civilians, and 61 percent admit they don't always report 'even serious criminal violations that involve abuse of authority by fellow officers.'"[112] In other words, a pervasive conspiracy of silence among rank-and-file officers makes it difficult to even estimate the volume of police misbehavior that occurs. In this sense, rogue police behaviors are often hiding in plain sight, since their behavior is tolerated or accepted by their peers. These conditions go unchallenged by police executives, who are intimidated by the blue wall of silence. The rogue culture prevails not by enlisting a majority of officers in overt misbehavior, but rather by creating a taboo that prohibits the exposing of police misconduct to those who administer the department.

What is the potential damage from police misbehaviors engaged in by large numbers of officers rather than a few bad apples? At what point does a city administration confront not a few rogue officers, but a rogue department in which violent and even predatory police officers understand that they are free to act out their personal antagonisms with deadly force? The Albuquerque Police Department had reached this nadir by 2014, its officers having killed twenty-eight people over a period of five years.[113] In October of that year, the US Department of Justice announced that federal officials would appoint an independent monitor to oversee the department. The disbanding of a SWAT-like tactical unit was one result of the federal intervention.[114] These kinds of paramilitary-style forces within civilian police departments, which offer a special opportunity for intense male bonding, have long promoted overaggressive and vio-lent policing. In fact, it had been public knowledge for years that the Albuquerque department was out of control, as one controversial police killing of an unarmed man followed another.

What Do You Call a Rogue Cop?

Every police chief and commissioner knows that there are unstable personalities on the force. In fact, police culture and the academic observers who study it have generated a vocabulary to describe the spectrum of potentially violent personalities in police departments. This vocabulary is important in part because not all police violence can be characterized as misbehavior. "People who do police work understand that it's very messy," says Eugene O'Donnell, a former NYPD officer and prosecutor who now teaches at the John Jay College of Criminal Justice. "Brutality is part of the police job."[115] Containing that brutality within appropriate limits is a balancing act for every sizable department. A vocabulary that can legitimize or stigmatize police behaviors, and thereby situate them within or beyond the pale of acceptable police practices, confers real power on verbal formulas that are absorbed into everyday language and define rogue behavior.

At the pathological end of this spectrum of personality types is a kind of brute that an American newspaper columnist once described as follows: "A common thread of inhumanity runs through policemen in every city across the land. The potential for brutality is always there. Some psychologists say that this is a char-acter trait that draws them to police work in the first place . . . In too many cops the beast still slumbers, ready to enjoy another bout of sadism."[116] While the general characterization of policemen as latent predators is a caricature, it is important to recognize that a partial dehumanization of the police is a recurrent theme in American life, one kept alive by constant reports of "police brutality." Limiting the public impact of these events is one aspect of a police executive's job. How police chiefs describe the behavior of officers involved in violent incidents is thus an essential form of public relations for a police department. At the same time, police culture must have its own way of talking about deviant cops so that they can be classified and managed, to the extent that is possible.

How deviant or violent officers are portrayed is a matter of perspective. For the informed (and perhaps sympathetic) outside observer, what police officers must endure on the job can make them look like the victims, rather than the perpetrators, of brutalization. There is, according to one academic author, "the policeman's hard-bitten pragmatism," which corrodes his long-abandoned idealism and, in all likelihood, some of his capacity for empathy. Overexposure to human depravity and the dregs of society produces a "cynical outlook on life" and a "misanthropic world-view."[117] This is the emotional toll exacted by police work, resulting in abnormally high rates of alcoholism, domestic violence, and divorce. Interestingly, these topics do not seem to preoccupy ordinary police officers, who are focused on the demands of their managers and the challenges of patrolling the streets. Similarly, the police unions, which serve as ever-vigilant guardians of their members' well-being, address the physical rather than the emotional dangers of the job. It is police chiefs who express concern about the emotional toll of policing, not the patrolmen or their union representatives, since exposing an emotional vulnerability would violate the masculine ethos of the workplace. What is more, police officers are unlikely to assess the consequences of their "hard-bitten pragmatism" in the same way that outsiders do. For the uninitiated, cynicism and misanthropy are a fateful prelude to a callousness that produces police brutality. For most hardened officers, pragmatism leavened with a dose of cynicism is a coping strategy that promotes emotional survival in a profession that involves regular exposure to emotionally damaged or physically dangerous people.

Euphemisms are used to characterize "violence-prone" or "problem" officers who employ "excessive force." There are "officers who have a low boiling point," "officers who respond to [volatile situations] with unseemly enthusiasm or lack of grace," and "officers who engage in demonstrably unconscionable conduct." There is "a 'hot dog' syndrome that includes overaggressive or inappropriate proactivity."[118] Policemen can be "hard-nosed."[119] A New York judge once deplored a "cowboy culture" that had established itself inside a narcotics unit of the NYPD.[120] Police administrators are extremely reluctant to call into question the character of their officers. The use of euphemizing language makes it easier for them to acknowledge the existence of "problem" officers without having to dismiss them or put them on trial. A "problem," after all, has a "solution." Proper training can reduce "excessive" force to an acceptable level. The hard-nosed cop can be taught to respond with greater sensitivity to some of those he encounters in the line of duty. Inappropriate "proactivity" can be dialed back to a less aggressive style of policing. These responses are part of an ameliorative process that does not allow the issue of police misbehavior to fester in the public sphere inhabited by politicians, reporters, and community activists, along with other interest groups that have opinions about police behavior.

The "Cop's Cop"

A rogue policeman can be an outlaw version of "a cop's cop," one who takes special pride in "prowess with weapons and tactics, sur-veillance, vehicle pursuit, or number of arrests, which can result in frequent confrontations with the public."[121] In these cases, an intense and sometimes unhinged devotion to action-oriented policing takes on a rogue character when an officer's zeal becomes a taste for aggressive and perhaps brutal policing for its own sake. But it can be difficult to distinguish where legitimate forcefulness ends and rogue behavior begins, since every police action has its own context and not all observers, inside or outside police ranks, see policing styles in the same way. As the police scholar Jerome Skolnick once pointed out, "'Police brutality' has no real meaning in court; it is a newspaper term, not a legal one."[122] If an aggressive policing style is unusually forceful but also effective, it may win accolades from both commanders and the rank and file.

Some specialized elite police units operate in an ethical gray zone where the distinction between effective policing and rogue policing can disappear. During the late 1960s, the militarization of the Los Angeles Police Department included, in addition to newly acquired helicopters and tanks, elite felony units that came to be called "'Death Squads' because of the extraordinary number of suspects they killed." As three police scholars noted in 1993: "Two cops can go berserk, but twenty cops embody a subculture of policing."[123] How many rogue police subcultures exist in American police departments is unknown. This book argues that uncovering anabolic steroid use inside departments would enable investigators to find some of them. A case in point was reported from England in 2014: "There is a thuggish element in West Yorkshire Police who believe that throwing their weight around impresses people. It doesn't. . . . Cells of self-styled police hard men such as the bull-necked, steroid pumping 'Leeds City Boys' based at Millgarth Police Station do little to help the police's cause."[124]

Aggressive policing, excessive violence, and rogue behavior are associated with the actions of street officers. Police commanders are charged with preventing these behaviors and disciplining officers who engage in them. Nevertheless, a rogue commander can appear in any police force that rewards forceful personalities who provide charismatic leadership. The paradigmatic case of this type of "cop's cop" in the NYPD was Michael Marino, a deputy chief called by a former NYPD chief of department "a cop to the marrow of his bones" and "a great leader."[125] One group of officers he commanded gave him the nickname "Elephant Balls," and others spoke of "that glow" he radiated in action on the street.[126] The *Village Voice* described him in 2013 as "blunt-spoken" and "barrel-chested," with "a bullish persona" and "a matching physique" that came from a heavy weightlifting regime, an obsession that, according to his first wife, had transformed both his mind and his body.[127]

By all accounts, Michael Marino was a very effective commander, despite his periodic conflicts with police higher-ups. When he was caught up in an NYPD steroid scandal in 2007, it was revealed that he had prescriptions for both a topical steroid cream and HGH. Both drugs, he and his lawyer claimed, served legitimate medical purposes. (The NYPD eventually found the growth hormone use in violation of departmental rules.)[128] Many police officers, of course, have claimed that their testosterone use served a valid medical purpose. We will never know whether the hypermasculine Marino was actually suffering from a testosterone deficiency. It is also possible that Marino's taste for hormones was a marker of his attachment to the bulked-up policing style that made him who he was.

While a police officer's use of male hormone drugs can express a desire to intimidate, there is no specific evidence to suggest that Michael Marino's hormone use affected his behavior on the job. No amount of male hormone could have produced his outsized personality or his high-octane police career, which lasted many years. Marino's rogue temperament as a commander expressed itself as an authoritarian streak that led him to kidnap and arrange the involuntary confinement of one of his officers—a kidnapping that can be followed word-by-word on a secret tape recording of the abduction, which occurred on October 31, 2009. When Marino learned that Officer Adrian Schoolcraft had reported misconduct in Marino's Brooklyn 81st Precinct to the NYPD's internal affairs unit, Marino led a team of cops to Schoolcraft's apartment, pulled him out of his bed, and forcibly removed him to the psychiatric emergency room at the Jamaica Hospital Medical Center, where he was confined against his will in a locked ward for six days. Marino's police team told the attending doctors a false story about allegedly bizarre behavior that had prompted them to have Schoolcraft hospitalized.

Schoolcraft's charges of police misconduct were eventually confirmed by a secret police inquiry. The official response to Marino's misconduct was to transfer him to Staten Island. Neither Mayor Michael Bloomberg nor Commissioner Raymond Kelly was willing to comment publicly on Marino's rogue conduct. Silence from the top of the command structure legitimizes the abuse of authority it refuses to address, thereby legitimating a rogue and lawless element that can become embedded in a charismatic police career.[129] In 2010, Schoolcraft filed a federal lawsuit asking for $50 million from the City of New York. He settled in 2015 for $600,000 from the city and $350,000 from the hospital. The city paid his lawyers $1.1 million for their legal fees.[130]

The case of Michael Marino shows that rogue conduct can be considered professionally acceptable behavior if the perpetrator has sufficient status and prestige. It may also be the case that maintaining command status can be enhanced by the occasional display of an authoritarian personality. This implicit official approval of rough tactics may explain the low-profile official response to Michael Marino. The decision makers inside the NYPD did not see him either as emotionally unstable or as psychologically unfit for command. The premise was rather that while the deputy chief may have gone too far, his sort of rogue style was compatible with effective policing even if such conduct could not stand up to public scrutiny.

The outlaw street-level cop, in stark contrast with those of higher rank, belongs to a rejected group known as "crazy" cops. "Make sure the other cops know if another cop is dangerous or 'crazy'" is one of the informal rules of police conduct. However, a catch-22 arises from the fact that the police code of silence rules out informing on another officer, almost regardless of his misconduct or lack of emotional equilibrium. As the authors of a study of "the dark side of policing" put it: "Police are caught in a double-bind if they become aware that one of their fellow members is unstable or presents a safety hazard. The secrecy dictum prohibits a line officer from informing police supervisors of another officer's instability; at the same time an officer has an obligation to watch out for his peers." Resolving this conundrum requires the police colleagues of an unstable officer to spread the word about his unreliability while at the same time enabling the problem officer to stay on the job.[131]

The dysfunctional consequences of this strategy are underscored by "most officers' remarkable accuracy in ranking the interpersonal skills and violence potential of their peers."[132] Before Justin Volpe of the NYPD—a probable steroid user—raped his prisoner Abner Louima with a broomstick in 1997, his union delegate "had been getting complaints from other cops that they didn't want to work with Volpe." They were "concerned that if they partnered with him they'd end up in trouble." The union delegate took their concerns to a sergeant, and from there it went nowhere.[133] The result was a catastrophe for the NYPD that might have been prevented. The outcome was also catastrophic for the union delegate, who went to prison as one of Volpe's accused confederates.

How police personnel talk about problem officers—the violent and the emotionally unstable—is constrained by both the blue wall of silence and the public relations concerns that preoccupy the leadership. This dysfunctional dynamic cannot, however, be acknowledged by police officials. For example, according to a commentary by Laurence Miller on the Police One website: "Any employee who decides to take the law into his own hands presents a dangerous situation for supervisors, coworkers, and the general community—and law enforcement professionals are trained to regard these suspects with extreme caution."[134] What we have seen, however, is that the "training" that alerts police officers to their unstable comrades is an informal procedure that operates independently of police supervisors, who may know little or nothing about the potentially dangerous eccentricities of the officers under their command.

Years of media coverage of police brutality and the resulting rogues' gallery of violent cops, such as the Los Angeles Police Department contingent that applied fifty-six baton blows to the prostrate Rodney King in 1991, has not resulted in a public discussion of anabolic steroids as a part of police culture. The idea of a steroid rage that could take possession of a police officer and literally drive him out of his mind might have provided news media and the general public with a dramatic and simplistic explanation of otherwise inexplicable acts of police violence. The popularity of roid rage as an easily comprehensible triggering mechanism of violent outbursts by weightlifters and wife beaters—and the cops who lift weights and divorce at twice the rate of the general population—is a part of steroid folklore that is seldom associated with cops.

THE STEROID SCANDAL THAT NEVER LEFT NEW JERSEY

The New Jersey police steroid scandal that broke in December 2010 gave unprecedented, though only temporary, exposure to the scope of the police steroid epidemic. The *Newark Star-Ledger* reports offered disturbing behind-the-scenes access to a secretive steroid subculture over which police commanders exercised little or no control.[135] Such lack of control can result either from a police chief's unwillingness to restrain steroid takers or from a defiance of command authority among members of the subculture. This drug culture is aided and abetted by fellow officers whose adherence to the "blue wall of silence" ethos outweighs any concern they may have about serving alongside men who are on mood-altering drugs and may be consorting with drug dealers.

More dramatically than the police steroid scandals in New York, Boston, Phoenix, and Albuquerque, the New Jersey revelations demonstrated that society's highly publicized campaign against steroid abuse in other social venues has not gained traction within police departments. It is important to understand the sources and consequences of this resistance to regulation. Time and again, evidence shows that the failure of a police department is only one part of a large-scale administrative dysfunction. In fact, the police steroid subculture signifies a disturbing failure of the entire administrative system that combines politics, law, and policing into the apparatus that makes it possible for civil society to function.

Close analysis of the New Jersey scandal, which involved taxpayer-supported, illegal drug use by hundreds of public safety officers and other state employees, revealed that state institutions had been infiltrated by attitudes and practices that cohered as a system lying outside the surveillance, control, and, possibly, concern of officials responsible for regulating unethical conduct. Where was Governor Chris Christie when steroid use was running rampant inside public agencies under his supervision? Why did news of a health insurance fraud costing the taxpayers millions come as a rude awakening to New Jersey legislators, who were finally roused to issue full-throated condemnations of what amounted to routine fraud? How could police and fire chiefs be unaware of steroid cultures operating right under their noses?

The particularly striking aspect of this affair was that an entire cast of state officials, vested with investigative or disciplinary authority, found reasons not to take action against lawbreaking police officers, even when a flood of incriminating and uncontested information had been made public. As one official alibi followed another, it was possible to detect a choreographed operation whose single purpose was to put the scandal to sleep. The organizing principle appeared to be a determination that whatever the "disturbing" findings about police behavior, there were to be an absolutely minimal number of direct interventions into the lives of hormone-taking policemen, who, in addition to their illicit drug use, had committed massive insurance fraud at taxpayer expense. This operation amounted to collusion among people in positions of authority, a complicity to grant anabolic steroids an exemption from regulations that might deter steroid taking among police officers. In a word, the authorities' official condemnations of steroid use by police were not (and have not been) translated into any sort of preventive action that will deter abuse.

An examination of what transpired in New Jersey amounts to a guided tour through the dimensions of police steroid subculture that are presented in greater detail throughout this book. Let us begin with New Jersey's statewide administrative system, which includes the state attorney general, state legislators, mayors, and local prosecutors.

The police steroid scandal presented Attorney General Paula Dow with a major public relations crisis that could not be ignored, and her initial response was assertive but measured in tone. Rather than outrage, she displayed an aversion to prejudging the accused officers. She called the newspaper's report "disturbing" and promised that state officials would carry out a collective examination of the affair. She would appoint a committee to examine physicians' illegal dispensing of drugs, the costs to taxpayers, and the possibility of random drug testing. "Everything will be on the table," she said. "We will be looking at several angles involving the improper use of steroids in law enforcement." The state's prosecutors endorsed the idea of a sweeping investigation of the newspaper's allegations. "The concerns raised by the attorney general are echoed by all 21 county prosecutors," said Salem County prosecutor John T. Lenahan, president of the County Prosecutors Association of New Jersey. "It's a matter that is going to be taken very seriously."[136] In an editorial that ran three days after the story broke, the *Star-Ledger* referred to "seething legislators [who] now promise to inject a strong dose of justice: legislative hearings, mandatory steroid testing, investigations and possible arrests."[137]

One state official who expressed outrage was state assemblyman John McKeon (D-Essex), who asked the attorney general to consider filing criminal charges against police officers who had used taxpayer funds to purchase medically unjustified drugs. "These people should go to jail," he declared. "They shouldn't be on the public dole for substances that are, for the most part, illegal and might constitute insurance fraud. When only one in every 100,000 people suffers from adult growth hormone deficiency, there is no way such a disproportionate number of law enforcement officers would require the use of growth hormone supplements."[138]

These early statements marked the apogee of official indignation in New Jersey. Within days of the published reports, public officials were softening their tone and distancing themselves from the evidence. Bergen County sheriff Leo McGuire cautioned that big muscles were not always a result of steroid use, and he refused to judge the accused: "There were no specific allegations made against any officers. And I, certainly as the person in charge of the sheriff's office, cannot go on a witch hunt just because of blanket allegations." A spokesman for the Passaic County Sheriff's Department chimed in: "It's a very expensive test [that is, the one for steroids]. And if the individual has a prescription from a doctor, then it would appear to be legitimate."[139]

In 2007, Joseph Colao, the physician who wrote most of the fraudulent prescriptions for steroids and HGH, dropped dead of a heart attack. Hudson County prosecutor Edward DeFazio argued that the opportunity to prosecute steroid-abusing cops died at the same moment: "There was never a criminal investigation or criminal charges because, although there appeared to be abuse, as far as criminality goes, there was nothing that could be proved beyond a reasonable doubt. Once Colao died it closed the door on any criminal prosecution." It quickly became clear that DeFazio had no interest in prosecuting cops, no matter how incriminating the evidence might be: "The patients would claim that Colao had told them it was a proper prescription. We'd have no way to prove that. Is it an abuse? No doubt. Is it disturbing? Clearly. But every time there's an abuse in the system, it doesn't result in an indictment."[140]

Prosecutors were not the only public officials determined not to go after Colao's gun-toting "patients." The mayor of Jersey City, Jerramiah Healy, declined repeated requests for an interview to talk about the scandal and instead issued a statement through a spokeswoman, who reported that the mayor would be "troubled" if police officers were found to be using steroids. "Should the investigations of any law enforcement agencies determine that to be true, the city will demand restitution or civil action to recover those costs," his representative said. "However, the mayor cannot presume that the mere existence of a prescription for steroids that was written by a medical doctor and filled by a licensed pharmacy for a city employee is not medically necessary or otherwise a fraud."[141]

As for the regulation of medical practitioners, over the preceding five years the New Jersey State Board of Medical Examiners had disciplined exactly three physicians for improperly prescribing anabolic steroids or HGH. In response to the New Jersey scandal, the DEA, which focuses primarily on criminal drug trafficking, declared its lack of interest in how these doctors had conducted themselves. "We're not turning a blind eye to it, but we don't tell doctors how to be doctors," said Special Agent Doug Collier, a spokesman for the DEA's Newark office. "It's not our mission to stand guard at every doctor's door to make sure they do their due diligence. That's where the Hippocratic Oath comes in."[142]

At the core of the refusals to investigate this kind of police conduct is the assertion that anabolic steroid and growth hormone use by police officers results from legitimate doctor-patient relationships. Yet the reported facts make clear that Joseph Colao was a fraudulent doctor prescribing hormones to an improbable number of allegedly hormone-deficient "patients" whose physical fitness was a prerequisite for their employment as policemen and firefighters. That prosecutors and other state officials were willing to give this sort of "doctor-patient" conduct the legal benefit of the doubt points either to a cynical tolerance for nonmedical muscling up or to a blind faith in doctors that is neither common nor warranted. In either case, effective scrutiny and prosecution of illicit police steroid use was rendered impossible by a phalanx of public officials whose declarations were orchestrated for the purpose of suppressing meaningful inquiry into the police steroid subculture.

We may also speculate that the New Jersey prosecutors' refusal to pursue charges against police officers resulted from an unwillingness to offend police officers, with whom they must cooperate to secure indictments and convictions. Relations between prosecutors and police are complicated by conflicts that can arise after a police officer makes an arrest and before a prosecutor decides whether to bring criminal charges against the accused. They may be concerned about each other's priorities when it comes to enforcing the law. Each party may feel misunderstood by the other. The conflicts are built into working relationships that must operate effectively for the justice system to function. In this context, and given the latitude of prosecutorial discretion, police can see prosecutors' pursuit of steroid-consuming officers as a form of ad hominem abuse and as a gratuitous damaging of their collaborative relationship.

The public official who could not afford to be seen as participating in an orchestrated opposition to the investigation of police steroid use was Attorney General Paula Dow. Seven months after the brief uproar caused by the *Star-Ledger*'s stories, she announced a set of reforms based on the findings of the study group that she had empaneled when the crisis first broke. "The Attorney General's reforms," the official press release said, "address three key issues: misuse of anabolic steroids and human growth hormones, improper prescription of these substances by physicians, and increased health care costs linked to such conduct." Indeed, the study group found that "the total cost to the state benefit plan for anabolic steroid and HGH prescriptions in 2010 was a little more than $11.2 million"—a huge expenditure for "treatments" that clearly involved a substantial amount of insurance fraud.[143] One can only imagine the public indignation that a comparable food stamp fraud would have touched off among public officials and the general public.

The press release from the Office of the Attorney General directly confronts the issue of medical misconduct:

> The report notes that the State's ability to prosecute law enforcement officers for improperly using steroids and billing them to public health plans was hindered in the past by the officers' ability to claim that they thought what they were doing was proper because doctors were prescribing the substances, pharmacies were dispensing them, and insurers were paying for them. The Study Group concludes that one of the most effective ways to improve the State's ability to investigate and prosecute abusers is to force them out of the doctor's office, through the recommended reforms, and relegate them to black market sources. Prosecutors then can avoid defenses centered on the fact that the substances were prescribed by a medical practitioner.[144]

But this candor was not followed by new regulations with teeth. First, anabolic steroids would be added to the list of substances tested for under the attorney general's Law Enforcement Drug Policy, but the testing of officers would be "at the discretion of the law enforcement executive." Second, officers testing positive would be required "to produce a letter from the prescribing physician confirming that the substance is being administered for a medically recognized purpose after appropriate diagnosis and that the use of the substance does not render the officer unfit for duty." Third, the attorney general encouraged "local law enforcement to require self-reporting of anabolic steroids or HGH pursuant to her authority to determine fitness for duty."[145]

Despite being presented as "reforms," all three recommendations accepted the status quo, which allowed police officers to pursue what the attorney general's press release referred to as "muscle enhancement and/or 'lifestyle improvement'" without fear of investigation or prosecution. The reform allowing for steroid testing "at the discretion of" police chiefs barely amounted to a legal fig leaf: police chiefs had long demonstrated their reluctance to confront officers who might be using steroids. This aspect of police culture will not be changed by official pronouncements; what is required is tangible political will to change the culture. One effective countermeasure would be to follow every accusation of excessive force with a mandatory investigation that would include both steroid testing and a background check on the officer's possible involvement in weightlifting or bodybuilding subcultures where steroids may be available. But no police department has a policy that calls for the testing of officers for anabolic steroid use that might be related to the use of excessive force.

Investigations of weightlifting behavior or automatic steroid testing after excessive force episodes would provoke fierce resistance from police unions, which stop at nothing to protect the privacy of their members. For this reason, a department's authorization to investigate would have to be written into employment contracts. Investigations of hypermuscularity achieved over a short period of time would also be controversial. So-called muscle profiling in Sweden provoked resentment in bodybuilding circles inside and outside that country.[146]

The reform requiring a physician's letter confirming the medical rationale for hormone therapy is also ineffectual. As the New Jersey scandal confirmed, many doctors are willing to make false diagnoses and then write fraudulent letters. While the attorney general made it clear that she was aware of "improper prescription of these substances by physicians," her study group chose to leave the authority of physicians intact, perhaps because they saw no viable alternative to doing so. The proposed check on physician misconduct was a recommendation that HGH prescriptions and most anabolic steroid prescriptions "be filled by mail order only by Medco, the State of New Jersey's prescription benefits manager to ensure complete fidelity to its new protocols instituted on March 1, 2011."[147] Careful monitoring should produce quantitative data about how many prescriptions are being written by individual doctors, but it would not confirm the legitimacy of diagnoses resulting in prescriptions for hormones.

The third and least effective recommendation encouraged officers to "self-report" their illicit hormone use. Hundreds of reports from around the United States offer no evidence that such behavior has ever occurred. Instead, the evidence suggests that there is no personal motive, peer pressure, or inducement that would cause a self-medicating steroid-abusing officer to turn himself in. There is nothing in police culture that would promote such behavior. That the attorney general and her study group could even have proposed such a recommendation suggests that they fundamentally misunderstand police culture or that they decided to make a disingenuous gesture whose purpose was to promote a reassuring and misleading image of how police officers behave.

The New Jersey scandal confronted state officials with the certainty that steroid use is a contributing factor in some cases of police use of excessive force. Many studies have shown that anabolic steroid use can increase aggressiveness, particularly the violent outbursts known as roid rage.[148] Reports from New Jersey found that six of Joseph Colao's "patients"—four police officers and two corrections officers—"were named in lawsuits alleging excessive force or civil rights violations around the time they received drugs from him or shortly afterward." Criminal violence was not limited to officers' performance on the job: "Others have been arrested, fired or suspended for off-duty infractions that include allegations of assault, domestic abuse, harassment and drug possession."[149] The Trenton police director, Joseph Santiago, reviewed the records of a group of hormone-taking officers and found what he called a significant number of excessive-force complaints. "When you look at these records," he said, "you start to see where there might be a correlation. Is it absolutely clear? No. Would a complaint have been there regardless of steroids? Those are issues that need to be addressed."[150]

The behavioral effects of psychoactive drugs are difficult to measure and predict. This uncertainty adds yet another complication to the current failure of police departments to enforce their own anti-steroid regulations.

The revelations from New Jersey brought public attention to protagonists and behavior patterns endemic in the police steroid subculture. What is more, we now know that the 248 police officers and firefighters caught up in the 2010 scandal were only a small fraction of those involved. On January 11, 2017, Mark Mueller, one of the two *Newark Star-Ledger* reporters who won a George Polk Award for breaking the scandal, told me that the 2010 story had omitted a crucial detail. Although the 248 first responders were getting their steroids and growth hormones from a single pharmacy, there were in fact dozens of pharmacies supplying steroids to cops in New Jersey. After the story broke, Mueller got a call from a CVS pharmacist in northern New Jersey who asked him, "Don't you realize that you have missed a huge number of cops by limiting your reporting to a single pharmacy?"

CHAPTER TWO

POLICE CHIEFS AND THE STEROID DILEMMA

Police officers, their unions, and sometimes their commanding officers have used medical rationales to justify hormone use by law enforcement personnel. These rationales have nothing to do with the functional argument that street cops and elite assault units need steroids in order to bulk up for violent confrontations with criminal suspects. In fact, the officers' medical rationales overlap with the stated therapeutic goals of other male "patients" who seek out hormone supplementation.

It is important to keep in mind that police officers' well-documented appetite for anabolic steroids constitutes a very small fraction of the overall demand for these drugs among adult and adolescent males. Police use of these drugs occurs within a sociomedical context that encourages androgenic drug use by recruiting candidates for testosterone-based "antiaging" therapy and by glamorizing the muscular male torso through pervasive television advertising and popular action films. The long and global career of Arnold Schwarzenegger has served as the most important promotional vehicle for anabolic steroid use in history. This propaganda on behalf of the hypermuscled torso has captivated an enormous male population that includes police officers.

This means that cops, too, participate in the medical nonsense and commercially motivated dishonesty that permeates the anti-aging business and the many clinics that sell hormones to athletes, policemen, and the general public. These enterprises have proliferated like mushrooms in many states, and especially in virtually unregulated environments like the state of Florida. Police officers' access to the drugs, therefore, like that of the general population, depends on both illicit and legal markets. The black market for steroids is pervasive within the gym culture that serves many thousands of bodybuilders, other serious weightlifters, and recreational lifters, all of whom are represented within police ranks. In fact, exposure to gym culture is the most accurate predictor of illicit use of anabolic steroids by law enforcement personnel.

The medical rationales invoked by police officers seeking male hormone therapy fall into two categories: pain relief and the restoration of normal bodily functions, or sexual rejuvenation. While some of these cases involve officers in routine clinical experiences, others are complicated by the expectations or eccentricities of hormone-seeking "patients."

Officer Tom Foley of Suffolk County, Long Island, New York, wanted to rehabilitate the wrist that he broke when he tackled a fleeing suspect in 1999. At that point, an inability to handle his gun properly threatened to put an end to his career. In 2002, he was legally prescribed a steroid on the chance it might restore flexibility to his wrist. Besides providing pain relief, the drug added a gratifying amount of muscle mass. Foley began using steroids solely to bulk up, transforming a therapeutic procedure into an enhancement project. His illicit steroids were supplied by a retired cop who became a steroid dealer. When Foley was arrested later that year, the charges were steroid possession and arranging a cocaine deal; he pleaded guilty to both. Physical rehabilitation had turned into a bodybuilding project and then into operating beyond the law he had once been charged with enforcing. Not for the first or last time, male hormone therapy turned into a crime story; what had begun in a clinical setting eventually migrated to the pharmacological underworld.

Another case that followed this script involved Tony Macik, a decorated police officer in South Bend, Indiana, who received a prescription for steroids following surgery for a work-related injury incurred in 2002. The drugs were used to ease his back pain, and when the prescription expired, he continued to use them illegally. In 2010 he was sentenced to a 300-day prison term for possessing a suspiciously large quantity of human growth hormone (HGH); his attorney claimed the drug was meant solely for Macik's personal use. Here, too, what seemed to be a routine case of rehabilitative hormone therapy somehow mutated into illegal involvement with synthetic hormones.[1]

A closer look at Macik's record of misbehaviors shows a disordered personality of which steroid use was only one aspect. Macik pleaded guilty in 2007 to a misdemeanor battery charge after getting into a fight with another man during a "domestic dispute" in July 2006. The charges included intimidation, battery, criminal trespass, criminal mischief, and disorderly conduct. The formal charge stated that Macik "lost his temper and knowingly touched in a rude, insolent or angry manner" another man, who suffered "physical pain" as a result of the assault. Macik was then arrested in 2009 for possession of a controlled substance as well as weapons violations (possession of a Taser and firearms).[2]

Police steroid use, as in these cases, is frequently associated with other forms of lawbreaking. In 2003, for example, an officer in Boca Raton, Florida, Anthony Forgione, a former NYPD officer, lied to his superiors about both his steroid use and his shoplifting.[3] In 2009 Forgione admitted to being a trafficker in steroids and HGH and to providing fraudulent prescriptions to his customers.[4] Forgione demonstrated an unusual degree of entrepreneurial ambition by establishing an antiaging clinic through which he supplied steroid prescriptions to boxers and professional wrestlers with the assistance of a doctor who was paid to write the prescriptions.[5] The cases of Foley, Macik, and Forgione suggest that steroid use by police officers is often a marker for a broader range of socially deviant behaviors that are incompatible with the requirements of law enforcement.

In 2010, for example, three FBI agents, one of whom was a body-builder, were arrested for concealing their use of anabolic steroids and HGH. According to the prosecutor, a part-time emergency room doctor had provided them with fake diagnoses, including pituitary dwarfism. Employing fabricated terms such as "hormone modulation therapy" and "adult onset growth hormone deficiency," this doctor had built a thriving practice that produced more than 5,000 anabolic steroid prescriptions between September 2005 and January 2010 for a variety of recognized growth hormone defi-ciencies.[6] Since the only patients affected by pituitary dwarfism are undersized children, the prescribing doctor was as careless as he was dishonest. In this case, federal law enforcement personnel were participating in unmistakable medical fraud.

Situated between the legitimate clinical treatment of a genu-ine testosterone deficiency and the kind of fraudulent "therapy" intended to camouflage the use of steroids for bodybuilding pur-poses is the ambiguous territory where ostensibly honest people resort to extralegal means to find relief. In 2003, for example, Troy Flohr was an exemplary officer in Medina County, Ohio, described as "a role model because of his dedication and commitment to excellence." His performance earned him the honor "deputy of the year." Following his service in the Marine Corps during the Gulf War, Flohr suffered from a chronic fatigue disorder; he found relief in illegal steroids that he imported from Yugoslavia. "I never wanted to look like Arnold [Schwarzenegger]," he said. "I was tired of being tired, I wanted to feel better." Flohr resigned from the police force and was sentenced to ninety days of house arrest for possession of illegal steroids.[7] This case appears to involve a person of good char-acter who did not exercise the necessary judgment that would have prompted him to seek out a legal prescription for a drug to treat his chronic fatigue.

Some steroid-seeking police officers, like many members of the adult male population, are looking for sexual enhancement. Large-scale interest among police officers in using synthetic male hormone drugs for this purpose was on display in December 2010 in *New Jersey COPS*, a publication read by officers throughout the state. The magazine featured two full-page ads that asked readers the following question: "Would you like to be able to lose fat, gain muscle, recover faster from physical activity, and possess the sex drive you had in your twenties?" The licensed chiropractor who owned the Signature Health and Wellness Center explained why he thought a magazine read by police officers was a logical advertising venue: "From what we heard, there were a lot of cops doing it, so we thought, 'Let's market it to that demographic.'"[8] The steroid-promoting advertisements stopped after the *Newark Star-Ledger* exposed the massive fraudulent prescription operation of Dr. Joseph Colao, which, as detailed in chapter 1, enabled hundreds of policemen and firefighters to buy millions of dollars of anabolic steroids and HGH at taxpayer expense.

Because very few law enforcement personnel qualify for male hormone therapy on strict clinical grounds, nearly all of those seeking and acquiring prescriptions are medicated in an ethical gray zone where physicians employing clear clinical criteria for treatment can be hard to find. The resulting ambiguity—and frequent medical dishonesty—about diagnosing "low testosterone" and prescribing anabolic steroids to "treat" it creates dilemmas for police executives, who find themselves having to monitor their officers' medical relationships. A 2008 newspaper story from Arizona, for example, notes that law enforcement agencies "are raising questions about what to do with officers who have obtained such drugs using methods described as 'quasi-legal,'" such as "officers [who have] ordered the muscle-building drugs online or have lied to doctors in order to get a prescription."[9] Indeed, police supervisors often confront the question of what constitutes a legitimate doctor-patient relationship, one that would justify issuing a prescription to the officer who wants it. Commenting on the new politics of medical steroids in Arizona, the steroid advocate Millard Baker argued that political pressure in response to cops-on-steroids reports coming out of Phoenix had forced the Arizona Peace Officer Standards and Training Board to adopt rules that "give the State authority to intervene in the doctor-patient relationships of police officers and define the acceptable medical treatment should an officer's physician prescribe anabolic steroids." Baker complained about biased enforcement that singled out officers for discipline while exempting the prescribing doctors from censure or punishment. "If the steroids are illegally prescribed, why aren't the physicians targeted? Why are the medical records of officers invaded instead? Why are local police departments given authority to dictate acceptable medical treatment for their officers?"[10]

This inequity aside, these officers, like countless others across the country, could have been indicted on felony charges of illegal possession of anabolic steroids. What we have seen, of course, is that police officers are virtually immune to prosecution when they violate the Anabolic Steroids Control Act of 1990. And medical alibis, legal or quasi-legal, have played a major role in shielding them from prosecution.

Despite the medically dubious (and often tawdry) nature of the male hormone therapy market, police chiefs and their official spokesmen, along with police unions, have defended police officers who are prescribed anabolic steroids. For example, when sheriff's deputies in Colorado were being investigated for steroid use in 2009, the Arapahoe County sheriff deflected potential criticism: "We have no indication that these [drugs] were for anything other than personal use."[11] The purpose of this statement was to assure the public that the officers were not drug dealers; the potential crime issue it did *not* address was the fact that officers committed a felony by simply possessing the drugs without a legal prescription.[12]

When fifteen Broward County (Florida) sheriff's deputies were relieved of duty during a steroid inquiry in 2009, an agency spokesman defended the legality of their steroid use: "The policy indicates that if there is a legitimate doctor-patient relationship, and they were prescribed in that situation, then they would be allowed." To this he added an inaccurate endorsement of steroid use: "There are a lot of legitimate therapies and medical reasons for a doctor to prescribe anabolic steroids, and we can't very well tell our deputies they aren't entitled to the same treatment as anyone else."[13] In fact, there are only a few medically legitimate reasons to prescribe anabolic steroids to adult males, and relatively young and physically fit policemen are less likely to need these therapies than the general population. For this reason, police department rhetoric about equal entitlement to androgenic drugs is either intentionally or unintentionally misleading.

At the same time, another police chief in southern Florida was making headlines by running medical interference for officers charged with using steroids. Chief Larry Massey of Plantation, Florida, announced his findings thus: "[I] concluded the persons involved were under medical care. That is all there is." He exonerated the officers because he believed that they had valid prescriptions and that steroids were "often dispensed for legitimate reasons." These officers, he said, rather than conducting dubious medical business online, had "put forth an effort to appear in person at an actual brick and mortar medical facility, to establish a doctor/patient relationship," meaning "nothing irregular" had occurred.[14] The chief seemed to be aware of less orthodox medical arrangements than visiting a doctor's office to get a diagnosis and a prescription, which is the usual procedure for most patients.

One of the exonerated officers was a bodybuilder, Joseph Alu, whose attorney, Scott Rothstein, claimed Alu was undergoing steroid therapy for injuries suffered in 1995 when, as a police officer, he entered a burning house to save its inhabitants. Both exonerated officers resigned from the force to work as bodyguards for Rothstein, who in 2010 was sentenced to fifty years in federal prison for having operated the largest Ponzi scheme in Florida history.[15] A year later, Alu applied for a job at the Fort Lauderdale Police Department.[16]

Police unions, too, have routinely defended steroid use that appears to meet medical criteria, despite abundant reports of medical fraud from many venues. In the wake of a 2005 steroid scandal at the police department in West Palm Beach, Florida, the president of the Palm Beach County Police Benevolent Association, Ernie George, defended the motives of thirteen officers whose steroid use led to charges of "engaging in conduct unbecoming an officer, failing to notify a commander of their use of controlled substances and failing to establish a proper doctor-patient relationship." The accused officers, he said, assumed that they were receiving lawful treatments for genuine medical problems. The union president then offered a different, and almost plaintive, argument that echoed the many print and television advertisements that hold out hope for more vigorous and virile living through hormone replacement therapy: "Everyone wants to push back aging," he said. "Everyone wants to feel 20 years old."[17]

Five years later, the president of a senior police officers' union in Hoboken, New Jersey, commented: "I'm not condoning use of steroids, but I think there are legal drugs out there that help people maintain their youthful vigilance." Sergeant Ed Drishti "said he could see why older police officers would want to return to how they felt in their younger years, especially cops who work in prisons and deal with criminals who 'have all the time in the world to work out.'" "I think," Drishti said, "the older they get, they're just trying to offset what they've lost."[18] While not expressing approval of illegal drug use, this union official clearly subscribes to the pharmacological folk wisdom about the aging male that has driven the expanding hormone replacement industry in the United States. For the leader of a senior police union, the primary appeal of steroids was their reputed antiaging role. The advantage of invoking this quasi-medical justification for male hormone therapy is that it offers a motive other than mere bodybuilding or creating an intimidating appearance to explain police officers' interest in the drugs.

A union's argument of last resort is that the officers who get steroids from antiaging clinics have been manipulated. "The officers thought they were doing the right thing, " Ernie George said in 2005. "The company was doing something fraudulent, not the officers."[19] "Officers thought they were getting medical treatment," George said. "They submitted blood tests and found out later the doctor giving the prescription wasn't legitimately a doctor."[20] An NYPD police union official offered the same argument in 2007 when some of his members were caught using steroids provided by the notorious Lowen's Pharmacy in Brooklyn, New York, via the prescription pad of Dr. Richard Lucente. "These guys relied on a doctor's advice," the union man said. "He did tests, blood work. What they hell do you expect them to know about it? They're just cops."[21] In 2010, Lucente was sentenced to five years' probation for his role in a drug ring that illegally supplied steroids and HGH to hundreds of patients, including police officers and bodybuilders. One of his patients was a bodybuilder who had undergone a heart transplant and later died following gallbladder surgery. The New York State Board for Professional Medical Conduct ruled that the steroids and growth hormone provided by Lucente probably contributed to his death.[22] In their zeal to defend almost any conduct by their members, police unions tend to ignore the medical incompetence that appears repeatedly in reports about the conduct of steroid doctors.

The loss of privacy that can result from contesting a steroid suspension became evident in 2010 when seven Jersey City, New Jersey, officers filed suit against the city and Chief Thomas J. Comey. In 2008, an NYPD captain had informed Comey that fifty Jersey City officers were among those obtaining illicit steroids from Lowen's Pharmacy in Brooklyn. The Jersey City officers under suspicion were required to disclose the medications they had taken in the last sixty days and to provide urine samples, which would be tested for steroids. The legal record of their lawsuit contains the following passage:

> Plaintiffs allege that they suffered from various medical conditions that required them to seek medical treatment. (Kramer Am. Compl.) For example, Kramer alleges that a licensed medical professional prescribed him hormone replacement drugs to treat erectile dysfunction and hypogonadism. McGovern alleges that he was diagnosed and treated for hypogonadism, erectile dysfunction, impotence, and fatigue and also was prescribed hormone replacements. Fay alleges he was diagnosed and

treated for hypogonadism, erectile dysfunction, arthralgia, and fatigue and was similarly prescribed hormone replacements. The plaintiffs in the *Bado* action allege identical allegations as to their diagnoses and medical prescriptions.[23]

The publication of such diagnoses of intimate medical issues stands in sharp contrast with the secrecy about police steroid use and its motivations that prevails in police departments across the country.

In fact, the release of these "private" medical details was triggered by the lawsuit brought by the officers against their commander. At that point they encountered a court that flatly stated: "Police officers generally have a diminished expectation of privacy compared to other government employees." The court cited a 1987 ruling that "police officers had little privacy interest in their medical information because they were being selected for highly stressful and dangerous positions." The court also ruled that "Chief Comey had reasonable suspicion to mandate drug testing of the police officers. The reasonable suspicion standard is not difficult to meet, and is a lesser standard of proof than probable cause." In 2014 a state appeals court ruling affirmed this decision.[24] While the court's assessment of the reasonable suspicion standard suggests that police chiefs should be able to use it frequently, there is no evidence to suggest that they actually put it to use.

The courts' affirmation of a police chief's right to order the testing and disciplining of suspected steroid users on the force should have marked a turning point in the ongoing contest between those police administrators who want to eliminate steroid use and the rank-and-file officers who do not. Up to that point, police officials had tended not to pursue strict enforcement of antisteroid rules (and federal law) because they did not know how to handle the medical claims presented by officers. But the judge in the Jersey City case refused to allow medical claims about "low testosterone" to dictate the outcome of the case. His decision called into question the reliability of doctors who claim to have diagnosed police clients and found them to be testosterone deficient.[25]

POLICE CHIEFS' LENIENCY TOWARD STEROID USE

The predominant attitude of police commanders toward subordinates who have been caught using or selling steroids has been leniency or, in some cases, command negligence amounting to dereliction of duty. At the negligent end of the spectrum is Greg Kroeplin, the former police chief of Canby, Oregon, who resigned from his position in 2009 after an FBI investigation and independent city inquiry found he had failed to investigate steroid use by an officer who, while in uniform, had ridden his police motorcycle to a nearby town for the purpose of making an illegal steroid purchase. With the chief's knowledge and complicity, the officer bought drugs while on duty and informed his drug dealers about ongoing police investigations into drug dealing. The chief and other police supervisors had failed to investigate reports of the officer's steroid use, and they concealed what they knew about it. The officer was eventually sent to prison.[26] The chief received a severance payment and did not face prosecution.

In summary, action against an officer who was both a steroid user and an informant for drug dealers required intervention by a federal agency. It should be noted that this rogue chief, who escaped unpunished, acted with the knowledge of other senior officers, who likewise did nothing to prevent the treacherous officer's illegal drug use. The federal investigation eventually extended to steroid use in the Greater Portland area. In May 2010, the FBI described the investigation as follows: "The public safety employees identified by [the steroid dealer] included law enforcement officers, corrections officers, fire and rescue personnel and university public safety officers. Several spin-off FBI public corruption investigations were initiated as a result of these allegations and are ongoing."[27] All too evident here is the wide range of action-oriented male first-responders accused of using steroids.

The question why police chiefs and commissioners have been unwilling or unable to eliminate steroid use in their departments points to the multi-institutional environment in which police executives operate. Shielding police officers from the legal consequences of steroid possession requires both a shared attitude toward police immunity from prosecution and cooperation among the actors who have jurisdiction when legal judgments are made about these officers. Police executives, district attorneys, civil service boards, departmental internal affairs units, city attorneys, federal agencies, and doctors—all of them can and do play roles in these cases.

Police chiefs have employed a variety of rationales to justify not taking action when they suspect or know about steroid use by their subordinates. One such rationale is the claim that going after steroid use is simply impractical. In 2014, investigators in the state of Washington learned that a King's County sheriff's deputy had been using and selling steroids to others both inside and outside his department. In response, "the sheriff told news outlets he suspected members of his SWAT team bought steroids, but he would not try to prove it because he needed the 20-man team intact."[28] Indeed, the elevated fitness standards required for admission to elite units such as SWAT teams can drive steroid use among those seeking to join them.

In 2010, Chief Jeff Hadley allowed an eleven-year veteran of the Kalamazoo Department of Public Safety to resign rather than be fired after he was accused of obtaining steroids and HGH without a prescription. Hadley found himself caught between his obligation to condemn police misconduct and his personal sympathy for the officer. While deploring the officer's "betrayal of public trust," he also offered some exonerating arguments. He claimed the steroid use had not affected the officer's conduct on the job, since there were no "[citizen] complaints relative to Sgt. Milton during that time frame that would cause us to believe that his use of any substance affected his behaviors at work." "He's a good guy," the chief continued. "He means well. I think he has some personal issues he needs to deal with and I don't believe Public Safety was the place for him right now."[29]

Who is to say this chief did not handle the case correctly as he tried to balance a presumed hazard to public safety against the officer's best interests as a troubled person? After all, Sergeant Milton had received commendations and had stayed out of serious trouble. What Hadley's presentation did not address, however, was the fact that Milton had no prescriptions for the drugs. When police officers get their steroids from drug dealers, they become potential targets for blackmail and thus may leak confidential information about drug enforcement operations to their suppliers. The chief redacted the information at his disposal in order to present the officer and the department in the best possible light. Once again a steroid-using officer was granted leniency by the law enforcement agency that employed him.

Versions of the leniency scenario have played out in many departments. In 2011, Chief Ralph Dawe of Scottsboro, Alabama, explained that he could not terminate four officers who confirmed that they were using steroids because he had no evidence other than their admissions. He and the assistant district attorneys he consulted decided they did not have a prosecutable case.[30] In 2007, Commissioner Ray Kelly of the NYPD presided over the Lowen's Pharmacy scandal, which involved six NYPD officers among many other customers buying illegal steroids. By December 2007, the Lowen's affair had produced twenty-two indictments and nine convictions. None of the NYPD officers faced criminal charges. Kelly put them on modified duty and emphasized that the cops had bought the drugs for personal use.[31] Such leniency did not, however, exempt the commissioner from criticism from the police union that represents patrol officers. The president of the Patrolmen's Benevolent Association, Patrick Lynch, accused Kelly of favoritism because deputy chief Michael Marino's prescription for a testosterone cream and deputy chief Jack Trabitz's testosterone prescription had incurred no penalty at all. Both men were imposing physical specimens who looked like athletes. "Right now," Lynch said, "six police officers and a supervisor are accused of the same thing—yet the police officers are modified and the supervisor is not."[32] (In fact, twenty-nine cops were known to have received prescriptions for hypogonadism, known in the vernacular as "low testosterone.") The dynamic of the situation promoted leniency for everyone involved—it was just that deputy chiefs did even better than the patrolmen. While ordinary citizens faced prosecution, police officers were exempt, for reasons that were not subjected to skeptical public examination outside the pages of the *Village Voice*.[33]

The 2007 NYPD case was only one of many in which a police commander decided not to discipline steroid-consuming officers who appeared to be following valid medical guidelines. In 2005, the Broward County Sheriff's Office found that two deputies on the SWAT team had turned up on a list of customers of a drug company raided by federal agents searching for mislabeled anabolic steroids and human growth hormones. The important legal point was that these drugs were being sold without valid prescriptions. But after federal investigators gave the names of eight deputies to the sheriff's office, it declined to pursue the cases, claiming: "If a deputy is legally prescribed a prescription drug, they're not required to notify their supervisor."

This justification for the deputies' steroid use is suspect on several counts. First, the federal agents contested the validity of the prescriptions. Second, corrupt doctors have issued many legally "valid" prescriptions to police officers and others on the basis of invented diagnoses of "low testosterone." Third, state health officials had suspended the license of PowerMedica, the Deerfield Beach–based pharmacy that provided the prescriptions to the deputies, in June 2005. Despite the evidence of improprieties, the sheriff's office simply exonerated its personnel, citing a lack of wrongdoing: "We didn't find any violations of our policies and procedures."[34]

Several months later, in nearby Delray Beach, Florida, Chief Larry Schroeder found himself dealing with officers' steroid purchases from PowerMedica. "It was found that although PowerMedica was operating illegally, they portrayed themselves as a totally legitimate and legal corporation," he wrote in an internal affairs report. Federal investigators found that the pharmacy had been "selling human growth hormones and steroids on its Web site without the patient submitting blood work or visiting with a doctor."[35]

Schroeder professed incomprehension that police officers would be obtaining drugs from a shopping-mall clinic that was, as a local newspaper put it, "operating in a murky area of the law."[36] "I find this extremely difficult to understand and even more difficult to accept that members of this department would not have those same concerns," he said.[37] Apparently, the chief was in over his head, unaware of the tawdry network of antiaging clinics that litter South Florida and can legally be managed by felons. In fact, police chiefs all over the United States have found themselves dealing with the question of whether the purported doctor-patient relationships between their officers and doctors of uncertain integrity are legitimate enough to justify the dispensing of male hormone drugs.

Many officers across the country do not share Chief Schroeder's concerns. In West Palm Beach, for example, the police chief dealt with thirteen police officers who were facing suspension for buying steroids. They believed that their prescriptions were valid because they had "doctor-patient relationships." The department's internal investigators said the relationships were not legitimate, but the police union's attorney begged to differ: "All a doctor needs to prescribe medication is a medical history and lab work," a rationale that was good enough for countless clients of the antiaging industry. As a story in a local newspaper put it: "When questioned by skeptical investigators, the officers expressed no qualms about buying anabolic steroids not covered by their medical insurance, as well as syringes and needles, and injecting themselves." The irony of this story is that the founder of PowerMedica had the temerity to turn the tables on law enforcement regarding the legitimacy of his operation. Daniel Dailey claimed that his clients included fifty to sixty law enforcement officers and firefighters from across the country. "Do you think," he asked indignantly, "I would invite police to do business with us if we thought we were doing anything wrong?"[38]

Chief Schroeder's response to his officers' behavior was atypical in his skepticism and disapproval of their medicalized lifestyle. In fact, police chiefs across the country have had to deal with the credibility of prescriptions for testosterone and other anabolic steroids dispensed to officers by physicians. They have heard a wide variety of medical and pseudomedical claims about the need to use these drugs. They have sometimes argued that officers who obtained prescriptions were misled into believing that their prescriptions were legitimate. Police unions have invariably defended drug-seeking officers on the grounds of medical privacy. Officers who tested positive have argued that they were the unwitting victims either of "supplements" contaminated with anabolic steroids or of supplements that metabolized into banned substances. The collective effect of these claims and contested judgments has been to shield officers from the possible legal consequences of their use of androgenic drugs.

Because district attorneys are reluctant to prosecute police officers for almost any reason, their rationales for not pursuing steroid charges against them deserve close scrutiny. A case in point is the outcome of an investigation of a dozen active and former police officers in Trenton, New Jersey, who in 2006 ordered large amounts of anabolic steroids and HGH over the Internet. The prescriptions came from a dentist who later pleaded guilty to unlawful distribution of drugs. State prosecutors estimated that the officers' drug purchases had cost state taxpayers $300,000. The director of the New Jersey Division of Pensions and Benefits called this scheme "a clear-cut case of insurance fraud" and expected the officers to be prosecuted. But neither the Mercer County prosecutor nor the state attorney general would issue indictments, the latter on the grounds that there was no way to prove the officers had intended to break the law. "I am commenting on the difficulty we would have had in proving the requisite mental state," a spokesman claimed. "The mental element can be the hardest part of a case to prove."[39]

But the Trenton police director, Joseph Santiago, was not interested in shielding these men from the law. Concerned about the potential for steroid-related aggression, he examined the officers' records and found a "significant" number of citizens' complaints about the use of excessive force. In one case, the City of Trenton paid $500,000 to a fifty-three-year-old man who had been beaten in 2004 by one of the officers implicated in the steroid scheme. In September 2008, Santiago took away the officers' weapons and assigned them to desk duty. Following his resignation because of a city residency requirement, the officers were reinstated.[40] Once again it became clear that most state officials in New Jersey were not sufficiently concerned about steroid use by officers to pursue legal action against them. The tacit but unmistakable attitude of the legal apparatus was that retaining the services of officers in whose training the state had invested was more important than purging the force of potentially hazardous drugs.

The reinstatement in 2010 of a Lafayette, Louisiana, officer who had been fired for testing positive for steroids in a random drug test followed this pattern. Corporal Trampus Gaspard was fired in 2006 along with Corporal Keith Richard after testing positive for the anabolic steroid stanozolol. Both blamed dietary supplements for the result. (In addition, Richard was criminally charged with the illegal possession of steroids and a stolen firearm.) The officers appealed their terminations to the local civil service board, which rules on disputes between police departments and officers. A forensic toxicologist testified that their claims were highly improbable. Yet a board member explained that while the board had endorsed the firing of Richard, it ruled against the firing of Gaspard because the ordering of the test did not meet the "reasonable suspicion" standard outlined in the city's *Policy and Procedure Manual*.[41] In this case, the reasonable probability that an officer had used illicit steroids was judged to be less important than exempting the officer from the consequences of an improper procedure. The drug testing in Lafayette had consequences only because the civil service board upheld Richard's firing.

In the Trenton case, prosecuting the apparent use of steroids was deemed less significant than bowing to the evidentiary problem caused by the purported need to be certain about the "mental state" of the accused. One might ask why the district attorney's office chose to focus on the need to establish the "requisite mental state" in order to indict officers whose behavior, including illicitly ordering large quantities of drugs and possibly committing insurance fraud, suggested that their "mental state" would have included an awareness of wrongdoing. The sheer quantities of drugs suggested these men were not simply interested in the standard medical treatment for "low testosterone," but also wanted to bulk up in order to look buff and intimidating on the street. Prosecutorial discretion in both the Arizona and Trenton cases gave the accused officers the benefit of the doubt, the result being that steroid-using officers were allowed to continue to work as policemen. The district attorney's office in Trenton and the civil review board in Arizona followed the tacit but clear consensus among authorities that cops who use steroids will not face prosecution—or often, indeed, any serious consequences.

The Civil Service Board in Phoenix issued a similar finding in 2010 when it returned to the ranks an officer who had tested positive for steroids in a random drug test. Following his termination by the police department, he appealed to the board, which unanimously accepted his attorney's argument that "her client tested just above the allowable threshold for officers because he had been taking body-building supplements that he had no idea metabolized into steroids when processed in the body."[42] The city attorney argued that only a valid prescription could adequately explain a positive test result. Several months later, the board overturned another positive steroid test. In this case, a Phoenix Police Department officer who was a former professional football player, Cedric Tillman, had tested "off the charts" for the anabolic steroid nandrolone. The officer claimed that a "supplement" he was taking had metabolized unexpectedly into an anabolic steroid, and once again the board exonerated him.[43] In both cases, the board accepted a metabolizing-supplement argument made by nonscientists, speculation that favored the officer over the city attorney, the police chief's zero-tolerance policy, and the department that wanted to fire him. Once again an extradepartmental body had undermined a random testing program. This is one more reason to be skeptical when departments announce they have instituted random drug testing for anabolic steroids.

Most penalties applied in police steroid cases confirm that these matters are not taken very seriously by those who assess punishments. For example, Cedric Tillman was ordered to serve a thirty-day suspension. In 2006, two Palm Beach, Florida, deputies were handed one-day suspensions for concealing their steroid use from their supervisors.[44] In 2011, two Scottsboro, Alabama, officers were given suspensions of three and four days for unauthorized use of testosterone.[45] In 2010, the first officer to test positive under the NYPD's random testing program for steroids was allowed to continue working; but he was required to work an additional two years before collecting his pension.[46] A police department again demonstrated that its random drug testing had only minor consequences for those testing positive for steroids.

An alternative to dismissal or prison for police officers caught having or using steroids is to be put on probation. In 2011, for example, a police officer in Michigan found in possession of steroids was put on probation for one year; upon successful completion of the probationary period, his conviction was to be stricken from his criminal record. Like many officers, this one had found his steroid connection at a local gym.[47] Two years earlier, a former state trooper in Wyoming who faced a possible sentence of five years in prison—the sort of draconian sentence that is never imposed on police officers—for possession of steroids had been given two years of supervised probation.[48]

In 2010, Brady Valentine, who had once been honored as Tennessee narcotics officer of the year, was sentenced to three years of probation for failing to report a steroid delivery by a known drug dealer. Valentine faced up to three years in federal prison, but the judge and prosecutors made sure that did not happen. "This is an especially tragic case because Mr. Valentine was a very promising officer," said US District judge Samuel Mays. "He was a model narcotics officer, but then he himself was engaging in steroid use. This was an aberration for Mr. Valentine." The prosecutors agreed to dismiss an eight-count indictment charging the officer with buying and selling illegal steroids. His attorney offered a version of the functional argument to account for his client's interest in steroids.

Officer Valentine had begun using steroids, his attorney said, after being "kicked around in the field a little," and he decided "to change that."[49]

Two similar cases were adjudicated in 2010. A former New York State corrections officer who admitted to selling steroids was spared a prison term and sentenced to five years' probation instead.[50] A former Immigration and Customs Enforcement special agent in Washington State who was caught importing steroids from China was spared prison time and sentenced to serve a two-year term of probation. In this case, mentioned briefly in chapter 1, the defendant and the US Attorney for the Eastern District of Washington agreed that his career as a law enforcement officer was over. In his statement to the court, former special agent Sean Ganley claimed that the drug culture was endemic in his workplace: "Steroid use was very common within my own police department, as well as neighboring agencies, so I again mistakenly felt it was 'no big deal' to use them. I was obviously sorely mistaken."[51] In 2014 a twenty-year veteran of the Jefferson County sheriff's office in Colorado pleaded guilty to steroid use and was sentenced to fifteen months of probation. Prosecutors converted a felony drug charge into a misdemeanor, and the deputy was allowed to resign rather than be brought to trial.[52]

POLICE HEROES WHO TEST POSITIVE

In the summer of 2009, a Paul Bunyanesque police officer named Chris Weaver, fitted out with a shoulder harness, pulled a 15,000-pound ambulance across a parking lot in Clinton Township, New Jersey, in front of an admiring crowd. The popular policeman-athlete was training for the USA Powerlifting Deadlift Nationals in Miami sponsored by USA Powerlifting, formerly called the American Drug Free Powerlifting Association, which tests all competitors for performance-enhancing drugs.

Police colleagues admired Weaver's enormous strength as well as his integrity. Fellow officers accompanied him to a local gym, where they helped him do his workouts. "Anyone could lift heavy weights on steroids," one of them said. "The fact that he does it all natural is more impressive." What is more, his size did not affect his temperament. "His demeanor is more laid back and easy-going," his colleague added. "When you look at him, he's a big guy, but he doesn't have that aggressive attitude to go with it." At the same time, Weaver acknowledged that his muscularity could be useful on the job, since "it helps to be big; you have a better presence."[53] Weaver emphasized that he was proud of his drug-free status: "It proves that with some hard work . . . you can accomplish things without drug use," he said.[54]

Almost three years later, the inspiring story of the gentle giant imploded when Weaver was arrested and charged with possession of an anabolic steroid without a prescription, following a two-month investigation into his off-duty conduct. "It is a sad and difficult task when we investigate law enforcement officers," the local prosecutor commented, "but it is for the greater good."[55]

It is striking that Weaver is one of very few out of the many confirmed steroid-using officers who have been arrested and indicted for illegal steroid possession alone. One wonders whether Weaver's local celebrity, along with his false claims of being drug-free, played a role in driving the investigation that ensnared him. Local folk heroes should not betray their loyal fans. It is also worth noting that the investigation into Weaver's conduct came in the wake of the sensational revelations in December 2010 about the 248 New Jersey police and firefighters who had obtained steroids and HGH at taxpayer expense from a single corrupt doctor. Not one of those first responders was arrested or charged, despite the political uproar that resulted from the publicity around the case.

Dishonoring the steroid-using officer who has distinguished himself in the line of duty is a painful and disorienting procedure. What does it mean if an exemplary police officer later finds himself disgraced by the revelation that he used a muscle-building drug? Do violations of the drug provisions of a departmental code of conduct really warrant personal disgrace and expulsion from the police community? Even most elite athletes who are excluded from competition for a period of time after testing positive for performance-enhancing drugs are allowed to return to competition as officially rehabilitated people. Difficult questions of this kind arise because our society has never relinquished the idea that "drugs" are a sign of degeneracy.

Some of the police heroes who have used or tested positive for steroids have already been mentioned. Joseph Alu was celebrated as a hero in 1995 after running into a burning house to save people.[56] ⋅ In 2007, he was accused of using steroids, and after he tested positive, he resigned from the Miami force.[57] In 1999, Thomas Foley was named Suffolk County cop of the month for having run into a burning building to rescue an unconscious civilian.[58] In 2002, he was one of four from the New York area to be charged with the sale and use of anabolic steroids and cocaine.[59] Perhaps not coincidentally, both Alu and Foley were weightlifters and fitness buffs.

In 2008, three Nashville, Tennessee, police officers—Danny Cage, Stephen Reece, and Mike Evans—were stripped of their badges while being investigated for steroid use. None had previously been disciplined for a serious offense. All three had received commendations for life-saving actions. Evans participated in a successful hostage rescue. Reece saved a four-year-old boy from two armed kidnappers by charging the criminal who was holding the boy. Cage had received "life-saving" awards from the department.[60]

In 1995, Grant Chambliss, a sergeant in the Mobile County (Alabama) Sheriff's Department, was commended for chasing down a bank robber. He was awarded an official commendation in 2002 and the combat cross for heroism for engaging in personal combat with an armed adversary in 2003.[61] In 2004, he was put on paid administrative leave related to a federal investigation into shipments of anabolic steroids that included a package addressed to him.

The treatment of police heroes who become tainted by association with anabolic steroids raises difficult questions about the ease with which earned merit and special honors can be canceled out by unauthorized drug use of any kind. And it is fair to ask whether the cases recounted above demonstrate a lack of official gratitude for services rendered. This is rough justice when one recalls that most steroid-possession cases involving police officers are resolved by resignations, short suspensions from duty, or in-house procedures that impose no penalty at all. At the same time, it is not surprising that the thousands of US police departments do not treat their steroid cases consistently apart from offering the standard antisteroid rhetoric.

A stricter perspective is that succumbing to the temptation of using drugs is an automatic disqualification for membership in a paramilitary community such as a police force. From this standpoint, the wrong sort of drug use indicates a character flaw that merits social disgrace regardless of one's professional accomplishments, because it undermines the morale of the officers who swear an oath to a code of conduct.

How widespread in police ranks is instinctive distrust of any police officer who uses an illicit drug? And why does this strict standard not apply to the alcohol abuse, which is, by all accounts, the greatest drug threat to police work? When they are asked to explain official zero-tolerance policies on steroid use, police chiefs can be curiously imprecise in their responses. For example, when Chief Rod Knecht of Edmonton, Alberta, found that some of his officers were on steroids, he explained his disapproval by saying that "using steroids is cheating."[62]

Despite official rhetoric of this kind, police chiefs across the country have implicitly rejected the "disgrace and dishonor" response to steroid use in the ranks by showing leniency toward offenders, many of whom could in theory be indicted on a felony charge of possessing anabolic steroids without a prescription.

Similarly, the official line in the US military and elsewhere is that confirmed drug use means dishonor. "Four Australian special forces soldiers have been sent home in disgrace after being caught abusing steroids," the *Sydney Morning Herald* reported on June 8, 2010. The rationale offered by a Defence Department spokesman went as follows: "Australian Defence Force members testing positive to prohibited substances are normally discharged as the use of prohibited substances is not compatible with an effective and efficient defence force."[63] Such categorical statements about steroid use are open to challenge. These soldiers might have responded with the functional argument that steroid use promotes their chances of survival in an intensely hostile environment such as the mountains of Afghanistan.

FUNCTIONAL RATIONALES FOR STEROID USE

The functional argument for anabolic steroid use by police officers claims that the use of these drugs has a practical and therefore legitimate role to play in police work. From this perspective, steroid use is a strategy for dealing with the special challenges and hazards of the physically demanding situations that police officers often face. This type of steroid use was reported in Britain as early as 1998: "Police officers are using body-building drugs to give themselves added bulk and strength to deal with violent criminals. Many officers around the country have turned to steroids as a way of minimizing their chances of being hurt or humiliated."[64]

American police officers rarely talk on the record about the functional doping that some believe promotes their safety on the streets. Those who do speak out do so anonymously or defend their drug use after they have been caught. One anonymous officer stated in 2005 that steroids made him a better policeman: "What law enforcement needs is a little testosterone," he said. "*Every* cop should do a cycle a year." The commonly heard justification for drug use invokes physical confrontations with violent suspects whose strength can seem superhuman as a result of bodybuilding or drug use. A police officer in Iowa reported: "We've had crack and meth users fight two to four officers. We recently had a crack user break his leg and disarm one police officer, while he was fighting two other cops." This officer, a former steroid user, said he was tempted to start using them again so that he could deal with drug-crazed adversaries more effectively.[65] Officers who feel they are aging out of their former physical fitness may also feel they can compensate by bulking up. An unidentified policeman in Pennsylvania commented in 2007 that, looking back at the age of thirty-three on physical confrontations that had not gone well, "I was not nearly as tough and strong as I once was. . . . I kept thinking I am only getting older, and the criminals will always be young. I was looking for an edge." He was eventually caught, forced to resign, and served twenty-three days in jail.[66]

Policemen who are exposed as steroid users will sometimes offer rationales for using what they believe are performance-enhancing substances. In a case discussed earlier in this chapter, the Phoenix Police Department fired an officer in 2010 who had tested positive for an anabolic steroid. The officer argued that the positive test resulted from his having taken a legal "supplement" that produced a false positive, a conclusion that was supported by expert testimony provided by Dr. Don Catlin, a leading anti-doping expert. Why had he taken the supplement in the first place? Officer Ramirez told the court that he had picked up the idea from trainers at a gym where police officers lifted weights. He began taking the supplement after getting into a couple of fights with criminals while he was on patrol. The thugs, he said, "spend hours working out" and are "stronger and hungrier than me." His goal, he said, was to survive his shift and get home safely.[67] Images of weightlifting convicts who acquired their intimidating muscles in prison are displayed on the walls of some police departments to encourage job-related fitness.

A first-year officer named Chris Holden claimed that his fear of being outmuscled by criminals in Oklahoma prompted him to begin taking steroids in 2004. His fears resulted from the death of a fellow officer who had been shot with his own gun by a physically powerful criminal who took it away from him. "I wanted to do everything I could to prevent this from happening to me," Holden explained, "and that is when I started to use anabolic steroids." Holden, three other police officers, and a state highway patrolman lost their jobs for using steroids. The reaction to Holden's confession within the department was extraordinary in its hostility. The spokesman for the Norman Police Department said that Holden's explanation of his drug use "alienated the entire department," and that most of the other officers "took his letter as evidence of cowardice and some kind of inadequacy in himself." Public criticism of a fellow patrol officer seldom occurs within police culture. It is police chiefs who make public comments about officers' misbehavior, and even they are generally reluctant to do so.

One wonders what might have caused members of this department to breach the customary bonds of solidarity that rule out public comments of this kind. It is possible that his colleagues' rejection of Holden's alibi came from feelings about the tawdriness of illicit drug use. It is also likely that the ostracizing of a confessed steroid user would not have occurred in a large urban police department. The combination of peer pressure from the police union and the greater prevalence of steroid use on the force would tend to preclude exiling an officer for "functional drug" use.

Even a very fit and muscular officer can make unfavorable comparisons between his own fitness and the perceived fitness and "command presence" of some of his fellow officers. In 2011, Officer. com described the predicament of such a police officer:

> [He] works in a large urban area, riddled by bangers. His beat has one of the highest crime rates in the city. He has kept himself in incredible shape. He is muscular with chiseled abs and can bench 250. He continues to work out feverishly to remain in condition. Yet he can't help but notice that some of his beat partners are substantially more ripped than he is. Additionally they are more imposing on the street and more confident. He continues to obsess about his muscularity. He has to be bigger and stronger. Paradoxically, the harder he tries, the punier he feels.[68]

Weightlifting is often on the minds of officers who are worried about their size and strength, and weight training at the station or in a gym has become a part of police culture. "We have inmates who can spend pretty much all day working out and getting buff," a Florida correctional officer said in 2005. "Some of the younger officers, the ones who are still thinking they need to be able to look intimidating to be in control, are the ones that those steroids will appeal to."[69] A self-identified former law enforcement officer in the Phoenix area posted in 2007: "Unlike the hard-core crooks, cops don't get 5–15 year stints [in prison] to pump iron. Long, boring shifts are the norm. But cops try to get in some brief, intense workouts regularly. The use of anabolics aids this process and allows them to stay competitive with their 'enemies' despite having far less free time."[70]

Cops must also deal with frequent injuries. According to the former law enforcement officer quoted above, steroid therapy can be "the only way to keep an aging cop on the streets," and so "docs will do everything in their power to put him on his feet." From this perspective, a functional attitude toward officer performance is the rule, and the burden of proof is on arguments that would deny rather than provide the purported benefits of androgenic drugs.

For officers who think of steroid use as a defensive preparation for their confrontations with criminals, steroid-generated muscle is a functional strategy that inspires fear in those the officer wants to bring under control. Displaying an intimidating physique on the street can sometimes be an effective form of policing, since this raw version of "command presence" can prevent dangerous physical altercations that a smaller officer might not be able to avoid. Presenting a show of overwhelming physical strength can obviate the need for an officer to use a Taser or a gun, thereby reducing the likelihood of injuring or killing a suspect. Sheer muscularity is desirable in part because the use of these weapons can lead to complaints and lawsuits that a show of sheer strength might avoid. Atholl Malcolm, a Canadian psychologist who screens Royal Canadian Mounted Police officers for high-risk assignments, commented in 2008: "Life gets rougher on the street, and they're criticized more and more for the use of things like tasers, so what's the alternative?"[71]

A former British police officer who used steroids told Sky News in 2015 that his ability to intimidate on the street made him feel superhuman. "I'm a police officer and I look like a comic book hero, and I'm in costume. Nine times out of 10 my sheer presence alone was enough to defuse a situation," he said. "I will say, and I don't regret saying this, it made me better at my job. That's why people take it. It's a performance-enhancing substance."[72]

The same intimidating effect was reported by a physically imposing and steroid-boosted Canadian constable named Roger Yeo, whose drug use and weightlifting regime had packed 225 pounds of muscle onto his six-foot one-inch frame. At his disciplinary hearing in 2008, he described the steroid scene inside his department: "I don't know if it was accepted," he said, "but a lot of guys were on it, including myself." While nonusers sometimes called him a "juice monkey," they were always ready to call on him "in case things got out of hand." From the day he joined the force in 2003, officers talked openly about performance-enhancing drugs in the station house.[73] The uncertain status of—and uncertainty about—the use of steroids in policing is on full display in this officer's comments. What is more, this case demonstrated once again police authorities' lack of interest in digging too deeply into their officers' drug use. The internal investigation called for by Chief John Metcalf went nowhere, and the department stopped replying to outsiders' inquiries about what if anything had been revealed.

WHAT CAN POLICE CHIEFS DO ABOUT ALCOHOLIC COPS?

The single most destructive drug problem police chiefs around the country must confront is alcohol abuse. Interestingly, when police executives convene to talk about the drug problems they deal with, the medical toll of alcohol use doesn't even come up. The focus is rather on "harder" drugs. The meteoric rise in the abuse of prescription painkillers such as Oxycontin (oxycodone) among the general population has also infiltrated police departments. In 2012, the head of the Albuquerque force reported: "Many of these prescription drug problems actually started with an on-the-job injury, which means that the initial prescription came from our own city doctors. These addictions ultimately affect the officers' home lives, their quality of work, and all operations of the organization." The financial desperation caused by addiction forces some officers to sell their guns, boats, or motorcycles.[74] In the years since this chief made his comments, painkiller abuse has become a pathway to heroin addiction in large segments of the suburban American middle-class, which includes many police officers.

Alcohol is, of course, much more than a drug of abuse, and its benefits are embraced for practical reasons inside police culture. "Cops use alcohol for a variety of reasons," the police chief of Milwaukee said in 2012. "They use it to de-stress, they use it to relax with each other. In Wisconsin, alcohol use is socially acceptable in policing because it's a high-stress job." In this sense, drinking is functional drug use, though not in the same way that anabolic steroid use is considered a functional kind of workplace doping by officers who are into serious weightlifting. Alcohol use can reflect larger social norms as well, as the Milwaukee police chief made clear: "Alcohol is a big part of the culture in Wisconsin. . . . The problems of policing and alcohol are exacerbated by the culture from which we recruit and the culture that we inhabit."[75] Drug use does not originate in police departments; it is imported into them from other social venues that range from the socially respectable to the socially undesirable.

Alcohol consumption is so entrenched in law enforcement that some refer to group drinking as "choir practice." The social respectability of drinking outside and inside police culture promotes its deleterious effects within the force by making it a routine behavior and sometimes a ritual of inclusion for new officers. The nondrinking recruit may find it difficult to be fully accepted by the group. Indeed, one study found that "the officers most at risk for problem drinking were those who drank to fit in." "It's part of the macho image, part of being a cop," says John Violanti, a research associate professor at the University of Buffalo and a former New York state trooper.[76] Research from Australia confirms that nondrinkers encounter problems and may not be welcome among their peers, since "a significant proportion [of police] viewed non drinkers negatively, suspiciously or as antisocial." Abstinence is not a way "to be part of the team."[77]

An important characteristic of drug abuse inside a police force is that it is generally secretive. Because substance abuse often escapes the attention of police managers, the emotional health of the alcoholic or addicted officer can deteriorate rapidly in the absence of therapeutic intervention. "Because drinking has been an acceptable part of the police culture and has been a way for officers to cope with the stressors of their work," one specialist notes, "issues with alcohol often go undetected. Repeated exposure to trauma, suicide, domestic violence, and mental health [problems] takes its toll on even the most highly resilient officer. Repeated exposure to these types of stressors often produces frustration, depression, anger, and other emotions, which officers are taught to suppress."[78] Police officers' unwillingness to self-report even severe mental health problems is bound up with the importance of an uncompromised masculine identity within police culture. It derives also from the inherently problematic relationships with the supervisors who scrutinize their attitudes and behaviors. The police chief of Denver commented in 2014: "Police officers, like soldiers suffering from PTSD, are reluctant to seek help because they fear it will ruin their careers. Police, in general, are very reluctant to self-report that kind of behavior especially when it eventually gets to the administration and they think their career is going to be in jeopardy."[79] Reporting the drinking problem of a fellow officer is another way to imperil a career in policing.

The rate of alcoholism among police officers has been widely estimated to be double that of the general population, perhaps affecting a quarter of the force. An Australian study suggests that alcohol abuse affects as much as a third of the police population.[80] The well-known consequences of alcohol abuse by police are driving while intoxicated (DWI), domestic violence, and suicide. According to the chief psychologist of the Los Angeles Police department: "Almost every officer who commits suicide was under the influence of alcohol at the time and had a history of alcoholism."[81]

Police departments' responses to drug use, whether involving alcohol or anabolic steroids, have tended to be slow, reluctant, and ineffective, even when the alcohol-abusing officer engages in behaviors that put the public at risk. For example, when the police department of Fresno, California, did some research on how other departments disciplined officers who were arrested for drunk driving, it found "huge differences in how agencies address the issue." Some gave "three-day suspensions"; almost none fired "an officer for the first drunk-driving offense."[82]

By now, it should be clear that blaming police chiefs for inadequate antidrug abuse efforts is mistaken. Police managers do not simply impose regulations on the rank and file, and they may not even know about many police behaviors and misbehaviors. Indeed, the department management that wants to reduce stress among its officers may be unaware that patrol officers often regard management's practices as the most onerous source of stress in their professional lives.[83] The constant tension between the managerial culture and street cops with union representation forms a barrier that complicates attempts at therapeutic intervention into their lives. Union-enforced privacy, the blue wall of silence, hostility to informing on partners' conduct, and the fear of psychotherapy as a stigmatizing mark on their records combine to conceal most drug use from police managers.

The police alcohol culture is so entrenched that it goes unmentioned when the occasional media reports of police steroid use appear. The police department that suddenly confronts a steroid "problem" or "scandal" already has a "drug problem" far more destructive to police health and productivity than steroid use could ever be. The possible exception to this rule is the infamous case of Abner Louima, the Haitian immigrant who was tortured by the NYPD officer Justin Volpe in 1997. Speculations in the press about Volpe's rumored use of steroids were never confirmed. In fact, credible reports of a steroid-driven crime like the sodomizing of Louima with a broomstick could have given the cops-on-steroids issue the national platform it has never achieved.

WHAT SHOULD POLICE CHIEFS DO ABOUT TATTOOS?

In January 2013, a Philadelphia police detective named Keith Gidelson was sentenced to a term of four years in prison for selling steroids and HGH to fellow police officers and to clients he met in local fitness clubs. "He preened, he boasted, he bloviated," the judge declared indignantly, referring to secretly recorded conversations that made Gidelson sound like "a drug dealer who thought the world of himself." Gidelson's lawyer called him "more sick than sinister" and presented a psychologist who testified that the former detective's work as a police officer had resulted in post-traumatic stress disorder, which accounted for his behavior. "Highly dubious," replied the judge.[84] At his arraignment in a federal courtroom in April 2011, Gidelson had stood before the court, "a small man with a large frame," wearing "running shorts, flip-flops, and a sleeveless T-shirt that showed his tattooed arms."[85]

In the world of policing, anabolic steroid use and tattoos are related to each other. Both behaviors can signify a defiance of regulations or laws. Both police and military authorities have consistently identified nonmedical steroid use and the wearing of tattoos as problematic behaviors that raise questions about character and fitness to serve. While police authorities have officially banned steroid use, their reactions to tattoos have been more complicated, since the traditional aversion to tattoos in respectable society has in recent years been challenged by a younger generation that has largely disregarded traditional prohibitions and adopted tattoos as a lifestyle option.

Within the field of criminology, the abhorrence of tattoos was firmly established in the later part of the nineteenth century by the pseudoscientific, but enormously influential, Italian criminologist Cesare Lombroso, who regarded tattoos as a form of atavistic behavior that disproportionately occurred among criminals and members of the lower orders. "In modern times," he wrote, "this custom has fallen into disuse among the higher classes and only exists among sailors, soldiers, peasants, and workmen."[86] This traditional disapproval has persisted among police commanders, despite the popularity of tattoos among the younger generation, from which new police officers are recruited. As we will see, this conflict between older and younger police officers over the displaying of tattoos continues in the form of restrictive policies that have provoked both challenges and compromises between police executives and rank-and-file officers.

One way that tattoos enter police departments is on the bodies of the many military personnel who are recruited for police work. The military establishment, too, regards tattoos as a potential threat to the discipline and conformity that are the basis of military life. The deputy commandant of the Naval Academy stated in 1997 that "tattoos are generally inconsistent with the high standards of personal appearance associated with officers of the Naval Service." And here, too, one detects a residue of the traditional view that associates tattoos with the lower social orders. "Although the military tolerates tattoos on the bodies of enlisted soldiers," Carol Burke wrote in 2004, "it frowns on officers who acquire them, reinforcing the stereotype of tattoos as lower-class adornment. A commissioned officer would tarnish his prestige if he were seen with tattoos in a short-sleeved summer uniform."[87]

Just as tattoos can enter police ranks from the military, tattoos can enter military ranks through infiltration by members of gangs or other fringe subcultures that express their alienation from society on their bodies. A 2007 assessment by the National Gang Intelligence Center states: "Military command policy generally prohibits participation in or association with extremist organizations or groups that advocate the use of force or violence. Regulations additionally prohibit the display of inappropriate or obscene tattoos, body piercings, hand signs, colors, and graffiti." Images prohibited by the US Navy and the Marines are further described as follows:

No tattoos/body art/brands on the head, face, neck, or scalp. Tattoos/Body Art/Brands elsewhere on the body that are prejudicial to good order, discipline, and morale or are of a nature to bring discredit on the Navy are prohibited. For example, tattoos/ body art/brands that are excessive, obscene, sexually explicit or advocate or symbolize gang affiliation, violence, supremacist or extremist groups, or drug use are prohibited. In addition, tattoos/body art/brands will not be visible through uniform clothing.[88]

Policies regarding tattoos are required by military and paramilitary organizations that enlist potentially aggressive and impulsive men into the regimented ranks of police or military life. As the military regulations cited above make clear, tattoos and other forms of "body art" are correctly seen as signs of potential trouble for any disciplined organization that confers on those it recruits the authority and the right to assault, confine, or even kill civilians. The navy rules governing tattoos recognize in recruits potential urges to commit acts that are excessive, obscene, sexually explicit, violent, racist, or politically extreme. All these potential behaviors are incompatible with wielding police or military authority.

Disputes over tattoos are an inevitable part of generational conflicts within police departments in any developed country. An assistant police commissioner in New South Wales, Australia, for example, commented in 2013: "Some of the older generation don't like tattoos. They feel a bit scared, there's a belief they might be from a criminal background just because they've got body art."[89] Here is more evidence that the theories of Cesare Lombroso linger on in the early twenty-first century. For the older generation, there are, however, more relevant sources of concern that have nothing to do with tattoos as signifiers of criminal instincts. A report titled "Recruitment and Selection of Police Officers" (2011) points out that whereas many police officers belonging to the baby boomer generation "had been in the military and were used to discipline and a hierarchy of authority . . . the Generation X and Y recruits have been exposed to modern liberalism, the passage of affirmative action laws, drug use, increased civil disobedience, and the breakdown of both the family and authority."[90] All of these "exposures" to modern life have contributed to the declining status of hierarchy and the social instincts that prop it up. It is, therefore, not surprising that the older generation can feel that younger recruits and their lifestyle preferences such as tattoos bode ill for professional discipline.

The traditional argument for a strictly disciplined police force was formulated as follows in 2011 by a retired Michigan state trooper named John J. Palmatier: "Law enforcement is about support of justice and service to the public; tats, grills and similar signs of individualism are generally interpreted as signs of rebellion or at least making an individual statement." He added, "The law and law enforcement is not about doing your own thing. If that is important, go drive a truck, sing in a rock band, but leave law enforcement to those who can conform."[91]

We should recognize here that this call for conformity is not an appeal for mindless obedience to authority. It is rather a call for self-discipline that also contains a warning against acting on impulses that are appropriate in, let us say, the entertainment industry but are "excessive" in the context of law enforcement. "Signs of individualism" are not limited to tattoos, intimidating dental "grills," and piercings. In a police or military context, the refusal to obey an illegitimate order, for example, is a sign of individualism that may amount to an act of heroism. Acting out obscene, sexually explicit, violent, racist, or politically extreme impulses is a different kind of individualism that many police officers have displayed, and tattoos are an opportunity to convey such feelings to fellow officers and to a public that may well be alarmed by displays of aggressive or antisocial feelings. A Florida officer who had a swastika tattooed on his leg was fired and then reinstated after his police union argued there was no evidence that this officer "was racist while on duty."[92] This case and similar ones demonstrate that police forces have tolerated and continue to tolerate many "signs of individualism" that violate, for example, the military standard cited above, which forbids indications of racism or political extremism.

Official concerns about eccentric or pathological "signs of individualism" displayed by police officers are legitimate in part because we know that some policemen participate in male subcultures where steroid use is common, such as bouncing, motorcycle clubs, security contracting (mercenary work), and bodybuilding. Tattoos and anabolic steroids appear in all these venues because body modification and hormone boosting can serve the self-expressive needs of the action-oriented male. Anabolic steroids that produce muscle and aggressiveness are masculinizing drugs, just as tattoos can have a masculinizing function as symbolic battle scars. As one commentator noted in 2013, "The military has a strong tattoo culture, and veterans wear their ink with pride."[93] And just as tattoos can be symbolic scars, scars can function as tattoos. The author of a study of violence and manhood puts it this way: "As tattoos, the scars of warriors become ways of gaining individual recognition from their peers, who know how to read the secret codes."[94] Many nonmilitary males, such as motorcycle gang members, have acted out the symbolic connection between scars and tattoos as a ritual that fortifies their identification with extreme masculinity and its antisocial values and impulses. Reading tattoos and steroid use as "signs of rebellion" is, therefore, a rational and legitimate response by police commanders to both behaviors.

Prompted by concerns that some police officers were not presenting to the public a "professional" and nonthreatening image, many US police departments began, after 2010, to institute restrictions against tattoos and "body modification" procedures such as piercing. (Des Moines, Iowa, began restricting police tattoos as early as 2008.) The police departments in New York, Los Angeles, and Baltimore have adopted such policies. Similar measures have been adopted in other countries. Senior police officials in Britain, for example, cracked down on "body art" in 2012 following "complaints from crime victims that some young officers appear 'thuggish.'" Police union representatives replied that associating tattoos with criminals was outdated thinking.[95] Police officers in New South Wales, Australia, were banned in 2013 from having tattoos on their faces, necks, scalps, ears, or hands. Messages conveyed by "body art" were forbidden to include "references to illegal gangs, criminal behavior, racism, graphically sexual images and/or slogans that are racial, religious, homophobic or sexually vilifying in nature." One official justified this policy and presented it as a compromise: "It's about maintaining professional standards and living up to the expectations of the community we serve, whilst recognizing the changing attitudes of some in that community."[96] Australian authorities' regulation of tattoos has been accompanied by intensifying concerns about steroid use by police officers and by motorcycle gangs, which invest in tattoo parlors and bodybuilding gyms and corrupt some policemen they meet there.

In the United States, the Honolulu Police Department in 2013 passed a regulation banning visible tattoos, piercings, and "dental ornaments" such as metal "grills" affixed to front teeth. This ordinance met with some objections after it was pointed out that Polynesian officers often wore tattoos as signs of heritage.[97] The "Tattoo Policy Notice for Police Applicants" in Great Falls, Montana, announces a ban on tattoos or body art displaying racism, sexism, obscenity, gang affiliations, allusions to drugs, or political opinions. Piercings and the displaying of tattoos on the neck, head, face, ears, or hands and fingers are prohibited.[98] The tattoo policy in McKinney, Texas, is identical to this one but adds to the banned list just about every conceivable body alteration that members of the public would be likely to find both abnormal and disturbing: gauges (large holes in the ears); pierced, split, or forked tongues; any foreign objects inserted under the skin on the hands, neck, face, and head; dental ornamentation (gold, platinum, silver, or other veneer caps for the purpose of ornamentation).[99] When Aurora, Colorado, insisted that its officers conceal their tattoos, the rationale offered by the police chief was that "tattoos are a barrier to building trust" and are seen as "intimidating."[100] An absolute distinction must separate police officers from the deformed creatures that might appear in a horror film and the threat to human identity they represent.

The new restrictions on body modification are being implemented just as some departments are accommodating tattoos judged to be inoffensive and small enough not to provoke alarm among members of the public. Whereas the Tampa Police Department enforces a zero-tolerance policy, other departments in the area are more flexible. The Tarpon Springs department, for example, given Florida's intense summer heat, no longer requires officers with tattoos on their forearms to cover them with shirt sleeves. But there are limits that are enforced by both police and military commanders. The consensus in Florida and elsewhere is that tattoos must not appear on the face, neck, or scalp. To avoid giving offense to the local community, the St. Petersburg department allows tattoos not exceeding a certain size on the arms. While norms vary, the essential rule is that there must be norms to assure the public that police discipline is being maintained, that anarchic impulses are under control. The freak-show potential of body modification practices and their implied threat of social dissolution must be avoided at all costs.

Police unions in a number of American cities offered objections to the new anti-tattoo restrictions. The attorney for the Fraternal Order of Police in New Orleans invoked the heat factor: "As we reach temperatures close to 100 degrees on some days, it just seems like cruel and unusual punishment [to require an officer to wear long sleeves], just because you are proud that you served in the US Navy or you put the name of your child on your arm," he said in 2013. A department already plagued by morale problems would gain little from this sort of interference with an officers' right to avoid discomfort.[101] In the same year, the head of the police union in Oklahoma City and the police chief resumed their long-standing debate over whether the city's anti-tattoo policy was dissuading well-qualified applicants from applying to join the force. The president of the Fraternal Order of Police argued that the policy was driving away former members of the military with tattoos. The police chief replied that there was, in fact, an abundant supply of tattoo-free applicants, including military veterans. "Having tattoos and visible symbols is not appropriate for a law enforcement agency in my opinion," he said. "If people want to have tattoos and be police officers, they have to get them removed."[102]

Police authorities regard tattoos and steroid use, to different degrees, as threats to the core identity of the police officer. (Steroids get less attention than tattoos, for reasons this book explores.) What, after all, *is* a "professional" appearance for law enforcement personnel? Broward County sheriff's officials concluded in 2011 that tattoos on a police officer could be "unreasonably intimidating." "People want a neutral authority figure when they call an officer to the scene," a Miami-Dade police officer commented.[103] Although the variety of conflicting opinions about tattoos cannot be quantified, police chiefs across the country appear to favor substantial restrictions over liberalization of the rules. Asked about the feelings of his officers on this topic, the police chief of Aurora, Colorado, said in 2010: "It's mixed. I've heard some pretty vigorous complaints from officers that have tattoos, and I have a more quiet, affirming sentiment from the rest of the organization that we should have done this a long time ago, and it is an issue of professionalism."[104]

This nationwide trend toward tighter restrictions is surprising, given the growing acceptance of the idea that people are entitled to the pursuit of self-expression and its gratification. The most interesting aspect of the tattoo debate is the persistence of a cultural conservatism that continues the tradition of regarding tattoos as a form of cultural degeneracy or, at the very least, as a symptom of deficient judgment on the part of the officer. The online comment of one self-identified police officer nicely captures this point of view: "While in the academy back in '69 we had a Lt. who instructed a course connecting criminals and tattoos. With the way society has fallen apart in the last forty years it's understandable that police now take up tattoos."[105]

The display of tattoos and the use of anabolic steroids by police officers represent potential "signs of rebellion" on the part of cops. Officers must not be allowed to disregard the police and civilian authorities who set the standards of conduct for armed representatives of the law who have the power to question, detain, and imprison ordinary citizens.

As the conflicting views on tattoo policies show, these standards may interfere with an officer's freedom of expression. For example, a 2013 editorial in the *New Haven Register* on the rights of Connecticut state troopers called into question the emphasis on maintaining a uniform code of conduct on the force. "Our state troopers," it said, "deserve better than the recently enacted policy warning the rank-and-file that they can be disciplined for tattoos or for saying something on social media."[106] Perhaps this editorialist did not recall the New York City police officers who, a year earlier, posted Facebook comments calling black participants in the annual West Indian American Day Parade in Brooklyn "savages" and "animals." The officers who could be connected to the racist comments received minimal punishments.[107] Highly publicized police racism counts among the signs of rebellion that, like steroids and tattoos, police authorities must control.

WEIGHTLIFTING COPS VERSUS PUMPED-UP CONVICTS

One of the less visible contests between policemen and criminals occurs indirectly in station houses and prisons. This contest takes the form of weightlifting, of "working out," and although the law enforcers have the better equipment, the sheer ingenuity of the weightlifting lawbreakers makes it a fair competition, if a competition is what it is. According to an ex-convict who produced a fine anthropological analysis of the weightlifting culture behind bars, "lifting weights is practically a religion in American prisons."[108] Interestingly, a genuine devotion to pumping iron is evident on both sides of the legal divide that separates the guardians of the law from those who require guarding. It is hard to imagine that the "cultural acceptance of bodybuilding" in the police community does not have some kind of primal link to what animates the iron-obsessed prisoners.[109]

The idea that there is a cops-against-convicts bodybuilding competition under way is encouraged by graphic posters that hang in some police stations. "He's Pumping. Are You?" reads one that shows a well-built convict doing a bench press. "They Worked Out Today. Did You?" reads another; it is graced by a photo of seven thuggish-looking inmates, including a bare-chested muscleman with a tattoo-covered torso. This anxious concern about the heavily muscled adversary is not reciprocated by the men behind bars. The prisoners who bulk up do not display photos of hulking cops on their makeshift gym walls as a source of motivation to get hard. As the ex-convict anthropologist points out: "It's part of the macho prison culture to lift weights, and to be manly and tough." In practical terms, convicts aren't worried about what hard-muscled cops might do to them on the outside. But cops are apprehensive about convicts who seem to have all day to muscle up in preparation for the havoc they plan to wreak when they get out. The cops, who have about an hour a day to spend in the weight room, are well aware that the cons have a lot more time than that.

The balance of power between these weightlifting adversaries was thrown out of kilter in the mid-1990s by conservative politicians bent on removing certain amenities of prison life. In 1995, Congressman Richard Zimmer (R–New Jersey) introduced his No Frills Prison Act (HR 663), subtitled "Amendment to Prevent Luxurious Conditions in Prisons." The bill died in committee, but if it had been enacted, many prisons would have banned smoking, cable television, R-rated movies, conjugal visits, and pornography. Despite its contribution to inmates' physical and mental health, weightlifting was added to the list of banned "luxuries." As one Texas congressman put it: "There is a psychological mind-set to being bulked up and I don't like that mind-set in a criminal." More muscle made criminals more dangerous inside and outside prison. And where did this concern about muscled-up convicts come from? According to Alan Tepperman, the author of a study on prison weightlifting in the 1990s: "Politicians passed many of these measures as a response to popular portrayals of prison weightlifting in the media." Tepperman argued that the infamous Willie Horton ad of 1988, Robert De Niro's "iron-pumping redneck" character in *Cape Fear* (1991), the 1992 Mike Tyson rape trial, and the 1994 Rikers Island prison riot, during which prisoners were reported to have hit guards with barbells, all contributed to "the moral panic surrounding prison weightlifting."[110] And in 1996 the Princeton social scientist John

DiIulio popularized his hysterical prediction that (black) juvenile "superpredators" were about to unleash an unprecedented crime wave on American society. Muscle profiling had acquired a toehold in the popular imagination.

Interestingly, steroids played no role in the overheated public discussion of weightlifting criminals. At the time, almost no Americans had any idea of the sheer scope of steroid use in certain social venues. More important, however, was the ease with which popular media conjured up the image of the "muscle monster" behind bars. (The protein deficit that the incarcerated lifters had to overcome was never mentioned.) These days, steroid-pumped convicts do not seem to pose much threat. In 2013, for example, a strongman contest at Addiewell prison in Scotland was canceled after the contestants heard they would be tested for steroids. The private company that runs the prison expressed its regrets: "The gym is probably the main thing in prison that helps inmates pass their time."[111]

STEROIDS AND COMMAND PRESENCE

Command presence is the aura of physical and emotional self-confidence that police officers are expected to project when patrolling the streets. The police executives who represent a department at the highest level have their own form of command presence. When, for example, a senior FBI agent wanted to reconcile with NYPD commissioner Ray Kelly over a jurisdictional dispute, he told the commissioner: "I have profound respect for your command presence."[112] As a standard of conduct, command presence is the coin of the realm in police work. Although its essence can be conveyed with words and images, it is a unitary and authoritative doctrine that is accepted across the profession.

Command presence has physical and mental dimensions that are analyzed and extolled on police websites. "Physical presence is the first level of force in the use of force continuum," says one commentator. "Being confident in your abilities generally reflects in your body language. Walk tall, speak clearly and stand up straight just like your mother told you. Doing so will reflect your command presence and help project authority."[113] Another police source cautions that "two-thirds of what we 'say' is transmitted through non-verbal means: body language and appearance. The body doesn't lie."[114] The police officer must project the image of a predator to his prey.

"Physical stamina is the root of mental toughness," said Major Dick Winters, a celebrated World War II hero whose exploits were featured in the 2001 HBO miniseries *Band of Brothers*.[115] Paramilitary police are expected to emulate the physical and mental toughness of the military man as a way to promote their own survival in urban combat.

The role of body language in command presence includes how an officer carries himself: "Walk with your head up, eyes alert, and your expression intent. You do not want to appear weak or vulnerable. You want to project the image of someone that knows why they are where they are, and who is trained and knows what they are doing." How a police officer handles his body in public must convey a firm and unmistakable "'I am in charge of this situation' image."[116] It is about mental focus and the kind of self-awareness that projects quiet confidence rather than self-consciousness and the vulnerability that it conveys.

Command presence is a charisma that is recognized by anyone who is within the ambit of a police officer who radiates it. It is a professional aura that evokes terms such as "acting sharp," "maintaining the edge," and being "squared away." In short, it is both a functional and an aesthetic style that soldiers and policemen are taught to respect. Indeed, the aesthetics of a police officer's self-presentation have a function. As *Policing Magazine* put it in 2013, police supervisors do not want to see a cop who "just looks bad in the uniform."[117] Policing requires creating and managing the "first impressions" that an officer makes while patrolling public spaces.

The essence of command presence is to maintain the difficult balance between living a "warrior" ethos and maintaining self-discipline. It is "a demeanor that is *authoritative* rather than authoritarian."[118] Achieving this balance is the precise opposite of indulging in the machismo and the aura of intimidation that come naturally to motorcycle gang members and some policemen.

Anabolic steroids threaten policing because their influence on officers' attitudes toward discipline and self-restraint subverts respect for command presence, which is the practical and ethical core of effective policing. The "steroidal" attitude prioritizes self-assertion, intimidation, and the uninhibited pleasures of a "badass" mentality over the capacity to exercise self-control in stressful encounters with suspects.

It is important to understand that the steroidal mentality is not steroid rage. The steroidal mind-set is a declaration of independence from the self-discipline that underlies command presence. That is why steroid use by police officers can precede the commission of crimes ranging from harassment to murder. In this sense, steroid use is often an unspoken declaration of intent to deviate from a departmental code of conduct and other social norms, including criminal statutes. Command presence is, therefore, society's primary line of defense against the disintegration of law and order inside a police department.

DO ANABOLIC STEROIDS CAUSE VIOLENT BEHAVIOR?

The researcher who sets off to find irrefutable proof of the widely accepted cause-and-effect relationship between anabolic steroids and violent male moods and behaviors will return from this misguided expedition empty-handed. "You cannot predict one way or the other whether someone is going to have one of these reactions," says Harrison G. Pope, a Harvard-affiliated psychiatrist who has published widely on the psychogenic effects of anabolic steroid use.[119] While the medical literature has repeatedly found a correlation between anabolic steroid use and aggressive impulses and behaviors, one cannot verify with scientific certainty that anabolic steroid use caused a particular episode of violent behavior in a police officer or anyone else. This absence of certainty does not, however, disprove the link between these drugs and the murder and mayhem they have caused on many occasions. Like earthquakes, outbursts of steroid rage are no less destructive for being unpredictable. Extensive anecdotal evidence, along with psychiatric studies, confirms that steroid use by some people poses a clear and present risk to public safety. There comes a point at which anecdotal evidence acquires so much evidentiary weight that discounting it becomes an exercise in obfuscation and outright deception. This principle applies both to the prevalence of steroid use among police and to steroids' association with the violent behavior that has been ascribed to roid rage. What remains unclear is whether steroids are both "markers" of violence-prone personalities and the physiological cause of aberrant behavior.

The power of the roid rage stereotype derives from its dramatic and simplistic portrayal of drug-induced mayhem and emotional derangement. In fact, the assumption that steroid rage is real has served a variety of interests. It has been invoked, for example, as a pathological symptom of drug abuse in order to justify the US government's campaign against anabolic steroid use over many years. The Anabolic Steroids Control Act of 1990 was amended by the Anabolic Steroid Control Act of 2004, which modified the definition of "anabolic steroid" by eliminating the requirement to prove muscle growth and by expanding the number of banned substances. On July 25, 2012, two US senators introduced the Designer Anabolic Steroid Control Act of 2012 to further expand the list of prohibited substances as well as to target any drug or substance "created or manufactured with the intent of producing a drug or other substance that promotes muscle growth or causes a pharmacological effect similar to that of testosterone" or "intended to be marketed or otherwise promoted in a manner suggesting that consumption will promote muscle growth or any pharmacological effect similar to that of testosterone."[120] That bill was not enacted, but the very similar Designer Anabolic Steroid Control Act of 2014 was signed into law.

The correlation between steroids and violence achieved a kind of legal recognition in 2011 when several police officers sued the City of Jersey City, New Jersey, "alleging that their rights were violated when they were suspended from active duty for their use of legally prescribed steroids." In fact, the police chief who suspended them and ordered them tested for steroids had reason to believe they had been purchasing illegal anabolic steroids and HGH. In its ruling in this case, on December 20, 2011, the US Court of Appeals for the Third Circuit confirmed an earlier US district court opinion that "generally, high steroid levels [are] linked to aggressive behavior," and cited "the uncontroversial proposition that high steroid levels have been linked to aggressive behavior."[121] When the deputy assistant administrator of the DEA testified in 2012 before the Senate Judiciary Subcommittee on Crime and Drugs on behalf of the Designer Anabolic Steroid Control Act, he described "uncontrolled rage" as one of the "adverse health effects" of anabolic steroid use.[122] In short, repeated use of the steroid rage concept by members of Congress and governmental officials has made it a virtually uncontested hypothesis in the media, among the public, and in courtrooms, where it plays several roles, depending on who invokes it.

The steroid rage diagnosis has thus achieved an authoritative status in media accounts of steroid abuse and at the governmental level where drug policy is made. This quasi-official and quasi-scientific status has attracted the interest of those involved in courtroom proceedings. What follow are three courtroom scenarios involving police officers in which the idea of steroid rage played a role. The first involves an officer who claimed that his steroid use catalyzed his inappropriate violent conduct. In the second scenario, citizens who claimed to have been injured or traumatized by an officer alleged that he must have been experiencing roid rage in order to behave as he did. The third (unusual) scenario features a criminal defendant who argues that officers' steroid use made them unfit to investigate and arrest the defendant.

Some criminal defendants and their attorneys have invoked steroid use as a physiological alibi, an exculpating factor in the commission of violent crimes. This courtroom tactic has been encouraged by the sheer notoriety of these drugs, which has been driven in large part by federal antisteroid legislation dating back to 1990 and by medical warnings about the consequences of steroid abuse. As three medical authors noted in 2001: "because bodybuilding magazines as well as the popular press support the view that violent and aggressive acts are the inevitable consequence of AAS use, this may create a self-fulfilling prophecy and provide exculpatory discourses for those already predisposed to violence."[123]

The first exculpatory scenario of this kind involves a Petersburg, Virginia, police officer named Michael Tweedy, who in 2003 pursued and tackled a twenty-six-year-old male suspect and then proceeded to beat him to within an inch of his life. His victim suffered skull fractures and brain contusions and spent two months in a coma. Tweedy pleaded guilty to depriving the suspect of his civil rights and was eventually sentenced to nine years in prison. Witnesses testified at his sentencing that Tweedy was incapable of such brutality. But it was also reported that Tweedy was experiencing marital and financial problems at the time of the beating and was depressed. And he had been accused of using overly aggressive tactics on two occasions in the past. In April 2005, his attorneys argued in US district court that their client had used anabolic steroids while serving on the police force, that he "was suffering from emotional, physical and financial stresses," and that he "was using steroids for a long period of time."[124] The steroid alibi was not accepted by the court.

A similar steroid defense was presented by the lawyer for a murderous former law enforcement officer in 2013. Jonathan Agee, a former Franklin County (Virginia) sheriff's deputy, was sentenced to three life prison terms for first-degree murder, attempted capital murder, and aggravated malicious wounding for killing his ex-wife and wounding a Virginia State Police trooper who was attempting to apprehend him. Having advised his client to plead no contest to these charges, Agee's attorney, C. J. Covati, constructed a defense strategy based on Agee's illegal steroid use during the two years leading up to the shootings. Agee testified that within a few months, his steroid use had enabled him to bulk up from 170 to 230 pounds. At the same time, he became irritable, paranoid, and bitterly resentful of any attention paid to his wife.[125] "But for the steroids, this wouldn't have happened," Covati said. "He was an eight-year veteran of the Franklin County Sheriff's Office, and he never had a use of force problem there." Agee was using nonprescribed (and, therefore, illegal) steroids, he said, in order to deal with a "body image issue."[126]

To provide a scientific foundation for the steroid argument, Agee's attorney presented a forty-five-minute video deposition by Dr. Harrison Pope, the Harvard Medical School psychiatrist and steroid expert, who stated without equivocation: "If [Agee] had not been taking anabolic steroids in May of 2011, the murder would not have happened."[127] Pope's theory was that steroid use could induce violence in an otherwise normal personality, that "anabolic steroids may cause some law-abiding and psychiatrically asymptomatic individuals to develop manic and psychotic symptoms, culminating occasionally in violent crimes," as he wrote in 1990.[128] Almost twenty-five years later, Pope reaffirmed this claim in his deposition for the Agee trial. In his formulation, only "a small percentage of steroid users" become violent, but there is no other way to account for their transformations into bullies and killers. Among the violent young men he presents as case studies, "all of them reverted back to their baseline personalities after they were apprehended and were no longer taking steroids." For this "minority of people there really is a genuine effect that cannot be otherwise explained." Jonathan Agee, too, Pope testified, had undergone a "Jekyll and Hyde transformation in his behavior and in his personality during the periods of steroid exposure."[129] Agee's attorney offered his own version of the psychiatrist's theory: "While he's a flawed man," Covati said, "he's not a violent man." Judge Charlie Dorsey did not even attempt to argue the scientific merits of the steroid defense; he simply dismissed it as irrelevant to "the coldblooded execution of a mother."[130]

The second scenario occurs when citizens who believe that police officers have verbally or physically abused them use the steroid rage theory to explain what happened. In 2005, a fifty-nine-year-old unarmed man was shot to death in Salt Lake City by a police officer, Steven C. Ward, who was subsequently indicted for importing anabolic steroids into the United States. The dead man's family filed a federal lawsuit claiming that the officer was under the influence of the drug when the shooting occurred. A police spokesman denied that the officer was experiencing so-called roid rage when he fired his weapon. "The allegation that he was on steroids at the time of the shooting really wasn't an issue," the spokesman said. A private investigator working for the family claimed that an informant had told the police that Ward was using steroids he obtained from Eastern Europe; the family's complaint alleged that the West Valley Police Department had been aware of Officer Ward's use of steroids for nonmedical purposes.[131] The lawsuit further alleged that Ward had "boasted" about a fatal shooting he carried out in 2004.[132] There was no way for the family of the dead man to pursue the case further, and Ward was not held accountable for the shooting death. While the department claimed to do random drug testing, it refused to say whether this testing included steroids. It is highly unlikely that the West Valley Police Department was among the minuscule number of police departments that might have been testing for steroids in 2005.

The image of the oversized, steroid-fueled police officer has become familiar enough that a large number of ordinary citizens who have traumatic encounters with police officers use this image to explain the behavior of officers who frightened them. One example of this scenario comes from Ontario, Canada, just across the border from the United States.

In April 2012, Constable Geoff Purdie of Niagara, Ontario, was arrested and charged with conspiracy to export and distribute anabolic steroids and other drugs worth more than $500,000. He was arrested in Buffalo, New York, by the US Department of Homeland Security. Citizens had filed complaints against Purdie and other officers, alleging excessive force, false arrests, and steroid use. In 2006, Niagara police supervisors had received a large volume of printed e-mails "suggesting steroid use and trafficking by an entirely different group of officers attached to the elite Emergency Task Unit." But, as a news report suggested, "it appears police brass took little or no action."[133]

This was the fraught context in which a Niagara woman named Laura Crawford filed a formal complaint against Constable Purdie and his partner, Constable Ryan Woehl, after they responded in 2009 to a 911 call she placed during an altercation with her husband, Robert Cox. When Crawford met with Niagara police chief Wendy Southall, she alleged that the officers had lied, and she stated "her belief the cops were so bulky and aggressive that they must have been on steroids." "I begged her to suspend him from the force immediately, have him psychiatrically tested and drug tested," Crawford said. She also said, "[The officer] was stalking, going back and forth, pacing, pacing, pacing, pacing. You looked at his eyes and you knew he was on something, or he was nuts, and I was terrified." The formal complaint was ultimately dismissed on the basis of the officers' testimony.[134] This case and many others demonstrate that it is almost impossible for civilian testimony to prevail in a courtroom against officers' accounts of the same events.

The steroid rage theme and a possible correlation between steroid use and violent police misbehaviors became evident on the basis of information deriving from the largest police-steroid scandal ever to come to public attention in the United States. The details have been mentioned already in this book, but they bear repeating: in 2010 the *Newark Star-Ledger* revealed that at least 248 police officers and firefighters from fifty-three state agencies in New Jersey had been obtaining anabolic steroids and HGH from a single corrupt doctor at taxpayer expense.

The sheer number of steroid-using officers created a unique opportunity to correlate known steroid use with indications or accusations of excessive violence. According to the newspaper report: "Six of those patients—four police officers and two corrections officers—were named in lawsuits alleging excessive force or civil rights violations around the time they received drugs from him or shortly afterward. Others have been arrested, fired or suspended for off-duty infractions that include allegations of assault, domestic abuse, harassment and drug possession." One Jersey City police officer filled seven prescriptions for testosterone and human chorionic gonadotropin (HCG) in 2007 and later had a brutality lawsuit filed against him. A "patient" who filled twenty prescriptions for three types of anabolic steroids—testosterone, stanozolol, and nandrolone, as well as for HGH and HCG—was charged with assault in 2009. (Bodybuilders use HCG in conjunction with anabolic steroids.) A Jersey City resident described another steroid-using officer as a "wild-eyed thug." His lawsuit against Jersey City alleges that the officer, Victor Vargas, beat him while in a steroid-induced rage.[135]

How much can this sort of information teach us about the steroid rage hypothesis? Despite the fact that these data are quantitatively unimpressive, only suggestive and inconclusive, they are not entirely without value. As we saw earlier, in December 2010, the police director of Trenton, New Jersey, looked at his own officers involved in the steroid scandal and saw a "significant" number of excessive-force complaints. "When you looked at these records, you start to see where there might be a correlation," he said. "Is it absolutely clear? No. Would a complaint have been there regardless of steroids? Those are issues that need to be addressed."[136]

In fact, the etiological uncertainty about the status of steroid rage is less important than the violent behavior of policemen who are known to use the drugs, whatever its source. Even if steroids cause mood-destabilizing effects in only a small fraction of the thousands of officers who use them, this portends a significant number of dangerous, and potentially fatal, incidents. In the unlikely event that there is no causal relationship whatsoever between the drugs and behavior, there remains the association between an affinity for steroids and police misconduct, which includes illegal drug use and may also involve black market drug dealing. Once again we contemplate the possibility that steroid use may be a *marker* of disordered and trouble-prone personalities.

Police departments have adopted the consensus view of steroid rage as a threat to policing. A 2008 article in *Police Chief* magazine, for example, advises police leaders to be aware of roid rage as a potential hazard and to look for telltale signs of drug abuse: "If the officer's appearance indicated he was exceptionally muscular, would they consider the possible abuse of anabolic steroids? What would prompt them to believe that excessive use of force could be associated with "roid rage," a hyper-aggressive, violent state of mind supposedly brought on by steroid use? When and how would they confirm that their suspicions are true? What if a defense or civil attorney proposed that an officer was a steroid abuser based on the officer's appearance and witnessed behaviors?"[137] The Tweedy and Agee cases offer an unambiguous answer to that question: the defense attorney will fail to persuade judges or juries that steroid use is an extenuating circumstance when a police officer commits violent crimes.

Police departments have speculated about steroid-linked violence for many years. In 1991, only a few years after police use of steroids came to the attention of the American public, investigators in Santa Clara County, California, who were reviewing allegations of brutality against jail inmates raised the possibility that steroids might have fueled guards' aggressive behavior. The San Diego police chief argued, however, that steroid use was "a problem among certain people—not police officers."[138]

On many occasions, police departments have had to confirm that their officers were using steroids either legally (with a valid prescription) or illegally, a felony for which police officers are almost never charged. The following case confirms yet again that although the steroid rage hypothesis has established itself as a norm in law enforcement circles, police departments do not necessarily take it seriously. In 2006, sheriff's deputies in California beat a diabetic man to the point that an insulin pump became dislodged from his body. The thirty-three-year-old victim reached a financial settlement with Merced County. According to the Associated Press: "The Sheriff's Department acknowledged that at least four deputies used mood-altering steroids. They were disciplined in-house and their names never released."[139] In an oddly dissonant manner, this press story combines the standard caution about "mood-altering steroids" with an unapologetic cover-up on behalf of the steroid-using officers. These men had committed felony drug possession, but their department took care of the matter behind closed doors and without involving the law.

CHAPTER THREE

POLICE UNIONS AND STEROIDS

Police unions have consistently opposed steroid testing and any other effective measure aimed at restricting steroid consumption by the officers they represent. This sort of obstruction will come as no surprise to anyone who is familiar with how police unions represent their members. The fundamental principle is to preserve an officer's freedom of action and to protect him from disciplinary measures or punishments to the greatest extent possible, regardless of the offense with which he has been charged. From the perspective of the unions, genuine misconduct by officers is almost nonexistent, while false and baseless accusations against them are the norm everywhere. At times, the defensiveness of police union spokesmen can sound like a kind of calculated paranoia.

Police unions' opposition to steroid testing is only one aspect of the complex politics of policing. The constellation of power within any large municipality involves the mayor in city hall, a police commissioner who answers to the mayor, a police chief who is accountable to the mayor and the commissioner, and the rank-and-file police force, which is represented by one or more unions and is, formally speaking, accountable to the elected and appointed officials who outrank them. In New York City, for example, captains, detectives, sergeants, and patrolmen are represented by separate unions. The largest of the NYPD unions, the Patrolmen's Benevolent

Association (PBA), is by far the most powerful—it is in fact the most powerful police union in the United States. From a legal perspective, this hierarchical power structure is topped by the elected mayor. In reality, the distribution of power is more complicated. Large police unions, such as those in New York City and the state of California, can wield great political power against mayors, commissioners, chiefs, and even elected officials, who sometimes court the unions for their political support. Union officials can sabotage a job-hunting chief or assistant chief by spreading the word to other departments that the candidate is not "an officers' chief." They can attack or even vilify a mayor who is accused of being "antipolice." At their most extreme, police unions can simulate or constitute a threat to public order. In 2014, for example, the president of the PBA, Patrick Lynch, "was flexing his organizing muscle during contract negotiations, harrying the mayor outside public events with large groups of off-duty officers, whose chants and comments edged close enough to threats to draw the attention of the Police department itself, which sent a video team to record the protests."[1]

As this episode and others demonstrate, any large police union carries within itself a latent threat to civil order and political stability. Extremism in defense of police officers' "rights" is a total ideology that starts from the premise that cops do not make serious mistakes and almost never commit harm for which they can properly be held accountable. In fact, in police departments across the country, it is very difficult to dismiss an officer for any offense short of a felony. It is in this context that, on a few occasions, police departments have announced that they will carry out random testing for anabolic steroids. These actions have almost always run into fierce opposition from police unions.

THE PORTLAND POLICE BUREAU (2004–2013)

Police departments willingly tolerate, or are compelled by courts or arbitrators to tolerate, a wide range of eccentric and illegal behaviors that do not result in the termination of officers, despite their known offenses against community standards or the law. In many cases, as this book demonstrates, these improper but often unpunished behaviors have involved the nonmedical use of anabolic steroids, often accompanied by other misbehaviors. The latitude allowed police officers was evident in the Portland Police Bureau, in Oregon, for many years. For example, in 2004 a Portland officer named Mark Kruger admitted, following accusations, to wearing Nazi uniforms—because he was "a history buff." Former associates called him a racist and a homophobe.[2] In 2010 he was disciplined for erecting a Nazi shrine in a city park. In 2014 he won a mediated settlement from the city that wiped clean his personnel file. Chief Mike Reese wrote Kruger a letter of commendation and appointed him captain of the Portland Police Bureau's Drug and Vice Division. Portland mayor Charlie Hales claimed to have been unaware of the mediation deal and its terms.[3]

In 2010 the City of Portland proposed that police officers be subjected to random drug testing—including for anabolic steroids—and mandatory testing after deadly force incidents, suspects' deaths in custody, and serious traffic crashes. The Portland Police Association (PPA), a union attorney said, objected on the grounds that testing would violate officers' privacy and go beyond the "reasonable suspicion" standard that was then in force to trigger testing. Portland mayor Sam Adams endorsed random testing: "We must ensure that an officer's decision-making thought process including whether or not to use lethal force is not clouded by drugs."[4] In 2009 a senior counsel for the City of New York had offered the same argument in support of hair testing for drugs: "To ensure sobriety by the department for its own safety and to instill confidence in the community."[5] The unspoken but insistent demand from the authorities in both cities was that the government was justified in imposing drug testing on police forces (and police unions) that did not want it.

Some observers who appear to be unfamiliar with police culture wonder why rank-and-file police officers don't demand drug testing for their own good. When the City of Portland proposed the drug testing of city police in 2010, the editorial board of the *Oregonian*, while unaccountably ambivalent about the testing proposal, asked the public to consider its civic benefits: "Imagine the strength and self-confidence the Portland Police Bureau would project if officers, tomorrow, voluntarily embraced random drug testing," these idealists declared. "Such a move would show public spirit, and a welcome concern for public safety as well as public perception. It would also show that officers believe they have nothing to hide." Testing would give officers with drug problems an incentive to "come forward and get help ASAP—before their problem is randomly revealed." Finally, the editorialists wondered why police officers themselves did not embrace drug testing: "Drug use by one officer, after all, could put his or her colleagues at risk, so police officers themselves have a strong motivation for weeding it out. To be sure, the logic behind such testing is unassailable." It was time to expand drug testing beyond "reasonable suspicion" cases, which almost never occurred.[6] Two years earlier, on the other side of the world, the assistant commissioner of the Ethical Standards Department in an Australian police department had likewise wondered why the police union had not endorsed drug testing: "I would expect that the [Police Association] would, like we are, be concerned that its members who are coming to work can expect to come to work and not have to work with colleagues who are putting their lives at risk because they're [drunk] or on drugs."

The problem with the well-intentioned invitation to the Portland police force was that it did not take into account the police union and the peer pressures that unions enforce among their members. The drug testing that makes sense to the journalist will not make sense to union officials whose mission is to avoid exposing their members to any sort of outside scrutiny. The editorialists' hopeful suggestion that "police officers themselves [will join] in the debate" about steroid testing imagines that police culture tolerates a freedom of discussion comparable to that of a newsroom. The newspaper's refusal to call for testing is also consistent with its disconnection from how police culture works. A deeper understanding of how the union and its members think might have prompted an outright demand for testing. The mayor of Providence, Rhode Island, made a similar miscalculation in 2010 when he ordered immediate random drug testing of the Providence Police Department. Following the police union's angry reaction to this proposal, the mayor attended a police department promotions ceremony and told the assembled officers that he had assumed they would welcome random testing as a demonstration of their professionalism.[7]

Police union resistance to anabolic steroid testing of officers has been steady and adamant. The defensive attitude toward monitoring steroid consumption can take on the irrational tone that character-izes police unions' efforts to resist almost any kind of surveillance. When the Portland Police Bureau announced in 2012 that a random drug-testing program would include steroids, the PPA opposed the plan. The PPA president, Daryl Turner, offered several objections. He rejected the idea that the detection of steroids at any level, no matter how small, should be regarded as a positive drug test. The union demanded a special test for over-the-counter supplements if the officer tested positive for steroids, since many so-called dietary supplements have been found to be contaminated with anabolic steroids. The union president argued that it was patently unrea-sonable to expect officers to understand what they were swallow-ing: "To expect officers to read the list of ingredients on the back of a supplement bottle, many of which are in chemical terms, and then determine whether those chemicals might contain illegal sub-stances is to ask the impossible," he wrote to a city official. But this demand demonstrated only that the union president did not under-stand that there was no difference between the steroids that might be present in a supplement and steroids from other sources. As a medical steroid expert at the Oregon Health Sciences University commented: "They don't know what they're talking about. . . . To say that amino acids or different types of supplements will test positive when they're not steroids is patently false." The Portland plan even allowed for consideration to be given to "possible alternate medical explanations" if an officer tested positive for steroids.[8] The fallacy here is that the medical alibis for steroid use that many policemen offer are based on bogus diagnoses of invented medical disorders. Indeed, any accommodation for "alternate medical explanations" is problematic simply because there are so many doctors who are willing to write medically unjustified prescriptions for testosterone and other anabolic steroids.

A year later, the police bureau agreed to a three-year contract with the PPA that allowed the city to start random drug testing of officers, but not for anabolic steroids, on the grounds that steroid testing was still too costly. Departments in Phoenix, Dallas, Albuquerque, Boston, and New York were testing for steroids, but Portland would not. "What law enforcement is finding is that there's a whole lot more people who are going to test positive for this, than for cocaine or anything," according to Commander Kim Humphrey of the Phoenix Police Department, one of the few police executives willing to take on the steroid issue. (Even Phoenix's steroid testing, which was quietly ended in 2014, required a vastly elevated testosterone level to constitute a violation.) Portland did reserve the right to test for steroids on the basis of "reasonable suspicion" that an officer was using them.[9] The problem was the uncertainty regarding how often (and on what basis) police commanders were willing to declare that the body structure or conduct of an officer was "suspicious." Police unions' expected responses to such decisions to test are likely to discourage this process.

In November 2013, the Portland police union's tentative contract contained a provision that, in effect, rendered steroid testing null and void. Officers who took steroid-tainted supplements would be off the hook if they tested positive for steroids in random tests. As the union phrased it: "This change to the substance abuse policy protects members who take sports supplements that are tainted with steroids or prohormones." Any positive steroid test could (and would) be explained away as having resulted from the ingestion of a tainted supplement by an unwitting cop. Every steroid user who tested positive would have a ready-made alibi. The medical steroids expert Dr. Linn Goldberg questioned the union's logic: "I don't get it. They're using something that was placed in a product illegally, but that's OK. It essentially voids the drug testing." To this argument, the union would surely reply, as it had in 2012, that cops could not be expected to be responsible for ensuring that the supplements they took were untainted.[10]

Police union officials have never openly advocated the functional use of steroids to promote the safety of officers on the streets, even though their resistance to expanded testing protocols effectively preserves the option of steroid use for doping officers. Official endorsement of functional steroid doping would be a public relations problem for the unions. The moral authority attached to the war on drugs rules out police officers having this sort of autonomy and requires that the unions take politically correct positions on illicit drug use. "Obviously, we have zero tolerance for any kind of drug use," the executive director of the Fraternal Order of Police (FOP) said in 2010. With 350,000 members enrolled in 2,100 chapters across the country, the FOP represents most of the local police officers in the United States. At the same time, the union insists upon "due process" and the protection of officers from "unnecessary investigations."[11] In a similar vein, the vice president of the Florida Police Benevolent Association (FPBA) declared in 2006: "As professional law enforcement officers, it's important that the citizens of Florida and our fellow officers have complete confidence in the fact that we are performing our duties drug-free."[12]

The public relations strategies employed by police unions combine this drug-free rhetoric with hyperbolic denials of drug use by cops and a range of explanations of (or alibis for) steroid use. Accordingly, in 2003 a labor relations specialist working for the Michigan Association of Police used a claim of infrequency to justify the union's opposition to random drug testing: "I would venture to guess that 99.9% of officers working the streets aren't taking drugs. To me, it's really one more slap in the face to the police officers." This statement followed the police chief's call for random testing.[13] In 2006 the vice president of the FPBA estimated drug use by police at one-half of 1 percent.[14] Following the arrest in 2011 of several Philadelphia police officers for dealing steroids, the president of the Fraternal Order of Police commented: "We've got a lot of good cops. We just have a few morons out there, too."[15] This comment combines denial of drug use with the "bad apples" explanation of police misbehavior, which is frequently heard from members of the police establishment faced with the task of explaining to the public excessive-force incidents and other forms of police misconduct.

THE BAD APPLES THEORY

On October 2, 2014, New York City's police commissioner, William J. Bratton, bluntly addressed the politically sensitive topic of bad police officers at the opening of a conference of NYPD commanders. "We will aggressively seek to get those out of department who should not be here," he said. "The brutal, the corrupt, the racist, the incompetent." The counterpoint to this unhappy message was the commissioner's ringing endorsement of those he called "the vast, vast majority, that 99 percent" of NYPD officers who did their jobs honestly and well. It was the brutal, the corrupt, the racist, and the incompetent, he said, who were "poisoning the well."[16]

Bratton's jarring denunciation of the bad apples of the NYPD was made during a difficult period for the force. Only three months earlier, NYPD officers had inflicted what the New York medical examiner called a "homicide" on an unarmed black man, Eric Garner, who had resisted arrest for selling "loosies" (single cigarettes out of a pack) on the streets of Staten Island. Since that fateful day in July, the NYPD and Bratton had been engulfed by what the *New York Times* was calling "the national conversation over police brutality." This controversy was already well under way, having been catalyzed by the police killing of another unarmed black man, Michael Brown, in Ferguson, Missouri, two months before Bratton's address to his colleagues.

Public discussions of police misconduct have long oscillated between two opposing stereotypes. At one end is the reassuring image of a brave and competent police force on which the public can rely. As the *Los Angeles Times* once put it: "The majority of law enforcement officers do tough and valuable work. A few abuse their authority."[17] "I know most police officers are brave, extraordinary servants who put their lives on the line daily for us all," a Dallas minister wrote in September 2014. "Their service is dishonored by rogue officers whose bullying and violent behavior promote distrust, resentment and even hatred of the police." "All cops," the president of the NYPD's largest police union said in October 2014, "put their lives on the line to protect all New Yorkers—and for that they deserve the public's support."[18]

The antithesis of the good cop is the bad apple, otherwise known as the rogue cop. "There is at least one crazy cop in every precinct," says one retired NYPD officer. Their fellow officers know who they are, but they cannot be thrown off the force unless they commit an offense that is clearly beyond the pale.[19] (The NYPD police unions have negotiated employment contracts that make it almost impossible to fire most of the worst officers.) "We should not eliminate the ability of law enforcement to weed out the few bad apples that make the ranks," a California assemblyman declared in 2013.[20] The rotten apple metaphor is both a vernacular and an official expression. A US Department of Justice report refers to "the 'bad apple' theory of police corruption."[21] Deviance among police can take the form of doping while in uniform. "In most forces," a chief constable in England said in 2013, "there will be a police officer who will be into bodybuilding and the gym and would abuse steroids."[22] The chief constable's portrait of the solitary bodybuilding policeman may be an accurate account of steroid use in a small English town, but it does not comport with what is known about increasing steroid use among adolescent and adult English males. "There are certain jobs that attract users," one British public health worker said in January 2015—"Army, doormen, police."[23]

The constant oscillation between the two stereotypes, "that 99 percent" of incorruptible police officers and the solitary bad apples, paralyzes our understanding of how cops really behave when a force of 35,000 officers polices a huge and ethnically complicated metropolitan area like New York City. Assigning every officer to one of two categories, either a member of the "vast" wholesome majority or one of the few unwholesome deviants, has prevented the public from finding out about certain kinds of police misconduct, including anabolic steroid use. This lack of knowledge, in turn, raises a seldom-asked question, namely, how much is the public allowed to know about how police officers think and behave when they are out of the public eye? Lacking this knowledge, how can the public or the media judge the accuracy of the oft-heard claim that the "vast, vast majority" of police officers are beyond suspicion?

Politicians and police departments promote the stereotype of the "99 percent" because it serves their interests and is regarded as essential to preserving a working relationship between police forces and the ordinary citizens they protect. The 99 percent argument is a rhetorical device that requires public discussion of policing to avoid even the suggestion that police misbehavior extends beyond the small number of deviant bad apples who, in the words of Commissioner Bratton, "poison the well." In short, the 99 percent stereotype is one of those "operative social fictions" that make it easier for public officials to convince the public and themselves that the social order is intact and functioning satisfactorily.

The stereotype of the untainted 99 percent is factually implausible, for a number of reasons. First, police work exposes officers to many temptations to violate professional ethics and the law. "As the history of virtually every police agency attests," the Department of Justice report on police integrity points out, "policing is an occupation that is rife with opportunities for misconduct."[24] What is more, the rules of conduct for policing are flexible; officers must constantly adapt to new circumstances and innovate in unexpected situations that may be unpleasant or threatening. Distinguishing between the use of excessive force or police brutality, on the one hand, and forceful but defensible tactics on the other can be difficult; in fact, the use of physical force is inherent in the job. Some cops see policing as "a full contact sport between the good guys and the bad guys."[25] From this perspective, the idea that the "vast, vast majority" of officers manage somehow to avoid misconduct, and perhaps repeated cases of misconduct, is simply not plausible. It is worth noting that in the 2012 fiscal year, claims against the NYPD for police misconduct cost the city $152 million.

Second, limits on what outsiders are allowed to know about how police think and behave makes the 99 percent model unverifiable. "Hearing New York police officers speak publicly but candidly about one another and the people they police is rare indeed," the *New York Times* noted in 2011 in its coverage of an NYPD racism scandal. On those rare occasions when it happens, what the public learns may challenge the 99 percent model in uncomfortable ways. The NYPD officers who called black participants in the 2011 West Indian American Day Parade "savages," "animals," and "filth" on Facebook—and signed their names to these comments—apparently did not think their colleagues would find such racist terms offensive.[26] If such behavior is acceptable to a substantial part of the NYPD, then the presence of systemic racism alone invalidates the 99 percent stereotype. A black councilwoman from Brooklyn called the Facebook postings "police terrorism." The president of the Caribbean Guyana Institute for Democracy warned: ""The lives of Caribbean Americans are in danger with individuals like these on the police force."[27] This event made it clear that the 99 percent model promotes the illusion of racially impartial policing. Commissioner Bratton's invocation of the "vast, vast majority" formula thus offered differing messages to different audiences. The white audience heard an attempt to rally public opinion behind a majority-white police force beset by a public relations crisis. Many in the black audience may have heard calculated indifference to their experiences of police misconduct.

As mentioned earlier, police officers limit knowledge of their misconduct by enforcing a code of silence. The Department of Justice report calls it "inherent in the occupational culture of policing": "The Code or The Blue Curtain that informally prohibits or discourages police officers from reporting the misconduct of their colleagues."[28] According to academic experts: "The code decrees that cops protect other cops, no matter what, and that cops of high rank back up working street cops—no matter what."[29]

In 1995 at a Harvard forum, Bratton, then the police commissioner of Boston, responded to claims by some criminal law experts that cops lie routinely on the witness stand when they testify in court. While acknowledging that experts "have said police perjury is pervasive," Bratton tried to counteract the assertion: "If you asked the police unions, they would say it is minimal. I think the truth probably lies somewhere in the middle." The angry reaction from the president of the Boston police union to Bratton's violation of the code included his claim that cops, to the best of his knowledge, never, ever lie on the stand.[30] Twenty years later, Bratton was in New York attempting to placate the police unions by claiming that 99 percent of NYPD officers can be trusted to respect the rights of citizens and obey the law.

The blue wall of silence makes it extremely difficult to calculate or even estimate with any accuracy the frequency or severity of police misconduct. The differing perspectives of higher-ranking officers and street cops, not to mention the periods of estrangement between them, mean that information about police misconduct at the street level may never reach the upper echelons. Police union leaders can make this gulf unbridgeable when tension and hostility between the top and the bottom of the force suits their purposes. Besides enforcing the code of silence among their members, police unions can compel police executives to acknowledge its sovereignty. In 1996, for example, the chief of the Bureau of Internal Investigations of the Boston Police Department filed a sworn affidavit that confirmed both the existence and effects of the code: "Officers are reluctant to break the 'code of silence' and to testify against their colleagues."[31] Except, perhaps, for the most egregious cases of misconduct, such testimony amounts to professional suicide. As a Boston judge summed it up in 1992: "I have determined that because police officers are not likely to regulate police conduct, an outside sanction here is necessary for the public good."[32]

The demonstrated inability of some police departments to police themselves during periods of turmoil is another challenge to the 99 percent stereotype. In November 2011, for example, the NYPD found itself dealing with multiple corruption prosecutions that had been initiated outside the department's ineffective Internal Affairs Bureau. The NYPD was then receiving about 65,000 corruption complaints a year, a thousand of which it classified as serious. Neither Internal Affairs nor the mayor's Commission to Combat Police Corruption—a tiny office with no subpoena power—could begin to keep up with this kind of volume.[33] The veteran New York journalist Wayne Barrett argued that "such an avalanche of scandal" required "going beyond the 'few bad apples' basket of bromides" in order to rid police culture of "the incest inside this department that is at the center of a great city's life."[34]

This book's specific challenge to the 99 percent rhetoric regards the illegal or medically fraudulent use of anabolic steroids by an unknown number of police officers. That figure may be conservatively estimated to number in the thousands or, in all likelihood, in the tens of thousands across the country. The many clusters of steroid-using officers in departments all over the country exceed the bad apples threshold. The fact that random steroid testing of officers occurs in very few of the 18,000 state and local law enforcement agencies in the United States makes it impossible to defend empirically the argument that 99 percent of them are drug-free. More effective "targeted testing" of officers based on a "reasonable suspicion" standard appears to be rare. Police unions' resistance even to random steroid testing suggests that steroid use by cops may be more common than police commanders profess to believe. Steroid use by elite athletes was underestimated for years because the acceptability of drug use within sports subcultures was not fully understood, either by the public or by many better-informed observers (including this writer). What is more, anabolic steroid use is increasing across several social venues in the United States and around the world. Police officers who, through socialization, are exposed to steroid-affiliated US subcultures, such as weightlifting gyms, are as likely as (or, perhaps, more likely than) other young men to use performance-enhancing drugs.

REASONABLE SUSPICION FOR STEROID TESTING

The drug testing of police officers in the United States is now a routine policy in most departments. Widespread drug testing by public and private employers dates from the mid-1980s, when President Ronald Reagan was vigorously promoting the war on drugs initiated by President Richard Nixon in 1969. According to a small survey carried out in 1986, almost three-quarters of police departments were carrying out drug-screening tests of all applicants. (Testing police officers for anabolic steroids was not yet even on the horizon.) That year, the *Chicago Tribune* reported "what may signal the start of a national trend," namely, plans by the Boston and Miami police departments to begin requiring all officers to be randomly tested for illegal drugs. In March 1986, a special presidential commission issued a report calling on employers to drug-test their workers in order to strike a blow against the "voracious" public demand for illegal drugs, which was enriching organized crime. "Citing the sensitive nature of their professions," the *Tribune* reported, "police agencies and those companies engaged in public protection and safety have been among the first to respond to this appeal." A month later, the Miami police union overwhelmingly approved the testing of all officers via annual random urinalysis to detect marijuana, cocaine, and other illegal drugs.[35]

That a police union was willing to embrace a new drug-testing regimen for its members suggests how early this was in the politically mandated "national trend" of drug screening police officers and other workers. Yet the union resistance to testing that has become the norm today was already evident in 1986. An attorney representing the Boston Patrolmen's Association articulated the combination of antidrug rhetoric and resistance to the scrutiny of officers' behavior that has become the standard position of police unions today. "We're the first to agree that there's no place in police work for cops who use or distribute drugs," the attorney said. "But to require an officer to be tested when there is no probable cause or suspicion constitutes an unlawful search in violation of the 4th Amendment."

Commissioner Francis Roache, echoing the presidential mandate to pull out all the stops in the pursuit of eliminating workplace drug use, saw the matter differently: "I have an obligation to make sure our employees are drug-free," he said. "The one issue we remember is that we're engaged in public safety."[36]

At the end of the 1980s, many courts were still arguing that police officers "should not be subjected to drug testing in the absence of a 'reasonable suspicion.'" As one legal author noted in 1989, "the courts continue to resist the idea of mandatory drug testing even though the public seems to be in favor of it."[37] President Reagan's summons to wage a relentless war on drugs had not yet fully registered in the minds of many judges. Since that era, random drug testing has become the norm in many workplaces, including police departments, and the concept of reasonable suspicion for targeted drug testing has evolved in ways that reflect the transition from the pre-steroid era of testing to today, when very limited steroid testing of officers may be taking place. In March 2016, I was unable to confirm that such testing was taking place anywhere in the United States.

The reasonable suspicion criterion for testing was examined in *Lovvorn v. City of Chattanooga, Tenn.* (1988), a court case involving a drug-testing program for firefighters. The Sixth Circuit Court of Appeals concluded that "there must be some evidence of [a] significant department-wide drug problem or individualized suspicion" to justify the targeted testing of individuals.[38] In the years since *Lovvorn*, the idea of a "department-wide drug problem" has appeared only sporadically, generally in the form of newspaper speculation following a local steroid scandal. And even in these cases, the bad apples model has prevailed, based on the assumption that a hard core of drug-using officers has tarnished the image of the entire force. There is some justice in this claim, since department-wide steroid doping is unlikely to occur, given the many personality types who serve in a department. If steroid use is suspected or found, some questions then arise: How large a subgroup within a department is interested in using steroids? To what extent does peer pressure play a role in promoting a steroid subculture? Will this subculture mutate into a cell of rogue cops? And what constitutes reasonable suspicion on the part of the chief who might want to investigate them?

When three Arlington, Texas, police officers came under federal (not local) investigation for steroid use in 2013, Chief Will Johnson asked: "Were there things we could have seen? Were there things we could have done? The answer is, I don't know." None of these officers had been drug-tested, because they did not serve in undercover units such as narcotics. And in any case, the tests in use did not check for steroids. In fact, less than 2 percent of the Arlington police force is ever tested. Not far away in Dallas and Fort Worth, all officers are subject to random drug testing, and special units are subject to additional testing. In the meantime, the City of Arlington's legal department was wondering whether it could come up with a testing plan the police union would accept.[39]

An effective reasonable-suspicion procedure should eliminate situations in which police chiefs unable to detect the dopers on their forces can only ask, "Were there things we could have seen?" The answer to this question in the year 2013 was an unequivocal yes. For one thing, the department demonstrated almost no interest in administering even conventional drug tests to its officers, and there was no attempt to detect steroid use. Police administrators showed no interest in steroid abuse or in what it could signify about mental stability. (One officer committed suicide shortly after being accused.) So what can a police chief who *is* concerned about steroids look for as signs of potential trouble?

Formulating a reasonable suspicion procedure is not a simple exercise, because identifying the signs of drug use that justify suspicion can be difficult. A Phoenix police academy recruit who fainted during training and then went on "a cursing tirade against his supervisors" made detection relatively easy by acting out the anger and irritability often associated with steroid use. He failed his steroid test and was expelled from the academy.[40] Most trainees and officers do not, however, create such a convenient reasonable suspicion of drug abuse. As the *FBI Law Enforcement Bulletin* noted in

1991, "police officers who use drugs generally do not come to work visibly under the influence."[41]

The concept of reasonable suspicion has taken two forms over the past few decades. The first relies on information about the suspected officer, the second on observable behavior. The *New Jersey Law Enforcement Drug Testing Manual* (2001), for example, says that reasonable suspicion "requires objective facts" in the form of information that may consist of "direct evidence or is hearsay in nature." Is the informant or source reliable? Is there corroborating information? Is the information current or out-of-date?[42]

The reliability of information became an issue in 2009 when the police union in Plantation, Florida, challenged the department's right to require the targeted drug testing of an officer unless he was able to face his accuser. The conflict between the union and the leadership originated in the department's interest in protecting the identities of confidential sources. The president of the police union argued that accused officers were defenseless against claims by the department that confidential informants were real and credible. Confounding this argument, an arbitrator had ruled that only a drug test could determine the credibility of the informant. The union's position was that its existing contract allowed for drug testing only on the basis of a reasonable suspicion based on verifiable information.[43]

The second source of reasonable suspicion is observed behavior. In the absence of overt misbehavior, what is required, according to the 1991 FBI report, is "a more subtle analysis by the police supervisor." Indicators of a substance abuse problem could include "a drop in performance, increased use of sick time, and excessive tardiness."[44] At the time, a "subtle analysis" of officers' behavior did not include the signs or symptoms of anabolic steroid use. In the steroid era, however, the physical appearance of a bulked-up officer can be regarded as evidence that justifies the "reasonable suspicion" of steroid use. The town of Upper Darby, Pennsylvania, for example, "will test for steroids if a supervisor notices an officer suddenly get overly muscled, especially if the bulk-up accompanies citizen complaints or reports of aggression," according to a police spokesman.[45]

Making potentially damaging judgments about musculature raises civil liberties issues that remain unresolved in the United States. In Sweden, however, police investigating the use of illegal anabolic steroids are allowed to detain citizens based on "muscle profiling."[46]

In 2008, a *Police Chief* magazine symposium on police use of anabolic steroids confirmed that both muscle profiling and certain behavioral disorders could constitute grounds for reasonable suspicion:

> If the officer's appearance indicated he was exceptionally muscular, would they consider the possible abuse of anabolic steroids? What would prompt them to believe that excessive use of force could be associated with "roid rage," a hyperaggressive, violent state of mind supposedly brought on by steroid use? When and how would they confirm that their suspicions are true? What if a defense or civil attorney proposed that an officer was a steroid abuser based on the officer's appearance and witnessed behaviors?

Furthermore, the symposium pointed out problems with both drug testing and behavioral observations related to steroid use:

> Compared with alcohol and other illicit drugs, anabolic steroids (also known as anabolic-androgenic steroids, or AASs) are not easily detected. Supervisors typically are trained to look for inappropriate behaviors that might justify a "just cause" drug screen; however, with AASs the behaviors and other indicators might not be as easily recognized.[47]

Precisely because the vague reasonable suspicion criterion has been generally disregarded, only a clear threat of dramatically harmful behavior can revive its use. For example, the Miami-Dade Police Department (MDPD) announced in October 2014 that after years of relying on the reasonable-suspicion-of-abuse standard, it was on the verge of testing all its officers for steroids. "Theoretically,"

one journalist observed, the department could test an officer suspected of steroid use, "but apparently that's never happened." This
impression was seconded by Miami–Dade County's labor relations
manager: "I've been here 21 years and I don't recall anyone ever
being tested for steroids." The police union chief saw no drug problem: "I haven't seen any blatant abuse." But an MDPD spokesman
offered a different story: "The move came after concerns had been
raised about 'rage-like' outbursts from cops using the drugs."[48] The
spokesman did not (and perhaps could not) identify the concerned
parties or the precise basis on which they had made their claims
about steroid-induced outbursts. In the end, all the back-and-forth
about testing turned out to be meaningless. A year after the October 2014 announcement that steroid testing was just around the
corner, nothing had been done. The obstacle to progress, according
to the department, was the refusal of the police union to come to
an agreement.[49]

POLICE UNIONS AND POLITICAL ENDORSEMENTS

Law enforcement personnel at local, state, and federal levels, along
with their professional associations, are a potent political force in
the United States. Altogether, they represent some 900,000 voters.
Police unions endorsed the racist and authoritarian campaign of
Donald J. Trump during his successful 2016 presidential campaign. The Fraternal Order of Police, a national organization that
has 330,000 members, endorsed the Trump candidacy in September after more than two-thirds of the group's national board voted
for Trump. Hillary Clinton, who had declined to seek the group's
endorsement, received no votes.[50] The FOP president, Chuck Can-
terbury, told National Public Radio that Clinton's support for police
reform was misguided: "Reform in a profession that doesn't need to
be reformed is not the answer to fight crime."[51] Trump also won the
endorsement of the New England Police Benevolent Association
and the Cleveland Police Patrolmen's Association, the National Border Patrol Council, and other police unions.

Other groups criticized Trump's understanding of policing issues. A coalition of police chiefs and prosecutors representing 30,000 law enforcement professionals responded to the "law and order" candidate by rejecting his zero-tolerance approach to reducing crime. Norm Stamper, a former Seattle police chief, pointed out that rank-and-file officers were more likely to support Trump's hard line on policing than police managers, who are more concerned about community relations. Groups representing African American law enforcement officers protested the endorsements of Trump by the FOP and the Cleveland police union.[52] The National Latino Peace Officers Association's executive chairman, a former NYPD sergeant, denounced the "stupidity" of the FOP and noted that it represents less than half of the country's 765,000 local officers.

Such numerical arguments are, however, misleading, since the temperament of most white police officers resonates with Trump's unqualified refusal to back reforms demanded by civil liberties groups but rejected and resented by police unions. In summary, the Trump endorsements further intensified the bitter conflict between a "profession that doesn't need to be reformed" and the people of color who fear it. While the black population demands relief from excessive police violence, many among the Latino population live in fear of the deportations that Trump promised during his presidential campaign.

POLICE UNION INTIMIDATION OF PUBLIC OFFICIALS

Police intimidation can be directed at elected officials responsible for monitoring police conduct. In 2012, police in Fullerton, California, denounced city council members who demanded the reform of police procedures following the horrific killing of a schizophrenic homeless man, Kelly Thomas, who was beaten to death by city police officers. This grotesque incident was videotaped and subsequently attracted national attention. In the meantime, union members have repeatedly confronted the city council over its alleged "lack of concern about public safety."[53]

Police intimidation can take the form of following a public official to his home and subjecting him to a sobriety test and then hiring private investigators to harass him. Councilman Jim Righeimer of Costa Mesa, California, was targeted by city police in 2012. "What you have here," he said, "is police associations and their law firms hiring private detectives to dig up dirt on elected officials that they can then use to extort them, embarrass them, or worse, in order to get the elected official to vote against the best interests of the city to protect themselves. That's the definition of extortion."[54]

Police intimidation of elected officials can also take the form of mob action by large numbers of officers in indoor or outdoor venues. Perhaps the most notorious police riot in recent times occurred on September 16, 1992, in New York City. The Patrolmen's Benevolent Association staged a demonstration to protest Mayor David Dinkins's proposal to create an independent civilian review board that would investigate police misconduct. Other grievances against the African American mayor included his handling of antipolice riots in a black section of the city and his refusal to issue semiautomatic weapons. Chants and shouted insults from the crowd included "The mayor's on crack!" and racial epithets. The *New York Times* described the chaotic scene as follows:

> Thousands of off-duty police officers thronged around City Hall yesterday, swarming through police barricades to rally on the steps of the hall and blocking traffic on the Brooklyn Bridge for nearly an hour in the most unruly and angry police demonstration in recent memory.
>
> The 300 uniformed officers who were supposed to control the crowd did little or nothing to stop the protesters from jumping barricades, tramping on automobiles, mobbing the steps of City Hall or taking over the bridge. In some cases, the on-duty officers encouraged the protesters. . . .
>
> At 10:50 A.M., a few demonstrators chanting "Take the hall! Take the hall!" flooded over the barriers and into the parking lot in front of City Hall, meeting no resistance from the police

on guard. Cheering and screaming, thousands of others poured through from every side of the park and seethed up the hall steps. Some mounted automobiles and began a raucous demonstration, denting the cars.[55]

Rudolph Giuliani, the Republican mayoral candidate who would soon defeat Dinkins in the next city election, thanks in part to massive political support from the police unions, "repeatedly shouted a barnyard epithet ["Bullshit!"] to the wild cheers of protestors."[56]

Recalling this "rally-cum-mutiny" a year later in a detailed investigation of the PBA, the *Village Voice* reported: "Almost every source the *Voice* approached in preparing this article was reluctant to speak. People intimately familiar with the PBA said they feared for their lives and those of their families if they talked. As one person put it: 'It would be suicidal for a police officer to speak out.'" A former NYPD investigator, Robert Hughes, pointed out that the PBA accrued power in part by outlasting police commissioners: "The turnover in the police department administration is so rapid, that nobody knows the whole story. And nobody wants to know. They are afraid of them."[57]

The NYPD's union-sponsored riot of 1992 was not the last of its kind. In February 2014, a group of Miami cops belonging to the Fraternal Order of Police entered the Miami City Hall "shouting, banging on glass partitions, disrupting the city commission meeting, sending commissioners fleeing from the dais, scaring the hell out of staffers." The Miami police chief had once declared that "disruption of a governmental official meeting" was "a prosecutable crime." The president of the FOP called this mob demonstration an "exercise of our First Amendment rights." In 2004, the *Miami Herald* had reported on a similar mob scene: "Let's call Wednesday's courthouse demonstration by Broward County police officers that masqueraded as a protest by its proper name: intimidation. It's a tactic favored by bullies, or, in this case, the union known as the Broward Police Benevolent Association." In March 2014 the police union returned to Miami City Hall. By that time, however, the Miami police chief had issued an order prohibiting off-duty cops from carrying fire-arms into city hall and warned that the next police-led disruption of a commission meeting would result in "punitive legal action, up to and including prosecution."[58]

The professional standards of police unions are called into question when mass actions of this kind are accompanied by the claim that crimes committed by police officers are not crimes. The major police union representing the NYPD mobilized hundreds of officers, in plainclothes and in uniform, to appear inside and out-side a Bronx courthouse in October 2011 when sixteen cops were charged in a ticket-fixing scandal. The journalist Wayne Barrett described the demonstration as "a mob takeover." The *New York Times* reported that demonstrating "officers were heard shouting slurs at welfare recipients at a nearby office."[59] Rather than claiming that the officers were innocent of the felony charges, PBA president Patrick Lynch declared that ticket fixing was not a crime: "Taking care of your family, taking care of your friends, taking care of those that support New York City police officers is not a crime." Many of the accused were also PBA officials. Small wonder that Barrett deplored "the incest inside this department." Lynch further rational-ized the alleged corrupt conduct of the accused officers by claiming that ticket fixing was standard operating procedure for the NYPD: "When the dust settles," he said, "and we have our day in court, it will be clear that this is part of the NYPD at all levels."[60] In the last analysis, and regardless of whether the accusation is true, this is pure ethical nihilism coming from the top of the union.

RESISTANCE TO THE REGULATION OF OFFICER CONDUCT

Police unions contest virtually any regulation of their officers' behavior. This resistance is applied to relatively innocuous proce-dures such as placing the names of troublesome officers on lists of those not to be called to testify in court, as well as to more serious matters such as investigations of police brutality and the surveil-lance of police conduct.

California's powerful police unions have resisted the publication of lists of police officers with alleged credibility problems, so-called Brady lists, which are kept by prosecutors who do not want tainted testimony by police officers to undermine criminal cases they bring to court. The unions want a role in determining how such lists are used in disciplinary decisions. Prosecutors place officers on a Brady list for violations that include falsifying reports and the use of excessive force.[61] Police unions dislike Brady lists and push back against their use, but they will vigorously contest charges of police brutality, and sometimes in ways that strain credibility. In one of the most infamous such cases in recent years, on July 18, 2014, members of the NYPD arrested Eric Garner, an asthmatic forty-three-year-old African American who weighed in excess of 300 pounds, for allegedly selling loose cigarettes on Staten Island. A videotape of the arrest showed Garner on the ground, apparently being subjected to an unauthorized chokehold, a tactic banned by the NYPD since 1993. Garner died as a result of the struggle with multiple officers, and the city medical examiner's autopsy report classified the death as a homicide caused by a chokehold.

This fatal encounter exploded into a widely protested example of alleged police brutality, thereby angering the police unions and further exacerbating their ongoing conflict with the liberal mayor of New York City, Bill de Blasio, with whom they had feuded about policing strategies. Patrick Lynch, the PBA president, flatly denied what others regarded as video evidence: "It was not a chokehold. He was a big man who had to be brought to the ground to be placed under arrest by shorter police officers. Sometimes the use of force is necessary. But it's never pretty to watch." In fact, Lynch objected to the fact that Garner's ordeal had been videotaped in the first place, on the grounds that it amounted to "demonizing the good work of police officers."[62] The videotaping of police officers' public conduct, it should be noted, is protected by the First Amendment. Lynch called the medical examiner's press release a "political" document. "Chokehold," he added, "is not a medical term." "The mayor," he said, "needs to support New York City police officers unequivocally."

Ed Mullins, president of the Sergeants Benevolent Association, also rejected both the video evidence and the medical examiner's autopsy report.[63] The mayor denounced the police union's assault on his competence as "fear mongering."[64]

Bitter conflicts between political leaders and unions representing armed men can leave an odor of insurrection in the air. This kind of strife is relevant to the steroid issue because officers' covert and illegal anabolic steroid use is a quiet form of insurrection against police managers' authority to set conduct standards for the rank and file.

Another way that unions fight the regulation of officers' conduct is to change the definition of misconduct or to minimize, even eliminate, punishment for certain infractions. After the Police Benevolent Association and the Fraternal Order of Police supported Jeb Bush's election as governor of Florida in 1999, he repaid the political debt by collaborating with state lawmakers to change the officer discipline system in order to make it more difficult to impose sanctions on wayward cops. The reforms even ruled out punishment for officers who lied while under investigation. Other evidence of serious misconduct could not bar compromised officers from employment. The director of the Florida Department of Law Enforcement, Mike Crews, said in 2011 that its disciplinary panel had once been "hardcore" when it came to revoking the certificates of dishonest officers. But new panel members were "not that hard-core," he said. "Some of them are saying: 'We don't care about lying on a timesheet. Yeah it's untruthfulness, a moral character violation, but perhaps this officer is salvageable.' They tend to give the officer the benefit of the doubt." As a result, officers who had committed assault, lied under oath, or stolen property regained their law enforcement certificates.[65]

Police unions' claims that officers rarely engage in professional misconduct goes hand in hand with the idea that surveillance of police behavior is unnecessary and intrusive. There is no clearer example of this than Patrick Lynch's assertion that videotaping the takedown of Eric Garner was equivalent to libeling policemen as a group. Only weeks after Garner's death, the police chief of Portland,

Oregon, announced that he wanted to put body cameras on police officers. In Rialto, California, over a period of two years (2012–2014), the wearing of police body cameras was accompanied by a 60 percent decline in the use of force and an 80 percent drop in citizen complaints. But the president of the Portland police union, Daryl Turner, was opposed to requiring his members to wear cameras. "When you are in a critical incident for instance, there are a lot of things that happen psychologically, physiologically, to officers that the cameras can't capture. The technology with the infrared light, that they don't see the situation the same as the officers do. The lighting may be different, the peripheral vision is different. There are a lot of things that are different that have to be taken into account."[66] In Florida, the Miami-Dade police union issued another rationale for rejecting body cameras: wearing them "will distract officers from their duties, and hamper their ability to act and react in dangerous situations."[67]

The hostile rejection of outside scrutiny of officer conduct typifies police unions' responses to any proposed surveillance that might limit the discretion of the officer on duty. Every perspective other than that of the officer is disqualified as uninformed or incompetent. The response to other perspectives can be violent. In 2012, a Las Vegas resident videotaping police during a routine traffic stop was confronted by officers, who threw him to the ground, as he screamed, and arrested him. He filed a federal lawsuit on the grounds that the officers had violated his rights, and he received a $100,000 settlement from the city.[68]

In fact, unions' rejection of the closer scrutiny of police behavior as invasive or disruptive is contradicted by evidence that body cameras have dramatic and positive effects on police (and, perhaps, civilian) conduct during street encounters. A study of the effects of body cameras conducted by the Police Foundation and published in 2013 reported: "We have detected a significant treatment effect on the use of force. . . . In terms of complaints against officers, we were unable to compute a treatment effect as planned, since the overall reduction was so large that there were not enough complaints to conduct any meaningful analyses." The officers who wore cameras used force only when dealing with people who were clearly physically abusive or physically resisting arrest.[69]

Police unions' arguments sometimes communicate a calculated defiance of authority, an unwillingness to accept the institutional hierarchy that vests ultimate power in the police administrators who run departments. Police unions expect to negotiate over the introduction of body cameras and other significant innovations in police work. So when William Bratton, the New York City police commissioner, declared in September 2014 that the cameras were "going to be an essential part of what an officer wants to wear on patrol," he was challenging the police unions in the arena of public opinion and placing a de facto bet on the proposition that they could not prevail in this debate. Highly publicized police shootings and the "homicide" inflicted on Eric Garner by NYPD officers appeared to have initiated a groundswell of public sentiment in favor of close surveillance of police behavior. PBA president Patrick Lynch saw it otherwise: "Police officers have nothing to hide, but there are many unanswered questions as to how this will work practically," he said.[70] By Lynch's standards, this was a moderate response. The fanatical aspect of the police union mentality is evident in the demonstrably false assertion that police officers never have anything to hide.

POLICE UNION ATTITUDES TOWARD FITNESS STANDARDS

An important factor in the growth of steroid use by officers is the recent emphasis on physical fitness within the police ranks. A 2012 article on Officer.com put it this way: "Beginning in the mid to late 1990's and early 2000's things began to change as the baby boomers became older. Department budgets increased; overtime pay, comp time, or vacations were allowed. Trends today are for police departments to hire young officers that [are] fit and trim. Those new officers work out daily and are muscular or 'pumped up' as they call it. Some departments pay gym memberships or have work out rooms to continue the officer's fitness."[71] Larry Gaines, chairman of the Department of Criminal Justice at California State University, San Bernardino, has pointed to the inevitable consequences of this trend. "This has become a great competition among officers," he said in 2010. "They want to be the biggest, strongest."[72] The police steroid culture flourishes in the gym, where the intersection of police officers with the bodybuilding culture can engender an outlaw temperament. In this environment, the line separating job-related fitness from cosmetic enhancement can be impossible to discern.

Police unions do not have a common policy regarding fitness other than that standards should be negotiated and that officers should not be treated in what the union sees as an arbitrary manner. The same police unions that passively facilitate steroid use by cops bent on achieving an intimidating muscularity routinely object to mandatory physical fitness requirements, since it is the officer's right to be left alone, not his physical ability to perform his job, that is the union's chief concern. Indeed, this preference for autonomy over fitness may be one reason why police unions have not openly endorsed the functional rationale for steroid use, which some believe enhances officer safety. Police unions that actually put safety first would do far more than they now do to promote physical fitness in the ranks.

In fact, police unions have demonstrated very little enthusiasm for fitness standards. "If the union believes as much as we do in wellness," the Portland, Oregon, commissioner said in 2012, "we wouldn't have to pay them overtime to take a physical fitness test." He refused to endorse the idea that taxpayers should pay cops to stay healthy. Most members of the Portland Police Association, however, had been paid to show up for a simple checkup, and now the city was attempting to force its officers to demonstrate their fitness to do nonsedentary policing.[73] In Killeen, Texas, in 2010 the local Fraternal Order of Police succeeded in blocking physical fitness testing, on the grounds that "persons who failed to meet certain requirements of the test could be punished." This defeat for mandatory testing caused celebration at the national office of the FOP.[74] A year later, the FOP of a small-town department in Indiana rejected "punitive" physical fitness standards that would have caused the termination of officers who could not pass the test after three tries.[75] In conclusion, police unions' resistance to fitness standards appears to contradict their widely broadcast concern about officer safety, which has become a part of the national conversation about policing. At the same time, the unions make no effort to discourage steroid-dependent "fitness" among the rank and file.

CHAPTER FOUR

THE GYM CULTURE, WHERE MUSCULAR COPS MEET

The global headquarters of the anabolic steroid epidemic is a social institution known as the gym. There are thousands of these venues around the world, forming a virtual community that extends from California to Qatar to Kabul. While all of them serve the primary purpose of providing a place for weightlifting, they differ according to the cultural, economic, and security conditions under which they operate: in some societies, muscled torsos must be concealed beneath loosely fitting clothes; in the poorer neighborhoods of India or Iraq, there are gyms that are nothing more than hole-in-the-wall spaces in basements or small rooms; during the wars in Afghanistan and Iraq, US troops worked out in gyms located in the relative safety of the Baghdad Green Zone or behind barbed wire at forward operating bases. Depending on their location, gyms may contain only the most rudimentary weightlifting equipment or a cornucopia of low-tech and high-tech devices. The glamorous elite gyms of Southern California are filled with barbells, dumbbells, kettlebells, EZ-Curl bars, trap ("hex") bars, safety squat bars, cambered bars, Apollon's Axles, Strongman logs, pull-up bars, lifting straps, weightlifting belts, weighted clothing, power racks, inversion tables, inversion boots, Teeter Hang Ups, dip stations, prowler/dragging sleds, plyo boxes, and weight machines: Marcy Combo Smith machines, cable machines, the Nautilus machines, Body-Solid GPR378 Pro Power Cages, the Powertec Fitness Workbench Leg Press Accessories, and Precor S3.55 Multi Gym Strength Systems.

Gyms are connected with the societies in which they operate in complex and interesting ways. The faithful clientele of an upscale gym can include members of every social and professional class. In swanky and lucrative urban and suburban gyms, lifting for upward social mobility can be more important than lifting to add muscle. A fundamental difference in purpose, ambiance, and drug consumption separates a hard-core "iron cave" bodybuilding gym from a "lifestyle health club" or a spa, where lifting plays a less significant role in the achievement of muscular fitness.

Bodybuilding gyms have spread the use and cultural influence of anabolic steroids in a variety of ways. They can, for example, serve as open or covert drug markets. A typical report from a narcotics squad operation in Queens, New York, in 2007 describes such places, which had names such as the Envy Us Gym and the Powerhouse Gym: "Far from being healthy environments for the body and the mind, the gyms were allegedly turned into drug supermarkets by many of the defendants who openly and illegally sold performance drugs wanted by body builders, as well as a cornucopia of highly addictive and potentially dangerous prescription painkillers and street drugs, in and around the two locations."[1] Those arrested included a female boxer, several competitive bodybuilders, gym employees, an aspiring female adult-movie star, and a police officer.[2]

The different backgrounds of the clients at a bodybuilder-type gym create networking opportunities that can promote steroid use. The steroid-buying clientele at Murphy's gym in Denver in 2005 included "office workers in their 30s who wanted magazine-cover bodies," "strippers who wanted to get lean," and "Denver police officers looking to 'stay on top.'"[3] Police officers meet drug dealers at gyms and may inform them of upcoming police raids on their operations. A gym trainer working as a bouncer meets a police officer who is providing off-duty security and teaches him how to inject himself. Customers can be referred to the corrupt doctors retained by corrupt pharmacies to write fraudulent prescriptions for testosterone and other anabolic steroids. Advice and gossip about steroids circulates among the clientele. "At the place I train," said a young man in Sydney, "every day I hear someone talking about what cycle of steroids they're on. No one is trying to hide it. It used to be very hush-hush, but now no one cares who knows."[4]

The undercover operation in Queens described above exposed a covert drug market. An open-market model is described in "The Steroid Subculture Expands," a 1988 report about a Gold's Gym facility in Pennsylvania: "With little fear of embarrassment—in fact, with tacit encouragement from other users—members of such gyms can sample the whole galaxy of muscle-expanding drugs." The on-site drug dealing attracted many customers to this gym. At the same time, the proprietor discovered that the drug market on his premises was a menace to his business. Bodybuilders constituted a small fraction of his clients, and many of the more civil and less muscle-fixated customers felt intimidated by the hard-core lifters. The proprietor, too, felt threatened by the unruly element among his clientele. Expelling the worst of the steroid exhibitionists did not eliminate the threat to his own safety: "I've got to watch what I say to these guys. We went through a phase where we kicked people out left and right. It's very much a clique, and when these guys are on steroids, they can be up or down. When they're up, they feel like they can conquer the world. When they're down, they can be downright nasty."[5]

The personal trainers who work at many gyms can be steroid dealers or facilitators or both. Sometimes clients demand that their trainers supply them with steroids. Trainers who abstain from steroids can find themselves competing against more heavily muscled rivals for clients, especially in gyms that attract well-heeled patrons. One trainer, for example, found himself in what he regarded as an unfair situation: "I am a personal trainer who is all natural and I find it a misrepresentation for bodybuilders, especially IFBB [International Federation of Bodybuilders] members who [are] 99.9% on roids, to be personal training in the same gym as me. Because they use steroids and are huge and cut, the general public believes they too can look like that." But muscle mass does not always determine who gets clients: "Of all the personal trainers in my gym, the one who is most sought after and makes the most is the one who keeps the clients interested in what they are doing and motivated to continue. He has trained some of our competitors, but he also trains some of the people who just want to tone up and know nothing."[6]

A trainer's physique sets a standard that some clients will want to emulate. Trainers "are the cognoscenti, the knowledgeable insiders, the gurus." As experts, "they instruct their clients in a wide variety of areas, including workout techniques, diet, nutritional supplements, and sometimes in the use of steroids."[7] Achieving an ideal physique may involve testing combinations of drugs and workouts to see which one produces the best results. According to a 1990 report: "Older PTs [personal trainers] used their own bodies as their laboratories, experimenting with various workout routines, nutritional programs, and drugs, including steroids."[8] In today's era of "low T" advertising and the indiscriminate marketing of testosterone products to millions of aging men, this model also applies to the bodybuilding doctors who both act as role models and prescribe testosterone products for "patients" wanting to physically resemble their superfit physicians. In this way, a trainer's role migrates out of the gym. Now it is doctors who are contributing to the medicalization of male aging by promoting male hormone replacement therapy for vast numbers of men who feel they lack the physical or sexual vitality to which they are entitled.

Anabolic steroids live their complex social life both inside and outside the gym. Their broad societal effects—projected out of the gyms where the muscles are made—take the form of aggressive and exhibitionistic social behaviors by young males or, in the case of motorcycle gangs, not-so-young males. In Perth, Australia, for example, the so-called shredder subculture consists of "young, often tattooed, men [who] are usually seen with arms and chest bulging through super-tight muscle shirts, if they are wearing a shirt at all." In November 2012 they were "expected to descend on the

Stereosonic music festival at Claremont Showgrounds, an event fast becoming the shredders' Olympic Games." This subculture has a substantial following: "More than 20,000 Facebook users have joined the online group called "Going to the gym cause u wanna be shredded for stereosonic," a site where many detail their plans to be in peak condition for the November 27 event."[9] Taking steroids before music festivals has become a routine part of this Australian subculture. Across the continent in the state of Queensland: "Music festival promoters are so concerned about the rise of muscled men at events they are introducing 'shirts on' policies. Onelove, which runs the Creamfields and Stereosonic music festivals, confirmed men were asked to cover up to keep other patrons more 'comfortable in their surroundings."[10] In Sydney, shredders are easy to identify: "The ones parading in shirtless packs at music festivals or down George Street on Saturday nights, often mixing their cocktail of steroids with booze, illegal drugs and Viagra. Or they're the guys on the doors at nightclubs telling these packs of men that they can't come in. When these two clash, it's explosive."[11]

Steroids thus fuel intimidating behaviors inside and outside of the gym. In Australia, the most serious threat to life, limb, and public order are the "bikies," motorcycle gang members who use and deal steroids and have begun investing in lucrative suburban gyms.[12] These criminal gangs, as we shall see, belong to an international network of motorcycle gang members who constitute one of the global networks spreading anabolic steroids around the world.

While the gym is the anabolic steroid's natural habitat, its social life—its invisible but pervasive presence in sports, entertainment, and police forces—takes two forms. The heavily muscled bodies of film stars, bodybuilders, martial arts fighters, comic book characters, and action-figure toys have become familiar within the cultural mainstream as a normative and even fashionable image of the modern male. Second, the anabolic steroid animates the public behaviors of steroid-using males who want to display their muscled torsos and sometimes act on the aggressive impulses these torsos represent.

GYMS, COPS, AND SOLDIERS

Working out in two kinds of gyms enables police and military personnel to develop steroid habits. In civilian gyms, cops and soldiers can make connections with dealers and learn how to use the drugs. In gyms reserved for police or military use, they can feel they are among their own, including other steroid-using officers. A police gym that serves cops provides a degree of privacy for steroid-using officers, who might be targeted by undercover agents in a civilian gym. Gyms on military bases can serve as emotionally important sanctuaries away from the combat zones. Both police and military gyms can expose personnel to personal trainers who promote steroid use. In 2011 a senior commander blamed trainers for the steroid problems that embarrassed the Australian military leadership. [13]

"For many New York City police officers," the *New York Times* commented in 2008, "a trip to the gym or the station house weight room is as much a part of the day as roll call or making notes in a memo book."[14] This sanitized presentation of police physical culture is one example of the media coverage that habitually ignores police forces' pathologies and underreports steroid use by officers. In fact, the police gym is a potential breeding ground for rogue cops because it facilitates the formation of steroid-taking cliques with access to drug-trafficking networks. For example, in 2007 a Brooklyn gym popular with NYPD officers turned up at the center of a nationwide investigation into a huge steroid ring that was also selling illegal drugs to professional athletes. Clients at the Dolphin gym were getting their drugs from the notorious Lowen's Compounding Pharmacy, located only blocks away. As one law enforcement source stated: "It was a closed circle. Lowen's processed thousands of prescriptions from a stable of doctors. Customers found out about these doctors. And the drugstore, through the gyms." The most prominent police customer was Brooklyn deputy chief Michael Marino, who confirmed that he had bought a topical steroid cream from Lowen's with a prescription.[15] Marino's tumultuous career as a famously aggressive police commander and bodybuilder was described earlier in this book.

Some police officers adapt easily to the bodybuilding gym culture, for the same reasons as their civilian counterparts. What can set the cops apart is the belief that steroids make them more effective against muscled-up criminals on the streets. John Wills, a former Chicago police officer and FBI agent, infiltrated gyms across the country with other undercover agents and described the scene in 2007:

> During the undercover assignment, my fellow undercover agents and I discovered a subculture consisting of gym owners, bodybuilders, and weightlifters that had no compunction about using steroids and other drugs. What we also discovered was that there were some police officers firmly entrenched in this lifestyle as well. As part of our cover we worked out daily, sometimes twice daily, in popular gyms like PowerHouse, Gold's, and the World Gym. Our networking took us all over the United States. During our travels we tried to make as many "friends" as possible, hoping that they would lead us to the dealers. In the process, we learned that the culture attracted cops for a variety of reasons. Some were competing as bodybuilders, weightlifters, and in other sports as well. Those who were truly obsessed about their endeavors bought into the notion that roids would give them that shortcut, that "leg up" as it were, to get them to the top. Indeed, a few were successful, winning amateur events and some even turning pro where the payoff came in money and fame, not just a trophy for the mantel.[16]

Two goals animate the deep affinity between US police culture and weightlifting or bodybuilding. Functional weight training promotes job-related fitness, whereas cosmetic lifting serves a personal desire for enhanced physical appearance and sexual appeal. The weight training is often intensified by means of a steroid regimen. In his penetrating essay on police use of steroids, the Baltimore attorney Philip J. Sweitzer argues that police officers are "functional strength-athletes," and that "both police officers and firefighters are occupationally predisposed to steroid use, because functional strength and fitness is a bona fide occupational qualification for each." At the same time, Sweitzer is well aware that however convincing the functional rationale for steroid-boosted weight training may seem, it "is largely undercut by an alternative reality: that discretionary use of steroids by most police athletes is primarily for cosmetic purposes." The dual nature of steroid-enhanced lifting thus complicates the assessment of an officer's motives to engage in this training regime. Sweitzer notes that like bodybuilders, "these cops want to be big, burly, and imposing, to have the physical proportions of comic book superheroes."[17] It is easy enough to imagine how this sort of command presence could deter physical challenges on the street and thereby serve a functional purpose. We do not know how much steroid use by weightlifting policemen is intended to be purely functional in this sense.

Police officers' interest in building muscles for sport has a history. As Sweitzer points out, "this culture of strength frequently manifests itself in police/fire/military athletic competitions, such as arm-wrestling contests, weight-lifting meets and other strength-defined athletic pursuits."[18] Sport and fitness competitions for police officers can be formal or informal; multisport Olympic-style athletic meets have been held over the past several decades. The California Police Athletic Federation held the California Police Olympics in 1967 and established the World Police and Fire Games Federation in 1983. The World Police and Fire Games take place biennially. In August 2013, 7,000 participants from sixty-seven countries competed in Belfast, Northern Ireland. Among the fifty-six sports contested was bodybuilding, which, as we have seen, is a problematic activity for police agencies to sponsor.

In 2005, I received the following account of a police bodybuilding contest held in 1983, the year the World Police and Fire Games Federation was founded:

My first body-building competition I ever saw which gave me the pumping iron bug was in 1983 in New York where the Tri-State Police department put on a show for a camp I was working in. These guys (and girls?!) were huge and as a young man I thought wow! I want to be big and powerful and these guys are all Police officers so it must be okay. I was in the National swim team at that time and had no idea of what steroids really were, I merely thought they were something that athletes in the Eastern bloc used to become monsters. Anyway, all the kids I looked after wanted to be like the Police officers they watched that night, the next day they were doing push-ups, lifting rocks etc. I was introduced to an ageing ex-pro bodybuilder that night who brought these officers to this camp for under-privileged children from the Lower East Side, he'd written books, trained champions, etc. and I was told that evening that bodies like this came from a good diet, hard work and plenty of sleep. I was also told they were chemically enhanced! At first I was disappointed but I thought, they're cops, the Nation's finest!

After the passage of three decades it is necessary to situate this lively memoir in its historical context.

Six years after Arnold Schwarzenegger appeared in *Pumping Iron* (1977), the mainstreaming of bodybuilding was already under way. The Ben Johnson steroid scandal that exploded at the 1988 Seoul Olympic Games was still five years in the future, meaning that the demonizing of the anabolic steroid had not yet become established in public discussions about drugs and doping. Police officers' status as lawmen made the bulked-up cops charismatic role models whose "chemical enhancement" was of only fleeting concern to this young admirer.

At the same time, some police athletes expressed their objections to steroid-distorted athletic competition. In 1987, following the 1986 Florida Police Olympics, twenty-five officers from around the state signed a petition demanding that steroids be banned in training for these events and that drug testing be introduced. This proposal was rejected by the president of the Florida Law Enforcement Olympics organization as being too expensive to implement.[19] This schism anticipated the relationship between steroid-using officers and the police executives who eventually, with varying degrees of sincerity and resolve, later declared their opposition to steroid use by police officers. Why they have failed to control steroid use is an important question this book attempts to answer.

The fundamental question that haunts any discussion of cops and steroids is whether steroid use is pathological behavior that affects police work. This book argues that an affinity for steroids is a marker of deviant personality traits that will eventually bring some of these policemen into conflict with the law. This hypothesis takes on added importance if an attachment to bodybuilding is an inherent part of a particular police subculture. For some of these men, according to Sweitzer, "it seems apparent that the reason that they chose to become police officers is psychologically inextricably intertwined with their bodybuilding impulse." One might ask whether there is "something inherent to policing that predisposes police officers to steroid use."[20]

Some bodybuilding police officers lead troubled lives that often involve anabolic steroids and a host of other complications. In 2003, the Denver Police Department found steroids, syringes, and fifteen guns in the home of Officer Thomas Lahey, a weightlifter who in 1990 was acquitted of domestic-violence-related assault and disturbing the peace.[21] The incidence of family violence among police officers has been estimated at about 40 percent, or two to four times the frequency found in the general population.[22]

The case of Anthony Forgione was discussed briefly earlier. In January 2011, the former police officer and bodybuilder pleaded guilty in New York to a fifteen-count federal indictment that included charges of selling anabolic steroids and human growth hormone through the mail. He had provided false information before being hired by the police department of Boca Raton, Florida. An entrepreneur as well as "an avid weightlifter with a muscular build," Forgione ran a "wellness referral service" and an antiaging clinic called Infinity Longevity. Following his sudden death in 2013, his family published an obituary: "Anthony was an avid body builder, nicknamed Pretty Boy. His love for life was God, family and his body building family. He was a professional in the sport as well as a gentleman. He was loved and respected by everyone in the sport he competed in since he was 16. He was a veteran of the Air Force as well as a former police officer with the NYPD and the Boca Raton P.D."[23]

New York City detective Constantine Chronis was a bodybuilder known for his "hulking physique." In 1996, he was at a nightclub drinking with bodybuilder friends when he became involved in an altercation with a twenty-four-year-old black man. He held a crowd at bay with his gun while an acquaintance, shouting racial epithets, bludgeoned the black victim into a coma with a metal steering-wheel lock. The civilian complaints on Chronis's police record "came from civilians who accused him of using racially or ethnically offensive language." Not long after joining the force, Chronis "began a rigorous bodybuilding regimen at BQE Fitness in Woodside, Queens, a health club popular with police officers."[24] Chronis was eventually convicted of assault with depraved indifference, official misconduct, and menacing, and sentenced to eight years in prison.[25]

Perhaps the most violent and dangerous criminals to have been involved with the police gym culture were members of a crime ring of bodybuilding police officers that was uncovered in the Atlanta area in 1993. Six officers from Atlanta-area law enforcement agencies, including two members from a suburban SWAT team, were tied to a murder, an armed robbery, and many burglaries. The formation of this rogue police gang was facilitated by the fact that some of its members worked out at the same Gold's Gym.[26]

How can we clarify the correlation between the police weight-lifting culture and criminal deviance? And how do bodybuilding and steroids figure into these scenarios? It is important to keep in mind that very few of the police officers who work out in police gyms, inside or outside police stations, pursue bodybuilding as an all-consuming lifestyle. There is a crucial difference between bulking up to feel like a tough cop and the obsessive pursuit of a perfectly muscled body. Sweitzer argues that for some men, the decision to become a cop "is psychologically inextricably intertwined with their bodybuilding impulse," and that police officers are "occupationally disposed to steroid use, because functional strength and fitness is a bona fide occupational qualification." This practical motivation fundamentally distinguishes the cop from the bodybuilder. The cop aims at becoming an action-oriented male, whereas the narcissistic bodybuilder aspires to become a perfectly proportioned human statue. It is true that, as Sweitzer says, many cops are out to create "a specific look," "big, burly, and imposing," and "to have the physical proportions of comic book superheroes." But part of the motivation to create this look is practical, since the desire to intimidate can serve a useful purpose in police work by creating a "professional aesthetic of physical imposition and deterrence."[27]

It is not difficult to see how the ambition shared by a group of men to be big and intimidating can cross the line into criminal behavior. A police gym on private premises is a kind of clubhouse where small affinity groups form and where a sense of impunity and a defiance of authority can germinate. The unusually intense male bonding that occurs among men who share a sense of danger and who trust one another with their lives can create a sense of entitlement that includes an exemption from judgment by outsiders. In this atmosphere, illicit steroid use demonstrates both self-indulgence and a willingness to break the law. The combination of weightlifting and steroids is a marker of a syndrome that originates in the temperaments of the cops who go down this road—and who may eventually turn to criminal deviance. The barbells and the drugs are thus accessories rather than causal factors in the making of rogue cops.

SOLDIERS IN THE GYM: WEIGHTLIFTING AND STEROIDS

The intensive use of weightlifting gyms by soldiers in war zones is invisible to the general public, but it has become nothing less than a lifestyle for a significant number of combat soldiers. An Australian newspaper described the scene: "At bases throughout the Middle East, many soldiers spend hours of down-time pumping iron, drinking protein supplements and watching body-building DVDs. Steroids are readily available in Afghanistan and throughout the Middle East."[28] "Any visitor to a military base," an American journalist, Spencer Ackerman, wrote in 2011, "quickly picks up on the particulars of its gym culture—the obsession (or, in some cases, laxity) with lifting or running or Crossfit. Some commanders are more hardcore than others. The Post Exchanges that serve as mini-Wal-Marts for the military often have entire shelves stocked with protein bars, Muscle Milk and weight-training powder. Think of what kind of performance the command is expecting if it thinks none of *that* is sufficient."[29]

Four years earlier the same journalist had spent an exhausting day with the legendarily fit General David Petraeus, the American military commander in Iraq. For a man in his fifties, Petraeus was in superb physical condition and fully capable of entering a gym and giving "soldiering lessons disguised as calisthenics." In practice this meant that "not a single push-up or bicycle kick went unmodified in that room: he had a critique of each standard approach to exercise." Petraeus the physical trainer and motivator conveyed the message that exercise, like the war itself, was all about endless training and the stamina it made possible.[30]

Enhanced by the tremendous prestige that Petraeus then enjoyed, his extraordinary physical fitness can be seen as symbolizing the army's official alternative to steroid-boosted fitness. Petraeus was "hard-core," not like the bodybuilder who stops at nothing to develop a freakish hypermuscularity, but rather in his capacity for self-discipline and his unshakable belief in the benefit of hard physical training for combat soldiers. Nonetheless, the idea of steroid-induced battle fitness has persisted, even if almost none of its advocates seem to have experienced combat. But the fundamental point here is the army's absolute distinction between drug-free fitness—which somehow allows for the use of numerous nonhormonal supplements—and steroid-dependent fitness, for which there is "zero tolerance." The Petraeus doctrine of fitness is an idealistic credo about character and the importance of physical training. "Physical and mental toughness," he has said, "are . . . essential [to] leadership. It's hard to lead from the front if you are in the rear of the formation."[31]

It has become clear that the Petraeus doctrine of drug-free fitness did not prevail in Iraq. There was too much evidence of widespread steroid use at forward operating bases to assume otherwise. "Steroids is a very big part of the war outside the wire in Iraq right now. . . . I've seen over 50% of my company using anabolic steroids," one self-identified soldier wrote in an online chat room in 2006.[32] The same 50 percent estimate of steroid use among the troops came from members of the Fourth Battalion, Twenty-Third Infantry Regiment, based at Joint Base Lewis-McChord in Washington State. By 2011 this base had acquired "a reputation as the most troubled base in the military"; there were reports of mental breakdowns, allegations of killing for sport, accusations of war crimes, and rumored steroid abuse.[33] A "kill team" based at Lewis-McChord had murdered three Afghan civilians and taken parts of their bodies as war trophies.[34] Five army Rangers from Lewis-McChord held up a Bank of America Branch in Tacoma. Two soldiers were accused of waterboarding their small children, one of them for not knowing the alphabet.[35] Army Staff Sergeant Robert Bales, a veteran of multiple difficult deployments, was eventually convicted of slaughtering sixteen Afghan civilians as they lay sleeping. (Bales's lawyer claimed that before the killings, his client had been "pumped" full of steroids by the special forces soldiers he was there to assist.)[36] In writing about Lewis-McChord, the journalist Mark Boal drew attention to what a prominent retired general, Barry McCaffrey, had called a severe leadership problem at the base. Stressed-out soldiers, he wrote, "were working under a commander who was incredibly aggressive—I shouldn't say incredibly—just aggressive, and so there may have been a false sense on their part that the command environment would look the other way."[37]

Anecdotal online evidence suggests that a perception among soldiers that commanders will tolerate rule-breaking behaviors contributes to covert steroid use among the troops. Any sense among the rank and file that the command structure lacks interest in punishing those who use muscle-building drugs subverts the army's official drug-free ethos. Different commanders convey different attitudes toward steroid use, thereby creating a sense of uncertainty about the degree to which the army's zero-tolerance policy will be enforced. Some soldiers suspect that certain officers are steroid users. A soldier who went to prison for steroid use in 2012 "reported that many in his chain of command—including his first sergeant and his battalion's executive officer—used the drugs."[38]

While I have seen no evidence that soldiers believe that the army *promotes* or *sponsors* steroid doping as official policy, there comes a point where apparent command indifference to drug use can seem like official approval. "It was generally an accepted form of drug abuse," a former soldier said in 2010. "The chain of command saw that as soldiers trying to become better soldiers. They really looked the other way."[39] Here we see the chain of command allegedly endorsing the functional view of military steroid use, which sees it as a potentially lifesaving enhancement.

The spread of bodybuilding culture on this scale into a military establishment at war is unprecedented. The military gym-and-body-building culture thus plays an ambiguous role in relation to the promotion or prevention of anabolic steroid use. The massive consumption of supplements in gyms on military bases as a legal surrogate for steroid enhancement is tolerated, even if not openly encouraged, by the military leadership. And how entrenched is the supplements boom? A former army captain argued in 2009 that banning supplements at stores on bases would hurt morale.[40] "What is unique about this theater of war," the US Army Iraq veteran Tim Hsia wrote in 2010,

> is the availability of body building supplements and the degree
> to which soldiers use them. I see gym injuries every day in my
> clinic because soldiers are working out every single day with-
> out allowing for healing time. Their rooms are brimming with
> supplements that make outlandish and unfounded claims about
> muscle building abilities. At best they are harmless and only

waste soldiers' money, at worst they can cause kidney and liver failure. The issue is real and should be examined in an intelligent way. Kneejerk banning of supplement use will simply drive their use underground (as with all bans). Perhaps it is time to assign an NCO (Non-Commissioned Officer) Athletic Trainer to each gym to supervise and monitor soldiers to keep them fit, sane, and healthy.[41]

But can the goal of keeping soldiers "fit, sane, and healthy" coexist with the gym-and-bodybuilding culture that has entrenched itself in military life? A study published in *Military Medicine* in 2013 reported that 81 percent of the US Marines who were surveyed believed that supplements had improved their physical performance. According to the report: "The majority of deployed Marines use multiple dietary supplements and perceive a high benefit. Given the high prevalence of supplement use and recent deaths associated with supplement use, recommendations are needed to guide the use of certain supplements by US Marines in the deployed environment."[42]

The problem here is that the logic of enhancement rejects guidance, because it is directed at expansion rather than moderation, and the muscle-building ethos of the gym promotes extreme rather than moderate behavior. Whether soldiers take a protein-based supplement or a testosterone-based drug, the presumed practical (as opposed to cosmetic) purpose is to boost physical capacity for the purpose of surviving on the battlefield. That functional rationale for steroid use by soldiers trumps any other position on steroid use, because what is at stake is survival itself. "It seems a growing number of infantry troops are using steroids," StrategyPage.com reported in 2010, "to help them build muscle mass, so that they can better handle the loads they have to carry in combat. For most of these troops, the additional muscle is seen as a matter of life and death." The military's response, according to this commentator, should be to implement new physical-training programs that can prepare the troops to carry the necessary loads. "The U.S. Marine

Corps and SOCOM (Special Operations Command) are already working on such programs, and so is the army, if only to discourage the perceived need to use steroids."[43]

Tim Hsia's description of the military gym scene is matched by a more dramatic account from the British press:

> Operations may be winding down in Afghanistan, but inside canvas tents, between sandbags and tangled barbed wire, a clandestine mission is under way. Soldiers call it "Op Massive": hitting the gym for hours at a time, lifting huge weights while sometimes "stacking," combining several types of legal—and in some cases contraband—muscle-building supplements, regardless of the dangers. For every free minute in the desert is spent sculpting bodies. This month our soldiers withdrew from the last of the Helmand Province patrol bases, where at night the clang of weights and throbbing music from makeshift army gyms would intermingle with the final call to prayer from mosques outside. Now they pump iron under a crescent moon in sprawling Camp Bastion. The fighting may nearly be over, but some of those on Op Massive are risking everything to have the body of a warrior.[44]

Bodybuilding in a war zone can be carried on as an officially steroid-free activity that conforms to the army's zero-tolerance policy for all illicit drugs. Given how many fighting men are attracted to bodybuilding, it makes sense for commanders to accommodate the widespread interest in lifting weights. "These days," a US Army publication commented in 2010, "you would be hard pressed to find a military base without some kind of weightlifting area, whether it is a full-sized gym or a bench surrounded by scrounged vehicle parts tethered to a makeshift lifting bar."[45]

On Contingency Operating Base Basra, a former professional bodybuilder and the Morale, Welfare and Recreation unit staged the base's first bodybuilding contest of the Iraq War. The soldier in charge, a former Mr. New York State bodybuilding champion, emphasized that the contestants would depend only on diet and exercise, abstaining from drugs and diuretics. On May 5, 2012, twenty-six bodybuilders serving in Iraq competed in the US Forces–Iraq Bodybuilding Championships for both men and women. The next show, scheduled for September of that year, would be the Baghdad Classic Bodybuilding and Fitness Competition.[46] It is understandable that weightlifting and bodybuilding are both tolerated and cultivated in police and military subcultures that put a premium on physical strength and self-confidence.

The bodybuilder culture has thus become firmly established in American, Australian, and British military cultures. Sharing military bases with American troops, according to the *Telegraph*, "has helped promote both a culture and availability of performance-enhancing drugs in the British Army."[47] The bodybuilding fad has driven up the number of British military personnel caught using sports supplements containing banned substances. Most of these soldiers were expelled under military law, thereby canceling the nation's investment in their training.[48] The official statement read: "The Armed Forces do not tolerate the taking of illegal drugs within their ranks, as it is incompatible with military service."[49]

As the American steroid proponent Millard Baker caustically remarked regarding these dismissals, "The soldiers had been deployed in four tours of duty in Afghanistan with over 12 years of service to their country. However, none of that matters to the Ministry of Defence. They used steroids. So, their service is no longer appreciated. And they must go."[50] Australian military authorities treated their own Afghanistan special forces veterans with comparable severity after they tested positive for steroids. Responding to this zero-tolerance policy, Baker objected to the traditional "demonizing" of the anabolic steroid and what he regards as the disproportionate penalty these members of the military paid for their use of a severely stigmatized drug. Given the long tradition in America of hysterical responses to some kinds of drug use, this perspective deserves a fair hearing, which it has not been granted by military authorities in any of the three Anglophone countries mentioned above.[51] We should also pay attention to the diction and rhetorical features of media coverage. For example, in 2013 the *Times* (London) described "a bodybuilding culture among troops" in Iraq involving "soldiers obsessed with bodybuilding."[52] Whether it is described as an obsession or a lifestyle will likely depend on the degree to which the observer is inclined to stigmatize certain kinds of drugs.

PRIVATE SECURITY CONTRACTORS AND STEROIDS

The Iraq War produced a paramilitary steroid subculture among private security contractors, a gentler term for mercenaries, who provided security alongside the much larger American military operation. Both paramilitary and military personnel participated in the weightlifting gym culture. "The popularity of steroid abuse has long been discussed as US troops and contractors in Iraq work out in gyms set up in bases and even in the mirrored halls of one of Saddam Hussein's former palaces," the Associated Press reported in 2005. "Private security contractors said that steroid use also is a problem among their employees, because the drugs are readily available in Iraq—as easy as buying a soda from the local stores, according to a contractor."[53]

Commentators on the contractor scene in Iraq have taken note of the heavily muscled body types and provocative appearance of these security personnel. Blackwater USA, the largest of these operations, was retained by the US government, at enormous cost, to provide security for its civilian personnel during the occupation of Iraq. "Blackwater's men," wrote one journalist, "embodied the ugly American persona to a tee. Its guards were chiseled like bodybuilders and wore tacky, wraparound sunglasses. . . . Some of them looked like caricatures, real-life action figures, or professional wrestlers."[54] The South African mercenary Eeben Barlow, a veteran operative who had participated in suppressing the opponents of African dictators, was particularly unsparing in his assessment of the disheveled Blackwater types: "The military and law enforcement contracting industry has no place for ill-disciplined, alcohol and steroid-fuelled, untrained, disrespectful and poorly led men wearing too tight T-shirts and dark glasses."[55]

At the same time, the British and American security companies operating in Iraq were hiring Iraqi bodybuilders to work as guards. "Many Iraqis," the *Washington Post* reported in 2008, "still join gyms to build muscle in the hopes of landing a high-paying job in security, which, like bodybuilding, is one of Iraq's few growth industries."[56] The recreational steroid doping among the Blackwater crowd was thus accompanied by the more utilitarian steroid doping of Iraqi weightlifters who were desperate for gainful employment.

Anabolic steroids manage to find their way into many violent, lawless, and criminal venues, including the bloody cockfighting competitions held secretly across the United States, as well as the war zones of Iraq and Afghanistan. Cockfights, which are illegal in every state, involve injecting steroids into the doomed birds and take place in conjunction with human activities such as gambling, drug dealing, illegal gun sales, and exposing children to the bloodletting. The supposedly secure Green Zone in wartime Baghdad provided British and American mercenaries with mayhem and bloodshed on a much grander scale. One contractor in Baghdad described the scene as "paranoid, competitive and fuelled by guns, alcohol and steroids."

The security companies—Blackwater, Aegis, Armor Group, Control Risks, and others—competed for lucrative government contracts. High daily wages for the dangerous missions attracted combat-seasoned ex-military personnel from all over the world. Leaving the relatively safe Green Zone in Baghdad to escort clients in the Red Zone outside or to man convoys across Iraq was a nerve-racking experience for men who knew they were expendable. "There is a management attitude," said one contractor, "that if you don't want to do the job, there is plenty more where you came from. There is a divide, open loathing, between the management and the men on the ground. There is no loyalty."[57] The only outlets for the anger and the boredom were drinking and working out in gyms where steroids were, of course, available. Indeed, the bodybuilding regimens and consumption of muscle-building products by the contractors and the enlisted soldiers were essentially the same. "Personally," another contractor wrote in 2009, "I don't use [steroids] because I am pretty satisfied with my fitness and body type. But for some guys who want to be big and look more the part of a muscle-bound protector, steroid use and heavy weight lifting is a big deal. Not to mention the massive intake of supplements like protein powders, energy drinks or creatine, along with plenty of gym time on the various FOBs that contractors live at. Like I said, you see a lot of big guys walking around out there."[58]

The steroid habits of the Blackwater contractors became known after a team of operatives carried out a massacre in Nisour Square, Baghdad, on September 16, 2007, unleashing a storm of automatic-weapon fire that killed fourteen Iraqi civilians. The Blackwater security personnel, moving slowly in their small caravan of four armored trucks, claimed they opened fire in response to a threat, which American investigators were later unable to verify. In July 2014, four of the Blackwater personnel involved in the carnage went on trial in Washington, DC, confronted by Iraqi eyewitnesses who had been flown in by the Justice Department to testify. In April 2015, a federal judge sentenced three of them to thirty-year prison terms for multiple counts of manslaughter and attempted manslaughter, and the fourth to a life sentence for murder.[59]

The steroid allegations directed against Blackwater derive from two legal actions brought against the company in the wake of these shootings, along with tawdrier forms of alleged corruption. On October 11, 2007, the Center for Constitutional Rights filed a lawsuit in federal court in Washington, DC, on behalf of five of the Iraqis killed in the Nisour Square attack and two of the wounded survivors. One of the allegations in the lawsuit concerned drug use: "Blackwater routinely sends heavily-armed 'shooters' into the streets of Baghdad with the knowledge that some of those 'shooters' are chemically influenced by steroids and other judgment-altering substances. Reasonable discovery will establish that Blackwater knew that 25 percent or more of its 'shooters' were ingesting steroids or other judgment-altering substances, yet failed to take effective steps to stop the drug use. Reasonable discovery will establish that Blackwater did not conduct any drug-testing of its 'shooters' before sending them equipped with heavy weapons into the streets of Baghdad." A Blackwater spokesperson replied: "Blackwater has very strict policies concerning drug use, and if anyone were known to be using illegal drugs, they would be fired immediately."[60]

In 2008, two former Blackwater employees, Brad and Melan Davis, filed a whistleblower lawsuit against the company, alleging fraudulent billing of the US government for a prostitute and strippers. In a deposition filed in the case, a Texas businessman named Howard Lowry, who had worked in Iraq from 2003 to 2009, claimed that he had attended Blackwater parties "where company personnel had large amounts of cocaine and blocks of hashish and would run around naked." Armed violence was also part of the celebrations: "At some of these parties, Lowry alleges, Blackwater operatives would randomly fire automatic weapons from their balconies into buildings full of Iraqi civilians." In his deposition, Lowry said that he was a close friend of Jerry Zovko, one of four Blackwater employees who had been brutally ambushed by insurgents in Fallujah, Iraq, in March 2004. According to Lowry, Zovko "provided me tremendous insight into the company and confirmed that the use of steroids and human growth hormone, testosterone, were pretty endemic to them and almost companywide." Lowry also stated that members of the personal security detail of L. Paul Bremer, the head of the Coalition Provisional Authority in Iraq from May 2003 to June 2004, were on steroids.[61]

How can we evaluate these claims about drug use by a private security force that included special forces veterans from American, British, Australian, and South African military units? It is important to keep in mind that mercenaries, despite their military experience, are not soldiers. In 2007, the head of Blackwater, the right-wing zealot and former Navy SEAL Erik Prince, "instructed Blackwater employees to recite and sign a military-style oath," and "the logo on the oath wasn't Uncle Sam's," but Blackwater's.[62] US military personnel in Iraq recognized the crucial difference between a real military and the counterfeit versions created by the private contractors. In fact, the mercenaries in Iraq were widely resented by active-duty troops, who knew the private contractors were making huge salaries compared with their own for taking on similar risks. The private-security types were resented by US intelligence agents, too, who regarded their unruly and threatening public conduct and their immunity from prosecution as threats to the safety of official US personnel.[63]

The idea that mercenaries operating in an ethical vacuum in the chaos of wartime Iraq would abstain from the use of illicit drugs, including anabolic steroids, beggars belief. Blackwater personnel openly defied the State Department, which had hired them, and the consequences of this rebellion were predictable: "Insulated from government supervision, the company degenerated into a militia." "I could shoot and kill you here in Iraq, and no one would do anything about it, because that's the way it is here," the company's project manager in Baghdad told a State Department investigator in 2007. As William Saletan put it in light of testimony about Blackwater and the Nisour Square killings: "Stripped of supervision and transplanted to Iraq . . . some of them absorbed the nihilism of their environment. They cheated, stole, exploited, threatened, and killed. Their story is much like that of Abu Ghraib, where American discipline collapsed even in the uniformed military."[64]

Lack of discipline on this scale in an action-oriented male environment was an open invitation to use anabolic steroids. In the absence of discipline, male bonding among these men was able to produce disorder, depravity, and debauchery, aided and abetted by whatever forms of drug abuse were available. The key variable in these scenarios was the presence or absence of a centralized discipline structure, which will always be tested by "action-oriented" personalities that constitute what the anthropologist Lionel Tiger called "men in groups." Two kinds of groups attract men of action: those that impose formal and effective discipline and those that don't. The military and police belong to the first group, while mercenaries and motorcycle gangs belong to the second. As a deputy commandant of the US Naval Academy phrased it in 1997, the midshipmen at the academy (and military men in general) constitute neither a tribe nor a gang.[65] These terms are more appropriately applied to the least disciplined men in groups.

We may assume that military commanders' seemingly instinctive rejection of anabolic steroid use derives from the crucial distinction between an army and a militia, between policemen and vigilantes. Commanders know how quickly hell can break loose in the absence of imposed restraints, and it is likely that for many military leaders, the anabolic steroid represents a catalyst of disorder analogous to tattoos. An anthropologist of US military culture noted: "Although the military tolerates tattoos on the bodies of enlisted soldiers, it frowns on officers who acquire them, reinforcing the stereotype of tattoos as lower-class adornment."[66] In fact, steroids and tattoos occur in a variety of action-oriented male cultures: military men, policemen, motorcycle thugs, bouncers. The military and the police regulate the wearing of tattoos in their ranks; motorcycle gangs and doormen do not. Once again, the difference has to do with whether discipline from above is a foundational principle serving a civilized social order. Gangs can accommodate codes of behavior and accept discipline from a dominant leader, but these are functional rather than ethical norms and serve the needs of criminal organizations. Military commanders, by contrast, regard steroids and tattoos as analogous threats to discipline in the ranks. Officers cannot allow their authority to be undermined by the ingestion of disreputable drugs or bodily markings that indicate defects of character associated with the lower social orders.

LEGAL STEROIDS: HOLLYWOOD'S HORMONE-BOOSTED ACTION HEROES

The entertainment industry's toleration of doping drugs like anabolic steroids and human growth hormone is matched by law enforcement's lack of interest in prosecuting drug use by police officers. This is a curious situation. Public knowledge of officially tolerated illicit drug use invites contempt both for antidrug laws and for the entire prohibitionist campaign against the illegal use of drugs, which remains deeply embedded in American law and public policy. At the same time, the kinds of workplace doping practiced by members of important social institutions constitute a management problem that requires the leaders of these institutions to assure voters and lawmakers that they are doing everything possible to bring their "drug problems" under control. Police chiefs and military commanders have declared their opposition to the use of anabolic steroids by police officers and soldiers. Zero-tolerance policies enforced by such government-sponsored institutions are a public relations requirement.

The social responsibilities assigned to the entertainment industry by politicians and the public are less significant than those assigned to public employees, including police officers. Unlike athletes and a handful of Hollywood actors, police and military personnel are not colloquially referred to as role models for youth. Their individual personalities are not projected into the public arena, whereas celebrity personae are available to be channeled by those whose emotional needs require that sort of vicarious experience. The police and the military rank and file are faceless "action figures" who take real risks, whereas the more celebrated Hollywood action stars and their steroid-boosted stuntmen do not.

It is important to recognize a distinction between two genres of popular entertainment. One of these genres is expected to enforce ethical norms, while the other is not. The managers of major American sports leagues and federations are expected to formulate and enforce codes of behavior that prominently include zero tolerance for criminal behaviors, including the use of doping drugs. Even as the use of hormonal doping drugs is increasing among the general population, the administrators of both professional and Olympic sports are intensifying their campaigns against doping. As the inheritors of a Victorian ethos that remains the basic sports doctrine of our era, these officials have little choice but to oppose doping as a mortal threat to the fairness and the "level playing field" that make athletic competition possible.

In contrast, entertainment products such as films and videos, or performed and recorded music, are essentially unregulated cultural commodities that are often celebrated for challenging or violating traditional social standards that condemn extreme levels of violence and the depiction of sexual behaviors. The same film industry that requires many actors to use doping drugs to acquire enough muscle mass to perform in action roles has created a sub-category of moralizing films that condemn steroid use. *The Program* (1993) is the story of a steroid-abusing college football player who turns into a raging lunatic. In *Rocky IV* (1985), Sylvester Stallone plays a gritty, hardworking boxer who triumphs in the ring over a steroid-boosted Soviet behemoth who at first appears to be an invincible and machinelike creature. Stallone's offscreen use of doping drugs is a matter of record. *A Body to Die For: The Aaron Henry Story* (1994) features Ben Affleck as a high school football player who goes crazy because of his abuse of steroids. In *Deadly Little Secrets* (2002), a sports physician who injects designer steroids into athletes starts injecting himself, succumbs to roid rage, and finally kills one of his athletes by administering a fatal overdose.[67] These moralizing melodramas are overwhelmed by the seemingly endless parade of hypermuscular heroes whose musculatures would appear to be impossible to achieve without the use of anabolic steroids. The glamour of steroid use promoted by superhero films is undiminished by the actors' less publicized assurances that they bulked up by training and eating to excess.

Some of the best-known male entertainers, including action stars in films, rock stars, and rappers, have been connected with the use of anabolic steroids and HGH. The use of these drugs—or the use of extreme diets or prosthetic devices to reproduce the effects of these drugs—are most evident in action films such as *Captain America: The First Avenger*, *Thor*, *Conan the Barbarian*, and *300*, which depicts the heroism of 300 heavily muscled Spartans at the Battle of Thermopylae. All the male stars of these films denied using illegal drugs to add prodigious amounts of muscle to their bodies.[68] Significantly, all these films are based on popular comic book heroes or villains—a lowest common denominator of character development. The cult of the steroid-boosted male torso is also evident on television. The HBO series *Game of Thrones* includes Khal Drogo, a seven-foot-tall warrior king who is a brutish tyrant, played by the American actor Jason Momoa, who also plays a bare-chested giant in the film *Thor*.

The MTV reality series *Jersey Shore* (2009–2012) became a cult hit across the United States and has been shown in more than thirty countries. One of its female characters describes her taste in men as follows: "Tall, completely jacked, steroids, like, multiple growth hormones . . . That's the type I'm attracted to." It was widely assumed that its heavily muscled male stars, Mike ("The Situation") Sorrentino and Ronnie Ortiz-Magro, were on steroids.[69] Ultimately, it is only the body and its charisma—not the actual use or nonuse of steroids—that counts. Every male torso that looks like the product of steroid use is propaganda that elevates the social appeal of the drugs.

How do celebrities manage their immunity from harassment by law enforcement? Drug-using entertainers have addressed accusations in ways that have ranged from blanket denials to an open acknowledgment of drug use that can take the form of an exhibitionistic pride in having done whatever necessary to be able to perform: the doctrine of libertarian pharmacology legitimates the artist's divine right to express his or her creative gifts through the use of any type of substance. The performer bears no moral responsibility for the content or consequences of the entertainments in which he stars.

The least candid performers opt for flat denials of drug use. "No way," protested Mike Sorrentino. "I'm 100 percent natural. I just have very good genetics."[70] When the R&B singer Mary G. Blige was alleged in 2008 to have received anabolic steroids from a corrupt pharmacist in New York, her spokeswoman said: "Mary J. Blige has never taken any performance-enhancing illegal steroids."[71] Such denials offer two benefits to the performer: the protestation of innocence is a hedge against potential legal problems, and being suspected of using the illicit drug can add outlaw glamour to a public persona whose drug use is unlikely to offend the fan base. The Situation "looks like the Incredible Hulk would if only his arms got angry," according to an entertainment writer, who added, "So what do you think? Are these guys on the juice, or just dedicated gym rats? And does it even matter?"[72] "If [the rapper LL Cool J] did turn to some chemical help," another fan wrote in 2010, "I don't think anyone would blame him."[73]

Performers can also take an exhibitionistic approach to drug use. Given their de facto immunity from prosecution, some celebrities have offered public testimonials to the benefits of performance-enhancing drugs. The middle-aged rock star James Murphy, for example, claims to have used steroids to sing a high note during a recording session after losing his voice while trying to sing in too high a register. "I had to sing it with a voice that was completely blown out, but then I took lots of steroids! So I juiced for this record! It's cheating, I'm cheating! I cheated to sing this song!"[74] The actress Jane Fonda let it be known in 2012 that "she's having great sex in her seventies—thanks partly, she said, to the testosterone she's been taking."[75] Such episodes point to the confusing legal and social status of legally prescribed hormonal drugs even as the rationales for the prescriptions are based on a desire for life enhancement rather than medical need.

Other entertainers offer medical alibis for their hormone use. The British singer Robbie Williams claimed in 2011 that a Hollywood doctor told him: "You've got the testosterone of a 100-year-old man." The singer then informed his fans that his testosterone injections had boosted his sex drive and changed his life.[76]

The most famous case of this kind occurred in 2007 when Australian customs officers found forty-eight vials of the human growth hormone Jintropin (somatropin) in the luggage of the action star Sylvester Stallone, whose bulging muscles have played starring roles in the hugely popular Rocky and Rambo films. "As you get older," Stallone explained, "the pituitary gland slows and you feel older, your bones narrow. This stuff gives your body a boost and you feel and look good. Doing Rambo is hard work." And the hard work put in by screen warriors and stuntmen, he says, often requires pharmaceutical support.

In the Stallone case, the workplace doping rationale was endorsed by both the defendant and the prosecutor. Even the deputy chief magistrate handling the case put in a mitigating word for the sixty-year-old action star: "There is no suggestion that the substances were being used for anything other than cosmetic or therapeutic purposes. He has shown contrition, he has expressed his remorse." Serving up the misguided notion that a patient should feel "contrition" over taking a "therapeutic" drug provided the magistrate with a politically correct cover to sweep the entire matter under the rug, where, apparently, everyone involved felt it belonged.

But do all actors who play superheroes benefit from this exemption? Are there, perhaps, certain iconic fictional characters who must not be tainted by the actor's drug use? "With Superman, well, that guy better be clean," one trainer told the *Hollywood Reporter*.[77] Unlike the hypermuscular action stars of more recent origin, Superman is an iconic figure with an American pedigree that makes him similar to sports idols. Iconic athletes are part of an American cultural tradition that represents ethical norms and thus offers an ideal of exemplary male character to American youth. If the actor playing Superman were to be exposed as a doper, the market value of the entire franchise could plummet.

In contrast, the comic book and cinematic superhero Captain America (Steve Rogers) represents a curious synthesis of heroic patriotism and an acceptance of pharmacological manipulation. The premise of the story is that drugs were required to create a superpatriot who could prevail over the Nazi war machine during World War II. The narrative of this legendary act of creation is presented as follows in an ad for Marvel Masterpieces trading cards:

In the darkest days of World War II, when a secret super-soldier serum transformed 90-pound weakling Steve Rogers into a physically perfect specimen of humanity, a legend was born—Captain

America! As the living symbol of his country and the principles it represents, he fought valiantly to help the United States and its allies win that long-ago war . . . but his personal war continues to this day. For as long as tyranny and evil exist, Captain America will never pause in his quest to bring liberty and justice to all!

This combination of martial heroism and pharmacological enhancement was uncontroversial when Captain America made his first appearance, in March 1941. Anabolic steroids had been introduced into clinical medicine only a few years before the comic book series made its debut, and steroid use by athletes was still many years in the future. By the time *Captain America: The First Avenger* (2011) appeared in cinemas, the stigmatizing of muscle-doping procedures had been under way for decades. But the film was spared public censure because of its honorable pedigree as a patriotic myth, and because the metamorphosis of the weakling into a superorganism was a familiar science fiction scenario that traced its origins back two centuries to Mary Shelley's famous story of Dr. Frankenstein. As the *New York Times* critic A. O. Scott remarked, the scientific transformation of the scrawny Steve Rogers "is not accompanied by side effects or public disgrace."[78]

Why is there a class of performing celebrities who use doping drugs yet escape public condemnation and are spared investigation and prosecution by law enforcement? The historian Richard Davenport-Hines has noted that a small group of creative types manage to elude the censure and oppression that can be inflicted on the drug-consuming majority: "Being 'on drugs' can be represented as a depraved appetite, a wretched obsession, escapism for fugitives; or as a search for transcendental visions and mystical excitement. . . . Many [drug users] are put under surveillance, and ostracized as members of a threatening underclass; but a few users (rock stars, fashionable models or poets) are allowed an aristocratic status."[79] But why is this the case?

There is a traditional belief that artists perform in a realm beyond good and evil. Audiences expect to see and hear from performers not the sights or sounds of virtue, but displays of virtuosity that inspire admiration, possibly even ecstatic identification. These uninhibited, shape-shifting creatures can transform a mass audience into a frenzied and adoring crowd that may be high on drugs itself. Awareness of a rock star's drug habit can enable an audience to share his pleasure or, perhaps, experience a vicarious degradation channeled through the addict who is performing on stage. It is easy enough to believe that performers who are paid enormous sums to enter into extreme emotional states have moved past a point of no return, and that some form of intoxication is both normal and expected. "Most of the time with drugs," the comic actor Robin Williams said, "if you're famous, they give them to you. It's good for business to say that they get you high."[80] The destabilizing and self-destructive potential of these self-inflicted emotional contortions is obvious. Thinking about Robin Williams's constant state of manic energy, the television personality Dick Cavett found himself wondering: "Can this be good for anyone? Can you be able to do all these rapid-fire personality changes and emerge knowing who you yourself are?"[81] Charismatic performances can thus involve an element of risk that may include drug abuse as a purported stimulant (dangerous but desirable) to creativity.

Some musical performers have believed that drug use might improve their artistic ability. The great jazz trumpeter Miles Davis once said of the drug-addicted saxophonist Charlie Parker: "When I listened to that genius night after night, being young and immature and not an educated person, I must have thought: 'If I crossed over that line, with drugs, could I play like that?'"[82] According to one psychologist, the explanation may be biological: "So why do so many young artists think that alcohol and drugs enhance their creativity? Poets, writers, composers, painters, musicians, etc. get caught up in this self-defeating misconception. Part of it has to do with the pleasure center of the brain that the chemicals impact—perhaps making one falsely believe they are more creative."[83] The consensus view, however, is that illicit drugs have a ruinous effect on musicians and their careers.

The protected status of celebrity doping is not lost on the young male population from which police officers and soldiers are recruited. Along with the general public, police and military personnel are fed news about the antics of the most conspicuous entertainers, see their pumped-up bodies, and hear the excuses that effectively insulate drug-taking celebrities from scandals and legal penalties that might damage their careers. Law enforcement officials usually lack proof that actors or rappers have broken the drug laws, since suspects must be caught with the drugs in their possession. In the hypermasculine world of famous rappers, Busta Rhymes may look like an NFL linebacker, and Dr. Dre may look like a bodybuilder, but these special people will escape the scrutiny that is directed at athletes and, less often, at law enforcement officers.

A major argument of this book is that muscled-up entertainers and bulked-up police officers are members, along with many other steroid users, of an "anabolic universe" that is now a global drug culture. Government agents, law enforcement officers, and military personnel have a legal obligation not to use these drugs. A significant but unknown number of these men, however, join the steroid subculture. The dominant role of comic-book heroes as the most popular protagonists of Hollywood films promotes the cultural prestige of the anabolic steroid by making these drugs indispensable to the production of commercially viable male superheroes. Their enormous market value derives from their global appeal, since supermuscled creatures engaged in violent combat constitute an action genre that transcends language barriers. The rise of the comic book franchise as a global entertainment genre exerts extreme (and unhealthy) pressure on male actors to submit to procedures that can produce the supermuscled torsos required by action films. "Now we expect actors who aren't action stars to transform themselves," a Hollywood producer said in 2014. "And we expect them to be big and powerful and commanding."[84] A similar requirement for super-normal bodies has resulted in the doping epidemic among elite athletes. But while athletic steroid use has provoked increasingly severe antidoping measures over the past two decades, the doping of actors occurs within an entertainment subculture in which amoral behavior is expected rather than resented. At the same time, nonjudgmental speculations about whether the heroic torsos are the result of hard training or drug use signal de facto public acceptance of steroid use by celebrities.

DOPING CONTROL AS FARCE: TESTOSTERONE REPLACEMENT THERAPY IN MIXED MARTIAL ARTS

Mixed martial arts (MMA) is a combat sport that combines techniques from boxing, wrestling, sambo (a Russian variant of judo), judo, Brazilian jiu-jitsu, karate, and kickboxing. Also known as cage fighting, MMA is the most gladiatorial of the legal combat sports and has rapidly achieved mainstream status in the United States and around the world. The Ultimate Fighting Championship (UFC) is the most powerful company promoting MMA. It broadcasts its major events to a global audience through a pay-per-view system and other programming formats.

Like enormous numbers of other young American males, some police officers are MMA fans and practitioners. Those officers are aware that along with its sheer entertainment value for the action-oriented male, the cage-fighting industry is an anabolic-steroid-doping spectacle. An unending parade of MMA fighters have tested positive for anabolic steroids; one steroid scandal follows another, yet somehow the dopers are allowed to stay in the sport, and business goes on as usual. Like the Hollywood film industry, MMA is an entertainment venue that indulges steroid use in full view of an army of fans that includes many cops.

The hugely successful marketing of cage fighting has affected policing in several ways. Comments posted by officers on police websites reveal a broad spectrum of feelings about MMA fighters and the potential value of their techniques. "I love to watch MMA. Those guys are nutz," says one enthusiast on Policelink.com. Some cops have found MMA fighting techniques useful in physical confrontations with suspects: "I've actually had some of it work for me on the streets!" says another commentator on the same site. "Being on the Swat team, it's actually a part of some of our workout."[85] Yet even MMA enthusiasts on the force can see "this new subculture of toughs" as a serious threat to police officers. "I'm a huge fan and a very amateur practitioner myself," one commentator says, "but MMA poses a threat to cops everywhere."[86] Another potential danger to the officer is that MMA tricks can replace standard police methods that better safeguard an officer during a fight.[87]

It is important to note that the charismatic appeal of MMA cage fighting is not universal among police officers. Some regard MMA as a venue for low-life types with whom they do not want to associate. "Many MMA studios cater to the Frequent Felony crowd," says one commentator. "That alone makes it distasteful to me." "There are a lot of unsavory characters that hang out at those places," says another.[88] Online comments suggest that officers can differ in their willingness to separate fighting techniques from the "subculture of toughs" who make MMA a way of life that may include criminal activity.

Like some other mass-audience sports, MMA has a long-standing doping problem that requires a public relations effort to convince the media and the audience that the UFC management is doing what it can to eliminate the use of testosterone and other anabolic steroids from the sport. This public relations effort is rendered difficult because the sporting entertainments promoted by the UFC are not affiliated with the International Olympic Committee (IOC) or the World Anti-Doping Agency (WADA). They are not required to employ (and do not currently employ) drug-testing protocols that meet international standards. The second and related factor is that the UFC presides over a global entertainment industry that operates in many countries and, therefore, in national jurisdictions that regulate performance-enhancing drug use to different degrees or not at all. Alongside the UFC, the International Mixed Martial Arts Federation has members from thirty countries, while the World Mixed Martial Arts Association has thirty-eight member states. There is no drug-testing arrangement in place that even resembles the IOC-WADA system, so the result is regulatory chaos. As antidoping expert Dr. Don Catlin has pointed out: "In boxing and MMA there is no central control. There is no set of rules that everybody has to follow."[89]

On February 27, 2014, the UFC announced that it would follow the lead of the Association of Ringside Physicians (ARP), which is affiliated with MMA and boxing, and ban the use of testosterone replacement therapy (TRT) by its fighters. "Steroid use of any type," said the ARP, "including unmerited testosterone, significantly increases the safety and health risk to combat sports athletes and their opponents. TRT in a combat sports athlete may also create an unfair advantage contradictory to the integrity of sport."[90] In light of the moral authority of the global antidoping campaign, the UFC's president, Dana White, weighed the public relations risks and presented himself as an enthusiastic supporter of a medical opinion that upended a permissive steroids policy he had supported for years: "The doctors came out and said they want to ban it? Well, that's the answer. It's legal in the sport. The [state] commissions let you do it. You get an exemption and you have to be monitored and all the stuff that's going on, but if they're going to do away with it? There you go. It's a problem solved."[91] And yet steroid doping continues to plague the cage-fighting business.

The UFC president had previously managed to address the doping issue in a way that defended both the TRT status quo and the ideal of drug-free sport. In 2012, for example, he defended TRT as an appropriate medical therapy that should not be abused: "Testosterone replacement therapy is something you can do and it's for guys whose testosterone is too low, but here's what you're supposed to do. You're supposed to get your levels to that of a normal guy your age and if you're even that much over, now it becomes illegal."[92] The same year, however, he also declared: "We don't want anybody doing this stuff. We don't want anybody using banned substances or drugs or anything else. It destroys everything—not only questions about the credibility of the sport and everything else, but it destroys big fights."[93]

A year earlier the head of the United States Anti-Doping Agency (USADA), Travis Tygart, had lambasted MMA's management of the doping issue. "They want, for public relations and marketing reasons, to say they have something that makes them look better than they truly are," Tygart told Reuters. "Why don't they have better rules to give athletes and sports fans comfort that there is not a rampant culture of cheating with dangerous drugs going on in their sport?"[94] The answer was, quite simply, that the manager of a combat-sport entertainment empire does not feel the same obligation to live up to the antidoping ideal as an antidoping official who is responsible to the WADA system. This distinction between self-styled Olympic idealists and pragmatic businessmen has always made WADA's evangelistic approach to professional sports leagues awkward and more or less futile. There are very few sports officials anywhere who are genuinely committed to trying to roll back the global doping epidemic.

MMA fighters have applied for and been granted therapeutic use exemptions (TUEs) for TRT in numbers that greatly exceed those of Olympic and other professional sports. The medical commission of the IOC almost never grants an exemption for testosterone. But in the absence of interference from the Food and Drug Administration (FDA) or even the harder-nosed DEA, MMA has issued testosterone exemptions that have frequently become topics of public debate. As the antidoping expert Don Catlin explains it: "There is a set of rules for each [state athletic commission], but they are kind of Mickey Mouse rules. So the route to being able to take testosterone is wide open. . . . You go in and say 'I have these symptoms.' The doc says, 'Oh yeah, you got low testosterone.' You get a TUE."[95]

The dubious diagnosis to which Catlin refers is hypogonadism, a condition where the male sex glands do not produce enough testosterone. A key question concerning any population of young and healthy male athletes would be, how many of these people might be expected to suffer from low testosterone levels? According to the ARP: "The incidence of hypogonadism requiring the use of testosterone replacement therapy in professional athletes is extraordinarily rare. Accordingly, the use of an anabolic steroid such as testosterone in a professional boxer or mixed martial artist is rarely justified."[96] According to the endocrinologist Richard Auchus, the incidence of hypogonadism in healthy thirty-year-olds is "vanishingly small," on the order of one man in a thousand.[97] The same point applies, of course, to the police officers who seek supplementary testosterone.

So why would MMA fighters apply for TRT exemptions? For Vitor Belfort, the reason was that he felt "tired and lethargic." "It's like a dysfunction of the hormones," he said, "and it can cause your immune system to go down and it can cover a lot of things. If I don't do it, I am actually at a disadvantage." "Quite frankly," said Dr. John Pierce, medical director of the Ageless Forever clinic outside Las Vegas, "he has hypogonadism. Now why is that caused? I don't know. More than likely it is secondary to repetitive head trauma over the years." Another fighter, Todd Duffee, got testosterone cypionate for "extreme fatigue," which was diagnosed as a consequence of "secondary hypogonadism."[98] In other words, MMA fighters claim to want supplemental testosterone for the same reasons that members of the general population do—to alleviate symptoms of fatigue and depression. One difference between MMA fighters and the rest of the male population is that they are young, physically fit, and at minimal risk of the low testosterone disorder some of them claim to suffer from. There is, therefore, a conspicuous discrepancy between the policy regarding synthetic male hormones that prevails in MMA and what the medical experts in this area claim.

More unsettling is the fact that the same discrepancy is evident in the general patient population. Millions of testosterone prescriptions for "hypogonadal" or aging men are written every year. The difference between TRT in MMA and in the adult male population is that the TRT dramas of celebrity cage fighters become part of a societal debate about the propriety of using of performance-enhancing drugs. This discrepancy between a popular therapeutic medical practice and what medical authorities judge to be the best medical practice undermines medical authority and normalizes testosterone use in a medically indiscriminate way.

This destabilizing of medical authority is both a causal factor and a consequence of the mass marketing of testosterone drugs. The apparent lack of a medical consensus on testosterone therapy for the general population creates room for misleading advertising that recruits many "patients." At the same time, the unfettered mass-marketing campaign undermines the authority of the best-qualified medical authorities, who regard the campaign as medically irresponsible. In the absence of a medical consensus that commands the respect of the public, the selling of testosterone products is subject to minimal regulation; in the state of Florida, in fact, there is no effective regulation at all.[99]

The pharmaceutical companies' advertising campaign about the alleged medical consequences of "low testosterone" has provided convenient pseudomedical alibis to MMA fighters and police officers, among many others, who claim to be looking for a hormonal tonic to energize their emotional lives—and in the case of some MMA fighters, to help them prevail in brutal hand-to-hand combat inside a cage. The doping of MMA fighters is particularly problematic, since it is widely acknowledged in MMA circles that the use of an approved TRT regimen (or undeclared anabolic steroids) creates an even greater physical threat to the brains being battered by steroid-boosted cage fighters.

Medical doctrine regarding testosterone use in MMA circles is a hodgepodge of hearsay about hormone therapies, but it can nonetheless achieve a degree of credibility among athletes and other laypeople. In MMA, this doctrine offers four major arguments. First, TRT is a legitimate way to restore the endocrine system of a fighter who has damaged his endocrine function by using anabolic steroids as doping drugs. As the MMA writer Zach Arnold paraphrases this claim: "An anabolic steroid user damages their endocrine system and, in turn, gets testosterone pellets or injections or creams & gels in order to make up for their damaged natural testosterone levels."[100]

The second argument is that the chronic use of painkilling drugs by fighters can lower testosterone levels. As Arnold put it: "In MMA circles, we have seen a scary [number] of fighters who are using cancer-grade, end-of-life-grade pain killers and are failing drug tests because of it. It is an alarming issue in combat sports because fighters often times are mixing different pain killing medications at once, sometimes combining it with alcohol consumption. It is a serious problem."[101] For this reason, steroid advocates say, the abuse of painkillers should be compensated for by allowing fighters to undergo TRT.

The third claim is that because MMA fighters absorb many blows to the head, they are vulnerable to sustaining concussions that lower their testosterone levels. "In MMA," Arnold says, "we are seeing a lot of older fighters who are using testosterone and getting a blessing from an athletic commission to do so. The reason it's a mistake is because older fighters tend to have more brain damage due to the amount of punishment they have taken in previous fights."[102] If this is the case, then giving TRT to older fighters is like prolonging the careers of aging boxers or professional football players: the likely result will be progressive brain damage that can culminate in full-blown dementia.

The final claim is that fighters' intentional sudden weight loss to qualify ("make weight") for a fight ("weight cutting") lowers testosterone production in the their bodies. "If you experience a bad weight cut to make weight for a fight and it's done improperly, you can damage your endocrine system and your body's ability to produce testosterone. While many people online debate the link of testosterone damage to weight cutting (especially in the amateur wrestling community), there's no question there's a link between the action and the outcome," according to Arnold.[103]

Evaluating the medical justifications for TRT advanced by those without medical credentials is an essential part of understanding how the "low T" industry operates. The widespread assumption within MMA is that supplementary testosterone is necessary to reverse "hypogonadal" testosterone levels that result from the abuse of anabolic steroids, the abuse of painkilling drugs, severe blows to the head, and sudden weight loss to qualify for competitions. In other words, four major occupational hazards of MMA create a need for supplemental testosterone. Given that MMA is, apparently, a TRT-dependent profession, it is striking that only fifteen fighters have been granted exemptions for TRT by the UFC. Many other fighters are assumed to be doping with anabolic steroids.

Advocates of TRT within the MMA community see the reparative use of testosterone as a legal, manageable, ethical, and medically effective procedure. One advocate criticized an athletic commission director who "said he wouldn't want anyone with prior steroid use to be licensed for TRT." The writer's argument was legalistic rather than medical: "This isn't part of the unified rules, nor is it an officially adopted stance even within the NSAC. Fighters with prior steroid use may well be licensed in the US for TRT."[104] For this TRT advocate, the therapy should be considered proper if it conforms to rules and regulations; and he objects to an unwarranted bias that would deny TRT to "anyone with prior steroid use." These fighters, he implies, should not be stigmatized as steroid "abusers" who, as people who have inflicted disease on themselves, are less deserving of treatment than those who have not. On the other hand, "why," Zach Arnold asks, "should fighters with low testosterone levels be given special treatment because they can't make it without drug usage in MMA?"[105] The answer to this question comes from a TRT advocate who presents TRT as nothing more than a medically appropriate therapy: "The purpose of testosterone therapy isn't to build giant and jacked super warriors, complete with comic-book-style physiques and powerhouse punching prowess. TRT is designed to bring people, typically men in their 30s and above who have seen the amount of testosterone their bodies produce dip, back up to normal levels of testosterone."[106] From this perspective, providing TRT to a fighter who has damaged his endocrine system by abusing anabolic steroids is a straightforward therapeutic procedure comparable to competent medical treatment in a clinic.

One question that TRT advocates never raise is whether a state athletic commission and the doctors who are willing to serve on it are competent to practice endocrinology. As Zach Arnold points out: "There's a reason why we're seeing General Practitioners and chiropractors outed as doctors who have supposedly led MMA fighters to get testosterone prescriptions, not endocrinologists."[107] The UFC and state officials, however, take the expertise and ethical standards of their doctors for granted. For example, in 2012 the former executive director of the Nevada State Athletic Commission, an organization that has overseen many MMA fights in Las Vegas, objected to what he saw as a widespread perception that his commission was presiding over a substandard medical program:

> I think there's an impression among the general public that everybody's getting exemptions for [testosterone replacement therapy]. I can't speak for other states, but for us it's probably about one a year asking and it's 50/50 whether they'll get approved. To even ask you've got to be able to prove that your testosterone is below normal—not just low—but below normal. Then you have to have a note from your doctor detailing your treatment plan, what the underlying cause is, showing that it's not going to put you at undue risk or give you an unfair advantage, and then our doctor talks to their doctor.[108]

Once again, TRT is described as a therapeutic regimen being managed by reliable medical professionals. Not mentioned is the fact that the Nevada commission is one of only a handful of state-level bodies that even attempt to manage a TRT program. In the many countries outside the United States where fights are staged, there is no regulation whatsoever. But the fundamental problem here can be heard in the commissioner's attempt to banish controversy by assuring his audience that when "our doctor talks to their doctor," medically responsible doctors have reached a medically legitimate decision.

Many physicians over the past half century have encouraged or participated in the steroid doping of athletes, police officers, and bodybuilders, thereby violating legal or medical standards, or both.[109] Many physicians have shown that they are willing to practice forms of rogue or substandard medicine, and some of these doctors manage TRT regimens for MMA fighters. Here is one insider's assessment of this physician cohort and how it practices medicine:

> When it comes to legitimate testosterone usage, a board-certified endocrinologist is the one who should be in charge of managing such treatment. After all, low testosterone levels indicate a damaged endocrine system. However, in the combat sports world, we see the sport populated with mark doctors. Mark doctors are fan boy doctors who are willing to write up prescriptions for drugs to fighters in exchange for a celebrity rub. Photographs, autographs, going out to dinner to socialize. As we have seen over the last few years in Mixed Martial Arts, the majority of doctors who are writing up prescriptions for testosterone to fighters are not board-certified endocrinologists. The mark doctors who are writing up these prescriptions are General Practitioners and Age Management Specialists, often who get referrals from chiropractors. The end result is that you have fighters getting their own prescriptions with little or no oversight and what oversight there is tends to be sloppy & dangerous. In some cases, fighters are getting prescriptions for injectable testosterone and are giving themselves the shots.[110]

Other commentators have pointed out the low quality of MMA doctors. "Interestingly," writes one, "most fighters granted a TUE for TRT were diagnosed by (often shady) physicians as having secondary hypogonadism, apparently secondary to repeated head trauma."[111] The psychiatrist and steroid expert Harrison Pope points to doubts about doctors who are attracted to muscle sports: "'Health professionals' writing in popular publications such as bodybuilding magazines may have limited or questionable credentials, no peer review and possible commercial interest."[112]

The owners and managers of MMA organizations promote bottom-of-the-barrel medicine for the purpose of keeping steroid-boosted fighters in the ring. It can sometimes be hard to tell how much naïveté or cynicism is in play. In 2011, for example, the UFC co-owner Lorenzo Fertitta said: "If you are going to have some kind of therapy, not only can you not be at the top of the range [of testosterone levels], you can't be anywhere near performance-enhancing. What you can't have are guys abusing this to the point where their levels are at some super-human factor, giving them this performance enhancement."[113] Did he really believe that UFC fighters on TRT were not seeking a competitive advantage? Given the medical confusion that prevails in MMA circles, he may have actually assumed that fighters see TRT as purely therapeutic.

Three years later, UFC president Dana White spoke with candor and exasperation after ARP called for a ban on TRT: "Here's the problem, nobody knows what the fuck they are talking about when it comes to TRT and the testing. It's the main reason it had to go away. If you talk to three different doctors, if you talk to different commissions, everybody has a different opinion on it. Nobody knew what the hell they were talking about. When it's like that it's got to go away, it's too big of a problem."[114] In other words, White was declaring MMA-affiliated doctors to be medically incompetent to manage TRT. The whole situation was simply out of control, in part because the problem of finding competent and reliable doctors was and remains an integral part of the TRT controversy.

The justifications one hears in MMA circles in support of the medical use of TRT are at variance with expert medical opinion in several respects. Are any of the purported reasons for using supplementary testosterone to reverse "hypogonadal" testosterone levels—abuse of anabolic steroids, abuse of painkilling drugs, severe blows to the head, sudden weight loss to qualify for competitions—substantiated in the medical literature?

The managers and regulators of MMA present TRT as a straightforward therapeutic procedure for repairing a damaged endocrine system. The damage caused by anabolic steroid abuse legitimates and requires TRT. The athlete is entitled to undergo treatment and to keep fighting. But Dr. Richard Auchus, an endocrinologist and professor of internal medicine at the University of Michigan School of Medicine, sees the matter differently:

If the athlete has been on [anabolic steroids] a short time they can just stop until their [endocrine] axis recovers. If they have been on for years at high doses, they might never recover. I would find it medically appropriate to offer these athletes chronic replacement testosterone therapy under medical supervision; however, they will not be able to compete. It is a tough problem since the longer you treat them the longer they need treatment. I have only been able to successfully taper one athlete back to normal function, and he was recreational not professional so TUE was not the issue. If the athlete wishes to return to competition, they will have to do without or with less for some time. This is why it is important to advise athletes to never start, because it will basically end your career when you are caught, and there is no going back.[115]

The medical syndrome being treated here—"anabolic steroid-induced hypogonadism" (ASIH)—is presented in the world of MMA as a simple deficiency disorder for which TRT is the treatment. But as Dr. Auchus and other medical authors point out, the situation is both more complicated and more threatening than the MMA narrative suggests. ASIH can be long-term or even permanent.[116] According to a study published in the *Journal of Urology*, "Depending on the cumulative dose and duration of AAS exposure, ASIH may last indefinitely." What is more, ASIH is a major cause of testosterone deficiency: one study "found that 43% of those with profound hypogonadism reported prior AAS exposure."[117] In other words, steroid use is often medically ruinous.

As managers of the one professional sport that operates a controversial TRT program, MMA personnel have no interest in—or, perhaps, little awareness of—the medical realities that call the therapeutic value of TRT into question. One result of this uninformed approach is an anabolic steroids policy that promotes steroid use rather than acknowledging that it is a medically disastrous behavior for large numbers of men. One TRT defender has pointed out that every announcement of a TRT exemption for an MMA fighter produces inquiries from "fighters and managers interested in finding out how to obtain a TRT exemption"—inquiries that cannot be based on medical evaluations of the prospective "patients," which have clearly not occurred.[118] The sudden interest shown by a host of eager candidates testifies to the virtual certainty that the number of MMA fighters who are or who want to be steroid users greatly exceeds the limited number who are granted public TRT exemptions for alleged medical disorders.

In a word, TRT in MMA is a medical soap opera that casts MMA fighters in the implausible role of hypogonadal males. The dramatic narrative of the show is driven by the question, will these medical unfortunates be granted the drugs they need in order to recover their health? This sentimental subplot of the TRT drama directs attention away from the medical harm done by steroid abuse and toward its alleged benefits. After all, the sports regulators who grant TRT exemptions are just "being responsive to individual health situations," and believe that "it's important not to punish the athletes that come forward with a legitimate need by banning TRT outright."[119]

A prominent narrative in MMA circles is that previous anabolic steroid abuse is not necessarily the cause of the alleged secondary (acquired) hypogonadism that causes an MMA fighter's subnormal testosterone level. This narrative is useful for public relations purposes, since creating a TRT program for steroid abusers is likely to offend a considerable portion of the sporting public. Why, they might ask, should the drug abuser be encouraged to return to his drug of abuse? MMA groups' diversionary strategy has been to focus on some of the other possible causes of testosterone deficiencies that would supposedly legitimate the use of TRT, particularly the continual use of opiates for pain and the need to lose weight quickly before a fight. But the idea that these practices should be banned for the sake of promoting the health of the athletes is never on the agenda.

The horrendous damage done by head trauma in MMA is regarded by management as another unfortunate but inevitable product of the cage-fighting industry, which has no intention of abolishing itself on account of the damage its fights inflict on athletes. "There are countless fighters in MMA who have been reduced to shells of their former selves," wrote a devotee of the sport who announced he could no longer bear to watch these brutal contests. His emotional farewell to MMA chronicles the brain damaged, the speech impaired, the opiate addicted, the depression afflicted, the suicides, the killings.[120] So why should the MMA fighter Vitor Belfort get a TRT exemption? "Quite frankly, he has hypogonadism," says Dr. John Pierce, an "antiaging specialist" who has advised the UFC. "Now why is that caused? I don't know. More than likely it is secondary to repetitive head trauma over the years." According to Belfort, it was a "UFC doctor" who started his testosterone regimen in 2011—similar to a 2012 claim by Quinton "Rampage" Jackson, who said a UFC doctor referred him to an "age-management specialist."[121]

By now it should be clear that the "UFC doctor" is likely to be an ethically compromised ("shady") doctor for whom testosterone prescribing has become a standard, and lucrative, practice. In all likelihood, the "UFC doctor" is an antiaging specialist whose clientele extends far beyond the ranks of MMA fighters into a patient population that includes police officers, firefighters, bodybuilders, and other men in search of muscular enhancement.

The key to MMA's complicated relationship to the regulation of performance-enhancing drugs is its cultural status as mere entertainment. Beyond that, it is a form of entertainment that lacks the cultural prestige of a traditional sport such as baseball, which is supposed to embody cultural values. The values that MMA represents do not matter to large numbers of people. While MMA has experienced a dramatic rise in popularity, the popularity of traditional boxing has sharply declined. Neither of these combat sports, however, possesses a cultural significance that creates effective demands for the imposition of drug testing on those who compete. Both MMA and boxing have doping problems, but the critical mass of concern that might put those problems on the social agenda is lacking. Baseball, football, and even track and field are regarded as sports worth regulating because a kind of integrity is at stake. Non-sporting entertainments are different in this sense. Steroid doping is widespread in Hollywood and elsewhere in the entertainment industry, but it operates outside the moral universe administered by the World Anti-Doping Agency, which establishes norms for Olympic sports, and outside the ethical authority of the police and military establishments.

OUTLAW MOTORCYCLE GANGS AND FREEWHEELING COPS

Motorcycle gangs belong to a transnational subculture of action-oriented males that has flourished around the world over the past half century. What began as a postwar version of "outlaw" American masculinity now has many thousands of imitators around the world, representing the globalization of both an extreme masculine style and a particularly violent crime network. The Hells Angels motorcycle club, founded in California in 1948, is now what its website calls "the world's biggest motorcycle brotherhood," comprising more than 100 chapters in twenty-nine countries.[122] The Bandidos Motorcycle Club, or Bandido Nation, formed in Texas in 1966, is said to have 2,400 members in 210 chapters spread across twenty-two countries. The FBI has identified both the Bandidos and the Hells Angels as outlaw motorcycle gangs.[123]

US outlaw motorcycle culture has been deeply entangled with the American military since the end of the Second World War. Combat experience in that brutal and protracted conflict served as a crucible that produced hardened, hostile, and antisocial attitudes in many men, who were then unable to make the transition back to civilian society, which seemed devoid of drama and the intense camaraderie of combat: "Thrill-seeking attracted some returning veterans to choose a saloon society lifestyle centered around motorcycles. Positive view of military experiences, and the intense camaraderie they bred, also made such a lifestyle attractive. In some cases, combat roles became master statuses for veterans who could not tolerate military discipline but linked their self-image to the small-group camaraderie and risking-taking of military service."[124]

This colorful and antisocial cast of misfits eventually acquired a kind of iconic and even charismatic status, in part because of Hollywood films such as Roger Corman's *The Wild Angels* (1966) as well as their association with the countercultural rebellions of the 1960s. What is more, their numbers have been replenished by subsequent military conflicts. A 2010 intelligence report from the Bureau of Alcohol, Tobacco, Firearms and Explosives (ATF) states that many members of outlaw motorcycle gangs (OMGs) "have previous military service; in fact, several prominent OMGs were founded by Vietnam veterans, and their current leadership still includes many veterans and personnel with military training." The ATF discovered that this affiliation was pervasive: "OMG members . . . belonged to clubs founded by former members of the United States military. For example, excluding the Hells Angels and Outlaws, which were formed before the start of the Vietnam War, the Bandidos, Sons of Silence, Warlocks, Mongols, and Vagos were formed by returning servicemen during the Vietnam era. Of the larger OMGs in the United States, the Pagans were the only OMG not started by a former member of the United States military."[125]

The men who join outlaw motorcycle gangs had a complicated relationship with the military culture that did so much to shape their identities. Combat under enemy fire forged the brotherhood and camaraderie that are frequently invoked as the core values that underpin the outlaw's life on wheels. In their postmilitary lives, they expressed this shared experience by displaying "some type of military insignia (pins, patches, placards, etc.) on their motorcycles and/or colors."[126] But these men will not accept military discipline or any sort of discipline that originates from outside their ranks. What they want is male bonding (brotherhood) and opportunities to engage in violent encounters, including crimes of violence, without regimentation. This sort of "freedom" is all that civilian life has had to offer them. The US Marines who belong to the Untamed Rebels motorcycle club in North Carolina, like the members of the

Special Forces Motorcycle Club, have found a way to combine their military and outlaw identities in both word and deed.[127] Military insignia placed on motorcycles are another way to create a symbol of these two "action-oriented" roles. It is, however, the Military Misfits, made up of US Navy and Marine Corps personnel in Southern California, whose name best expresses the contradiction between military and outlaw identities.

Many gang members have a variety of relationships with the American military. They are "employed on military compounds, bases, installations, and Federal buildings in the United States and abroad."[128] They may be serving in the National Guard or Reserves. Some have been sentenced to prison terms for offenses including the distribution of narcotics and firearms.[129] Some are discharged without pensions, while others hold top-secret clearances.[130] Some have served as soldiers or worked as Department of Defense contractors in Iraq.[131] While in the military, some recruit new gang members. At least one served in a Ranger (special forces) detachment.[132] One US Army veteran and motorcycle gang member receives disability payments because of injuries sustained in Iraq and is in the "Wounded Warriors" program.[133] The US Office of Strategic Intelligence and Information attempts to keep track of all military personnel who belong to or are affiliated with OMGs.

The complex interpenetration of the OMG and military communities has not eliminated conflict between the anarchic impulses of the one and the iron discipline of the other. For the Hells Angels, it seems that anyone who has agreed to enforce civilian or military law is to be regarded as a sworn enemy: "Per the Hells Angels By-Laws: As of June 15, 1996, anyone who has ever considered training for or trained for a Federal, State, or local law enforcement position of any type with the capacity to arrest or incarcerate individuals, or a position that keeps individuals incarcerated, shall be excluded from membership. Also, anyone who volunteered or chose to be military police or shore patrol, etc., shall be excluded from membership in HAMC."[134] For this reason, the social intermingling and sharing of identities that conjoin police officers with outlaw bikers occur on a smaller scale than is the case in the military. The Hells Angels' hostility toward law enforcement is indicative of this separation. Gang members' hostility to police officers is graphically shown by including in their regalia the so-called Dequiallo patch, a decoration that announces that the wearer has physically assaulted a law enforcement officer.[135] ("Dequiallo" is likely a corruption of "degüello," a Spanish word meaning "no quarter given.") It is a combat award of sorts that honors the kind of defiance police will not tolerate on the street.

The outlaws' categorical rejection of law enforcement has not been reciprocated by police officers. In fact, the emotional relationship between police and the outlaw motorcycle gangs is asymmetrical. While the outlaws reject the police, there are many police officers who belong to police-only motorcycle clubs in order to pursue their own form of brotherhood while riding the open roads. According to a 2013 NBC News report: "Across the country . . . the number of police officers joining and forming motorcycle clubs has soared. 'Within the last 10 or 12 years, there has just been an explosion of these clubs of law enforcement, firefighters and military,' said Terry Katz, a retired lieutenant in the Maryland State Police who is vice president of the International Outlaw Motorcycle Gang Investigators' Association."[136] Substantial numbers of police officers indulge in versions of the outlaw lifestyle. The sudden increase in the number of lawmen who aspire to some version of the outlaw life is not reassuring in a society in which police violence has become a national crisis. "In the last 15 years," said Katz, "I would say that we've probably seen a tenfold increase in these clubs. The first ones were pretty straightforward—they were family-oriented clubs. What we see now as a trend is biker by night and cop by day."[137] In other words, cops can turn into bikers in a Jekyll-and-Hyde fashion as soon as they put on their "colors."

Various observers have expressed concern about the sudden transformation of police officers into wannabe motorcycle thugs. The Associated Press reported in 2015 that "even some within law enforcement worry that too many officers believe bikers are just misunderstood Robin Hoods. And empathy from officers who emulate or even aspire to the outlaw life can put police or the public at risk, gang experts warn." Chris Adams, the police chief of Laconia, New Hampshire, the site of an annual bikers' festival, has witnessed this metamorphosis more than once. "Some of them won't look at you or talk to you," he said. In a similar vein, Jay Dobyns, a former undercover agent who infiltrated the Hells Angels for the ATF, has observed these transformations with concern. "I'm talking about the clean-cut law enforcement officers who wear a uniform and ride around in marked cruisers every day; then Saturday comes around and they put on a black bandanna and black T-shirt and scowl at everybody."[138] In 2016 a spokesman for the National Council of Clubs, which represents hundreds of motorcycle groups, commented: "It's almost like they are playing dress-up on the weekend and acting out what their perception of an outlaw gang is. They create aggressive situations with other motorcycle clubs" that sometimes end in brawls and the occasional fatality.[139] Like the police steroid subculture, the burgeoning motorcycle subculture within police ranks has never become a topic of public concern. Here, too, one sees a police leadership that is either indifferent or reluctant or afraid to take disciplinary measures against police behaviors that constitute a threat to professional standards and public order.

Police officers' explanations of their attraction to this lifestyle can be found in an online directory of law enforcement motorcycle clubs (LEMCs).[140] Their affiliation stems largely from fraternal spirit, the rejection of criminality and the OMGs, and ambivalent declarations that combine the lawman and the outlaw in a way that evokes the specter of the officer who is a "biker by night and cop by day."

The most frequently heard theme is fraternal bonding. "Upon acceptance into the club," say the Choir Boys MC (motorcycle club), "you will enjoy the camaraderie and brotherhood frequently associated with law enforcement and motorcycling."[141] The Blue Reapers declare that they "live brotherhood, honesty, loyalty, and trust."[142] For the Blue Breed MC, it is "brotherhood to the bone" for "active duty officers with a motorcycle addiction." The second theme draws a sharp distinction between LEMCs and OMGs. The Iron Circle Law Enforcement Motorcycle Club (ICLEMC) states: "There are no 1%ers [motorcycle gangsters] and no member[s] of the ICLEMC associate with or support these groups/individuals. Those who commit to the ICLEMC do not tolerate any activity which discredits the law enforcement profession or the ICLEMC."[143] The Blue Breed MC declares that "we do not associate with 1% clubs."[144] The Blue Thunder MC states: "We are law abiding citizens. We do not support any outlaw motorcycle clubs or criminal activities whatsoever."[145]

The growing appetite among police officers for the freewheeling life indicates that this hell-bent-for-leather lifestyle on the road expresses more than a need for simple recreational activity. Some police clubs proclaim an affinity for the aggressive ethos of "freedom" that is also the core doctrine of the OMGs. The Roughnecks MC invokes a latter-day cowboy ethos: "We all live by Old School values and the rule of the Wild West Lawman!" The Blue Iron Texas Original MC combines the demand for "freedom" with a therapeutic rationale: "We ride for the pure freedom riding provides, to support those in need and to escape the reality of what we see and deal with on a daily basis in our profession." LEMCs distance themselves from the uninhibited lifestyle of the OMGs. On the other hand, public behavior that reveals some officers' affinity for the gangster life is inevitable.

What can happen when LEMC members act out their fantasies of OMG-style behavior was evident on the evening of December 22, 2012, when the Whiskey Row chapter of the Iron Brotherhood MC held its annual Christmas party in Moctezuma's Bar in Prescott, Arizona. The club members were decked out in black vests and other regalia and flashed their police badges as they entered, since motorcycle gang members wearing their colors were routinely denied admission to the bar. The trouble started when a young man went up to one of the Iron Brothers at the bar and asked him about the patches on his vest. This club member, who claimed to police investigators that the interloper touched his vest while talking "crap" to him, turned out to be the Prescott Valley chief of police, Clair

("Billy") Fessler, president of the IBMC and nicknamed "Tarzan." Among his LEMC companions at this event were William ("Bill") Suttle, nicknamed "Mongo," a Yavapai County sheriff's sergeant, drug task force commander, and vice president of the IBMC; Bryce ("Deuce") Bigelow, the club's sergeant at arms and a Department of Public Safety officer; Marc ("Yoki") Schmitt, a Yavapai County sheriff's captain and the club's accountant; Troy ("Heat") Teske, a Bullhead City police officer; Jason ("Bull") Kaufman, a Prescott Valley police corporal and club sergeant at arms; and Tyran ("Budda") Payne, a Prescott Valley police officer. The young man was punched to the floor by one of the Iron Brothers and suffered a broken nose. Police investigations filled more than 350 pages of documents with testimony and evidence reports, but no charges were filed against any of the police officers involved.

Even though the black vests had brought along their wives and girlfriends, this Christmas event, held in a rented room behind the bar, was not marked by a family atmosphere. Witness statements described a rowdy crowd that was out of control. One witness said they "scared the hell" out of other patrons in the bar. Another said that if "you didn't know they were a police-affiliated gang, you would think they were a Hells Angels supporter." At some point the biker crowd moved down the street to Hooligans Pub. One employee there told police that night "many of the members were highly intoxicated and they had to cut off many of them from drinking because of their level of intoxication. [Witness] Bennett then said that some of the members were acting like they were 'Hell's Angels' and he didn't feel it was right that police officers would portray themselves like that."[146]

Given the reports of skyrocketing numbers of police biker clubs and officers eager to pursue brotherhood on wheels, the Jekyll-and-Hyde-like metamorphosis of lawmen turning into aspiring gangsters raises questions about the professional motives and emotional stability of the make-believe Hells Angels who are "bikers by night and cops by day." For one thing, applicants to police departments are vulnerable to pop-cultural romanticizing of motorcycle gangs.

One FBI special agent commented in 2012: "With the popularity of current television programs that glamorize the [motorcycle gang] culture, the desire [of] some law enforcement officials to maintain close, unprofessional and sometimes criminal relationships with [OMG] members" will continue to pose dangers to the confidentiality of police investigations of the gangs. Some officers' affinity for the gangs has led outlaw types to brag about how easy it is to manipulate their admirers in uniform.[147]

Another commonality between police officers and motorcycle gangs is the gym environment, where men from different walks of life train side by side. Many police officers belong to gym cultures outside station houses. Their devotion to weight training is shared by the many convicts and gang members who associate physical strength with survival. Since a readiness for brawling requires muscle, gym-culture affiliations that connect outlaw bikers with weight-lifting equipment and combat sports are to be expected. Lee Moran, a full-patch member of the Oakland chapter of the Hells Angels, was a national and international powerlifting champion in 1984 and the first man ever to squat more than a thousand pounds.[148] Steven ("Gorilla") Mondevergine, a heavily tattooed weightlifter and former Philadelphia police officer, became president of the South Philadelphia chapter of the Pagans motorcycle gang, a criminal organization involved in drug dealing and extortion.[149] Although most bikers who lift weights do not achieve such distinctions, many of them participate in gym culture, which brings them into contact with more mainstream members of society.

Widespread alarm in Australia about "bikies" and violent crime produced media coverage of the commingling of these criminals with police officers and other respectable citizens while working out at gyms. In 2011, the *Sydney Daily Telegraph* reported: "Bikies have spread their tentacles across Sydney and throughout NSW [New South Wales] with more than 2000 people now identified as members of 21 outlaw motorcycle gangs. And police have also told of how bikies are diversifying their legitimate operations beyond the traditional tattoo parlours, smash repairers and earthmoving work into lucrative suburban gyms and nightclubs." The official response to this threat was to unleash a special police strike force, called Raptor, to conduct an unprecedented campaign of harassment against gang members.[150] In 2013, the Liberal National Party government in Queensland, led by Premier Campbell Newman, introduced new laws in its "war" on OMGs that were so draconian as to provoke protests.[151] These measures, which became law, included the Vicious Lawless Association Disestablishment Bill 2013 and the Tattoo Parlours Bill 2013.[152] A law to drive outlaw bikers out of the gym industry was proposed.[153] Such laws are extreme attempts to drive an unwanted and stigmatized subculture away into the remotest corners of society. The immediate effect of these laws was to set off a migration of outlaw bikers from Queensland into the Northern Rivers area of New South Wales.[154]

What puritanical measures of this kind cannot do is to sever all ties between an outlaw subculture and the many members of mainstream society (including policemen) who choose to participate in the gym culture and its cult of muscle. In 2012 the *Sydney Morning Herald* reported that a "huge boom in illegal imports of anabolic steroids and growth hormone is fuelling a bodybuilding subculture with roots firmly in outlaw motorcycle gangs," which distributed as well as consumed the drugs for the purpose of producing "threatening muscular physiques."[155] In 2013, Victoria's police chief commissioner, Ken Lay, expressed concern about outlaw gang drug dealers corrupting police officers by offering them steroids.[156] Certain gyms were "among the few places where elite sportspeople rub shoulders with underworld figures, policemen—even judges. . . ." At one gym, notably, "magistrates, police and business executives pump weights alongside criminals and bikies."[157]

POLICE BIKERS AND BOUNCERS

In the United Kingdom, they are called "doormen," in Germany "*Türsteher,*" and in Norway "*dørvakter.*" The more kinetic American term for these "security specialists" is "bouncers." According to Merriam-Webster.com, a bouncer is "a person whose job is to force anyone who causes a problem in a bar, nightclub, etc. to leave that place." Bouncers, like police officers, enforce rules. But while it is fair to say that bouncing bears a resemblance to the physically violent side of police work, police work that is performed in accordance with rules and regulations has nothing to do with the inherently lawless culture of bouncing. In fact, bouncing occupies a legal and ethical gray zone somewhere between lawful policing and unlawful brawling. Bouncers can imagine that they have the status and authority of police officers. Conversely, police officers may want to indulge in the roughhouse tactics employed by bouncers or enjoy the freewheeling lifestyle of motorcycle gangs. In fact, when police officers employed as security personnel get entangled in (or provoke) alcohol-fueled mayhem in nightclubs, it is a serious problem for American police departments.

Social contact between bouncers and cops is facilitated around the world by their shared interest in weight-training facilities and, in many cases, by the use of anabolic steroids. As an Australian journalist pointed out in 2013: "We have this range of people running from very respectable police and security people right through to bikies and criminals and they're all meeting around the gym."[158] Potential problems arise because the standards of conduct that are assumed to separate the law enforcers from the lawbreakers can break down in gym culture. Police officers' interest in illegal steroid use does not necessarily derive from identifying with the criminal element with whom they share social space at the gym and in tattoo parlors. On the contrary, they may see weight training and steroid use as functional responses to the muscles they see on their lawbreaking adversaries. The gratification of unbridled aggression can eclipse all other norms and obligations. The public interest requires, however, that police officers adhere to higher standards of behavior than bouncers and motorcycle gangs.

Bouncers have long been notorious for their abuse of steroids. A 1990 Australian government report on illicit drug use noted the following: "The Committee heard on numerous occasions that it was commonplace for people using performance drugs to be employed as bouncers, particularly in clubs and hotels. This is the case because bodybuilders, powerlifters and weightlifters are the type of person required as bouncers for their size and strength. And most of these people are likely to use performance drugs, particularly anabolic steroids."[159] The connection between weight training and employment as a bouncer is hardly limited to Australia; for easily understandable reasons, it is an international subculture in entertainment venues where physical intimidation is a required job skill. The many police officers who moonlight as bouncers in the United States are often motivated to seek out this kind of work by an opportunity to supplement their salaries. At the same time, their absorption into the bouncing subculture opens up opportunities to socialize with criminals and acquire bad habits. As one Australian officer noted in the 1990 report, powerlifting police officers are already motivated to use steroids: "Should a policeman obviously be in that position he would be as susceptible as the next person to the side-effects."[160]

The overlap between policing and bouncing takes two forms. First, uniformed police may be called to a nightclub to deal with altercations between bouncers and patrons. These confrontations may pit bouncers against drunken and unruly customers, or they can take the form of bouncers' brutal and unprovoked attacks against clients who happen to catch the attention of one or more of the door staff. On some of these occasions, police have shown little concern about bouncers' potentially criminal assaults against innocent customers. The second form of overlap occurs when out-of-uniform police personnel work as bouncers. Shedding their professional identity for a less disciplined role can encourage what police managers regard as unprofessional behavior.

A potential conflict-of-interest problem arises when a police department is called upon to investigate the behavior of its own cops who get into trouble while working as bouncers. An analogous situation occurred in northwestern England. Prison officers in the area were reported to have "a shared interest in body-building and anabolic steroids." During an investigation into police and prison officers working as bouncers—which is illegal for police in the UK—a prison source summarized an uncomfortable encounter: "The problems began when police were called to a club after a fight and found that all the bouncers involved were prison officers. One prison officer got charged with hitting someone with a chair."[161] This venue had, in effect, experienced a complete breakdown of law and order, because the very men who were supposed to be enforcing the law were the cause of the mayhem. Indeed, taking a hard look at the intersection of policing and the other action-oriented subcultures, such as bouncers and motorcycle gangs, reveals how porous the boundary separating lawmen and lawbreakers can be. The action-oriented underworld and its macho style attract substantial numbers of policemen, who find ways to join the action or to create their own versions of the outlaw lifestyle.

CHAPTER FIVE

STEROIDS IN THE MILITARY

Anabolic steroid use enters police departments in a variety of ways. As we have seen, young men's interest in steroids for cosmetic enhancement of their bodies is a powerful cultural force that influences the ideals and behaviors of many action-oriented males, including prospective policemen. The most determined muscle builders, such as weightlifters and bodybuilders, bring their steroid habits into the police force with them. But the most heavily recruited young males are former military personnel, some of whom used anabolic steroids while on duty. What is more, former military personnel have the potential to further promote the militarization of American police forces that has been under way for several decades. This process includes the introduction of military equipment and a combative approach to policing that emphasizes the role of physical force at the expense of cultivating a more collaborative relationship with civilians.

The gradual infusion of military strategies, attitudes, and equipment into domestic police forces has undermined the civilian nature of policing in the United States and brought about a widespread transformation of the roles and conduct of police officers, especially in urban areas. In 1972, the chief justice of the US Supreme Court, Warren Burger, cited "a traditional and strong resistance of Americans to any military intrusion into civilian affairs."[1] Law enforcement responses to the civil disorders of the 1960s and the war on drugs of the 1980s and beyond have altered the balance of power between military and civilian approaches to maintaining domestic order. This shift in the direction of deploying overwhelming force to meet the challenges of civilian law enforcement has "masculinized" police identity by putting a greater emphasis on officers' use of physical force and the utilization of their recently acquired military-style equipment. "As inner cities have become increasingly violent with the proliferation of the drug culture," Philip J. Sweitzer noted in 2004, "the 'war on drugs' has fostered a parallel development in police conduct: the emergence of a militaristic, hyper-masculine cop," resulting in "the paradigm shift away from the community-caretaking police officer to violent 'soldier' cop."[2] Sweitzer argues that anabolic steroids have become an integral part of the evolution of action-oriented cops, who are "occupationally predisposed to steroid use" and "want to be big, burly, and imposing, to have the physical proportions of comic book superheroes."[3] An indirect acknowledgment of the potential role of steroids in paramilitary-style policing is a former agent's claim that the federal Bureau of Alcohol, Tobacco and Firearms (ATF) recruits by "hand-picking these superhormone guys."[4]

The transformation of American policing reflects the crucial kind of state-sanctioned power shared by the police and military establishments. An academic study of paramilitary policing put it this way: "The military and the police have an inherent political connection: both possess a monopoly on and the prerogative to exercise the state-legitimized use of force."[5] But because the hypermasculine traits of muscularity and aggressiveness, which can be essential on the battlefield, may be counterproductive or even dangerous in civilian environments, hyperaggressive forms of the legitimate use of force come to seem illegitimate. For example, the transition from community-oriented policing to increasingly frequent commando-style raids on private residences has become a widely recognized threat to American civil liberties. In this sense, an occupational predisposition to anabolic steroid use is likely to intensify police violence and its intimidating effect on targeted citizens. An officer's attraction to steroids may also signal a taste for confrontation that distorts genuine command presence—a self-confident take-charge attitude—into self-assertive pugnacity. In such cases, "male police officers may sometimes be tempted to turn encounters with male civilians into masculinity contests."[6]

Both the military and the police, traditional bastions of masculine identity, have developed codes of conduct that include an emphasis on courage, physical and mental toughness, and a capacity for aggressive behavior. The many police departments that recruit former military men often proclaim the deep affinity between police and military cultures, which in turn promotes the paramilitary identity that much of American policing has adopted since the war on drugs began to intensify during the 1980s. The Police Link website, for example, appeals to military personnel who might be considering a career in law enforcement: "Police Officers and Military Personnel are a special breed of people. For the most part, we have an attraction to action, conflict, and non-simplistic lifestyles where everything can change in a moment's notice. . . . Our co-workers are more like brothers and sisters. Our very lives are often placed in each other's hands."[7] "As a veteran," says a recruiting page for the Cleveland Police Department, "you are particularly well suited to law enforcement jobs such as police officer, as your military service has already taught you many of the skills required for the job. Police officers maintain law and order, and respond to calls for help."[8] And from Philadelphia:

> The Police Department is structured as a para-military organization. This means that we employ a culture and protocols that closely approximate those of the armed forces. Concepts like the chain of command, organizational hierarchies, military order and discipline, and others are ideas that are present in all police organizations. Because of this similarity to the military services, veterans have demonstrated an ability to quickly assimilate into

the police organizational framework and are, therefore, productive in their respective duties quicker and at a higher proficiency level than those who have no experience serving in such organizations. In addition, veterans are, on the whole, in peak physical condition.

Honorably discharged veterans received an extra ten points on the written examination they take to be admitted to the Philadelphia force.[9]

Many law enforcement agencies facilitate the recruitment of military veterans by streamlining or fast-tracking applications, waiving education requirements, adding preference points to exam scores, offering incentive pay, and offering service credit toward retirement.[10] These policies promote the masculinizing of a police force by favoring the hiring a disproportionate number of men as opposed to women, and by hiring of a disproportionate number of men with military training as opposed to other professional or educational backgrounds. Since only one in every seven members of the active-duty military is a woman, the recruiting of military personnel is an additional obstacle to more women becoming police officers.[11] Apart from gender equity, this discrepancy affects what we may call the temperament of a police force as it relates to the resolution of conflicts by means of negotiation or force.

Police department recruiting efforts aimed at military veterans do not address the gender issue in policing or the related issue of police temperament. "Law enforcement agencies," one analysis points out, "continue to heavily recruit ex-military personnel and at military bases, security agencies, and male-oriented sporting events, which are all disproportionately populated by men." (All of these groups include substantial numbers of anabolic steroid users.) "Recruitment departments have not adequately intensified their efforts to attract qualified women candidates or to portray policing as a profession that welcomes women."[12] While police departments' recruiting pitches routinely claim that soldiers and police officers share a common identity, they fail to point out that police officers and soldiers have different roles and obligations, and they ignore the differences between men and women altogether: "Many law enforcement agencies continue to promote an outdated model of policing by rewarding tough, aggressive, even violent, behavior. This 'paramilitary' style of policing results in poor community relations, increased citizen complaints, and more violent confrontations and deaths. Redefining law enforcement to a community-oriented model of policing would attract more women who are repelled by policing's trademark aggressive and authoritarian image."[13] Unsurprisingly, this aggressive and authoritarian behavior has been frequently linked with policemen's use of anabolic steroids, since steroid use in this group is a reliable marker of the kind of deviance that expresses itself in aggressiveness, a need to dominate, and a defiance of rules and laws.

Contact with charismatic military veterans can promote anabolic steroid use among police officers. "Police officers and military veterans are kindred spirits," says *Police Magazine*.[14] These kindred spirits are not, however, equal in prestige; in fact, the militarization of American policing has elevated special forces operatives to the status of being the most prestigious role models for paramilitary policing. Just as some small departments aspire to "having some sort of 'big department muscle,'" in the form of bulked-up cops, large police departments aspire to the paramilitary status and prestige that come with having access to military-style assault weapons, armored personnel carriers, and commando-style training provided by elite special forces soldiers.

The superior status of the military man is incarnated in the "warrior," an idealized figure for both groups. Here, for example, is a tribute from a Special Operations Forces nutrition guide: "The demands imposed by Special Operations Forces (SOF) training and missions are unlike any athletic endeavor. Success requires the mustering of all strength and endurance—both physical and mental. SOF are 'Warrior Athletes,' the ultimate athlete, at the top of the athletic pyramid."[15] While policemen, by comparison, are located further down the slopes of this Mount Olympus, they too pay tribute to the warrior ideal. "Command presence," says an official police website, is "about walking the path of the warrior: Displaying honor, possessing integrity and demonstrating teamwork."[16] The warrior, then, is a kind of spiritual figure revered by both groups.

The warrior is also an international role model celebrated at the annual Warrior Competition—"the Olympics of counterterrorism"—held annually in the Kingdom of Jordan at the King Abdullah II Special Operations Training Center, a facility in Amman operated by the Jordanian Armed Forces and funded by the United States. In May 2014, the six-day special-operations contest involved thirty-eight law-enforcement and military units from nineteen countries, including the United States, Russia, and China, the eventual winner of the overall competition. The American entry was a police SWAT team. "We are celebrating the warrior spirit," declared a Jordanian brigadier general, "the camaraderie that grows within those who suffer together to protect their homelands and their people." This warrior figure is a universal hero who is loyal to whichever political forces send him out on his patriotic missions. Subjecting these "warrior athletes" to drug testing appears to be unnecessary.[17]

US special forces depictions of the warrior are reverential to the point of hyperbole: "The SOF operator is the primary weapons platform. There is an imperative to extend the operational life and maximize the battlefield performance of the operator."[18] Here the emotional tension invested in the "warrior athlete" reaches maximum intensity.

The unspoken message of this supercharged language is that "warrior athletes" do not need to use anabolic steroids. According to *The Special Operations Forces Nutrition Guide*, performance enhancement is the name of the game for the special forces, but it is "appropriate nutritional habits and interventions [that] can enhance performance."[19] As we shall see, the US Army has been unable to enforce its zero-tolerance policy regarding anabolic steroids and has instead tolerated the massive use of dietary supplements as an alternative to male hormone doping. Minimizing the use of steroids for functional reasons depends on convincing soldiers that intensive training and good nutrition can keep them safe on the battlefield. Conventional athletes may dope, but athletes animated by the camaraderie of the warrior spirit presumably do not.

Special weapons and tactics (SWAT) teams are paramilitary units within civilian police departments consisting of heavily screened and tested volunteers who are comparable to special forces operatives. Some law enforcement agencies require "their [SWAT] personnel to be veterans of the armed forces, but this is usually not considered strictly necessary for such personnel."[20] Special forces, Army Rangers, and Navy SEALs are welcomed as applicants to the FBI's Hostage Response Team.[21] Early FBI SWAT teams usually came from military backgrounds,[22] and physical training was based on the fitness programs of elite military units such as the US Army Special Forces and Navy SEALs.[23] "We've had teams of Navy Seals and Army Rangers come here and teach us everything," an enthusiastic member of a police paramilitary unit said in the 1990s. At the same time, as the criminologist Peter B. Kraska points out, "the heightened ethos of militarism in these 'elite' police units is potentially infectious for the police institution."[24] Such concerns about a "military mindset" and a "general trend of heavy-handedness in a law enforcement community relying heavily on paramilitarism as police policy" are noted (and downplayed) in a long analysis of SWAT teams and constitutional law that appeared in 2001.[25] For this commentator, the mind-set of the elite police units he describes is not a matter of concern.

The alternative to this detached approach to action-oriented police personnel is recognizing that a heavy-handed mind-set is common in police work, especially among a subset of officers, and that paramilitary policing intensifies this syndrome. In one sense, the paramilitary style is a constant temptation for many ordinary police officers: "The allure of police paramilitary subculture stems from the enjoyment, excitement, high status, and male camaraderie that accompany the heavy weaponry, new technologies, dangerous assignments, and heightened anticipation of using force in most PPU [police paramilitary unit] work."[26] Kraska, an expert on police militarization, writes from personal experience:

The paramilitary culture associated with SWAT teams is highly appealing to a certain segment of civilian police (certainly not all civilian police). As with special operations soldiers in the military, members of these units saw themselves as the elite police involved in real crime fighting and danger. A large network of for-profit training, weapons, and equipment suppliers heavily promotes paramilitary culture at police shows, in police magazine advertisements, and in training programs sponsored by gun manufacturers such as Smith and Wesson and Heckler and Koch. The "military special operations" culture—characterized by a distinct techno-warrior garb, heavy weaponry, sophisticated technology, hypermasculinity, and dangerous function—was nothing less than intoxicating for its participants.[27]

It is possible for the emotional gratifications of paramilitary policing to become addictive. Philip Sweitzer noted in 2004 the hypothesis "that recurrent exposure to trauma in police work diminishes sensitivity to stress, establishes a permanent state of 'hypervigilance,' and establishes adrenaline addiction in many officers"; the authors of one study compared "this directly to war-related incidence of post-traumatic stress disorder in soldiers." To this diagnosis, Sweitzer added: "This addiction to the excitement of policing opens the psychiatric portal to steroid use, because testosterone and its derivatives directly ameliorate the recurrent stress to which cops are, necessarily, exposed, in the process of enhancing, rather than impeding, performance. As such, steroid use by police officers is likely far more pervasive than known, and will probably continue on an upward trend."[28]

Susceptibility to steroid use is not part of the official narrative about what happens when police officers experience extreme stress. On the contrary, the police officer who has undergone extreme stress is presented, and rightfully so, as a victim of difficult or even overwhelming circumstances. The *FBI Law Enforcement Bulletin* reports that intolerable levels of emotional stress can produce "vicarious traumatization" and the attendant symptoms: "hypervigilance, symptomatic reactions, relationship problems, lack of communication, denial, depression, isolation and dissociation." An officer's vulnerability on the job derives from a capacity to feel and identify with the person he or she is helping: "Vicarious traumatization results from empathetic engagement with traumatic experiences."[29] While the hazards of police work are constantly associated with gunfire, the far more prevalent emotional damage goes largely unpublicized. In 2015 the number of police officers killed by gunfire was 42 out of a total population of about 700,000 officers.[30] This deadly toll should be seen in relationship to the vast human costs of alcoholism, domestic violence, and divorce that afflict the lives and families of police officers.

The steroid narrative opens the door to a disturbing account of how police officers cope with the emotional consequences of the traumatic experiences they endure on the job. The effects of "adrenaline addiction," "addiction to the excitement of policing," or the "intoxication" caused by participating in a violence-prone paramilitary subculture are the very opposite of empathetic engagement with crime victims. Not all adrenaline addicts are steroid users, but steroid use promotes the paramilitary syndrome among police officers. One study shows steroid users as having "higher scores on measures of pathological narcissistic traits (exhibitionism, entitlement, and exploitativeness) and lower ratings for empathy, relative to non-AAS-using weightlifting comparison subjects." Weightlifting or bodybuilding policemen bring their own versions of narcissism and exhibitionism—and, in some cases, their steroid habits—into police forces.

This steroid use can put the people closest to the doping officers in serious danger. Compared with nonusers, male steroid users are more prone to violence, physical aggression, verbal aggression, and the abuse of female partners.[31] Three studies have shown that domestic violence is two to four times as prevalent among police families (24–40 percent of families) as among American families in general.[32] Things are even worse in the military, since domestic violence rates there are reportedly two to five times as high as the rates among civilians.[33] Domestic violence rates among police officers suffering from post-traumatic stress disorder are comparable to those of combat veterans and former POWs.[34] These data confirm what the Policemen's Benevolent Association of New Jersey declared in 1988, namely, that police officers "are members of quasi-military organizations"[35] who bear grave responsibilities and the psychological pressures that go with them.

What I have called the steroid narrative of the paramilitary police subculture, and its tendency to promote violent behaviors, does not propose a simple cause-and-effect relationship between anabolic steroids and police behavior. There is no question that anabolic steroids trigger violent behavior in a certain number of users, including some police officers. These violent outbursts are, however, unpredictable, and even most heavy users will not kill or maim while under the influence of these drugs. The more interesting hypothesis is that steroid use is a *marker* of troubled personalities, some of whom gravitate toward an entire range of action-oriented male subcultures that regularly engage in steroid use. For example, a finding that 25 percent of anabolic steroid abusers "had memories of childhood sexual or physical abuse" suggests that this type of drug use can serve as both a sign and a precipitating factor of certain kinds of psychopathology.

MILITARY USE OF ANDROGENIC DRUGS: PSYCHOTROPIC DOPING GOES TO WAR

The vast majority of Americans are unaware of the fact that the military personnel sent by the United States to fight in Vietnam, the Persian Gulf, Iraq, and Afghanistan were heavily medicated with psychotropic mood-altering drugs as a matter of military policy. Precisely how and when this new era of military pharmacology began is a matter of definition. "For the first time in history," *Time* reported in 2009, during the Iraq and Afghanistan Wars, "a sizable and growing number of U.S. combat troops are taking daily doses of antidepressants to calm nerves strained by repeated and lengthy tours in Iraq and Afghanistan. The medicines are intended not only to help troops keep their cool but also to enable the already strapped Army to preserve its most precious resource."[36] More recently, Lukasz Kamienski called the Vietnam War "the first 'pharmacological war' because both the prescribed and self-prescribed consumption of psychoactive substances by military personnel assumed alarming proportions, unprecedented in American history." Between 1966 and 1969, the US armed forces used an estimated 225 million tablets of "stimulants, mostly Dexedrine (dextroamphetamine), an amphetamine derivative that is nearly twice as strong as the Benzedrine used in the Second World War." (Benzedrine consumption by American troops during that global conflict has been estimated at 250 million tablets or more.)[37] During the Vietnam War, military psychiatrists also prescribed new medications such as the anti-psychotic Thorazine, Valium for anxiety, and Compazine, which works both as an antidiarrheal drug and as a tranquilizer.[38] Kamienski says the routine use of a powerful antipsychotic drug like Thorazine (chlorpromazine) was a first for military psychiatry. David Grossman has called Vietnam "the first war in which the forces of modern pharmacology were directed to empower the battlefield soldier."[39]

These accounts of the development of military pharmacology point to the differentiating characteristics of what we may call military doping during the modern period. For example, it is essential to distinguish between state-sponsored psychiatric doping and the self-prescribing of drugs to cope with the boredom, terror, and varieties of sheer suffering endured by the troops in Vietnam. While the US military promoted amphetamine use, it did not encourage the use of marijuana or heroin. A second distinction—between the relief of mental suffering and the "empowering" of a soldier by means of performance enhancement—is not so clear. Here we encounter the ambiguous distinction between performance-enabling and performance-enhancing psychoactive substances. It is reasonable, for example, to assume that a less anxious or less depressed (and, therefore, performance-enabled) soldier is going to perform better in combat than his anxiety-ridden counterpart. And that thinking has motivated the US military leadership to make military pharmacology a matter of national policy in wartime.

The psychopharmacological dimension of preparing fighting men for combat is as old as warfare itself. Alcohol has been by far the most commonly used psychoactive drug for the purpose of preparing men to go into battle. "For centuries," Kamienski writes, "alcohol has been so common before, during, and after battle that it has entered an almost symbiotic relationship with soldiering." The warriors of ancient Greece, the Roman legionnaires, Napoleon's army, the English sailors and soldiers who protected the empire on which the sun never set, the fighting men of the American Civil War, the soldiers of both World Wars—for all of them, drinking alcohol was both a source of "liquid courage" and "an almost universal liquid way of masking the horrible face of war."[40] Napoleon's men had their brandy, the English and George Washington relied on rum, Union and Confederate soldiers drank whiskey, the Russians consumed vodka, and the Romans and the French preferred wine. Government sponsorship of alcohol supplies ended with the Second World War, even if heavy drinking among the troops did not. It was also during the Second World War that governments' investment in military pharmacology shifted dramatically away from alcohol and to amphetamines, millions of doses of which were consumed by the soldiers and airmen of all of the major combatants.

The transition from mass amphetamine doping to major psychiatric drugs occurred during the early phase of the wars in Iraq and Afghanistan. "Prior to the Iraq war, soldiers could not go into combat on psychiatric drugs, period," the psychiatrist Peter Breggin, an expert on psychiatric drugs and violence, said in 2012. "Not very long ago, going back maybe 10 or 12 years, you couldn't even go into the armed services if you used any of these drugs, in particular stimulants. But they've changed that. . . . I'm getting a new kind of call right now, and that's people saying the psychiatrist won't approve their deployment unless they take psychiatric drugs."[41] Breggin believes that lobbying by the pharmaceutical industry has played a major role in putting psychiatric drugs into the many thousands of American soldiers who go to war.[42]

Which psychiatric drugs do soldiers take into battle? "You get a cocktail, and it's usually a sleeping pill, anti-anxiety medication, an anti-depressant, and an anti-psychotic—and sometimes even a stimulant like Ritalin or Adderall," Charles Ruby, a retired air force lieutenant colonel and clinical psychologist, said in 2013.[43] The journal *Military Medicine* reported in 2007 that "the modern Army psychiatrist's deployment kit is likely to include nine kinds of antidepressants, benzodiazepines for anxiety, four antipsychotics, two kinds of sleep aids, and drugs for attention-deficit hyperactivity disorder."[44]

Modern military psychopharmacology has long included amphetamines for US Air Force pilots, who are effectively required to take them when commanded to do so; refusing the medication can harm a pilot's military career. In fact, American military personnel "*are legally required to take medications if ordered for the sake of their military performance.*"[45]

The military use of psychiatric drugs has been driven primarily by the need to put into the field large numbers of combat-ready troops to fight two brutal wars at the same time. Two bioethicists commented in 2009 that "it may be that the military is at a point where there is no choice but to ask pilots or soldiers to use such drugs when their sleep/wake cycles must be manipulated because of added missions."[46] *Time* reported in 2009 that "the Department of Defense practice parameters in psychiatry are governed by a longstanding mandate requiring psychiatrists to use psychoactive drugs—even against their best professional judgment."[47]

The US military leadership has defended the use of psychiatric drugs, arguing that there are "few medications that are inherently disqualifying for deployment," and that psychiatric drug use in the military is comparable to that in the civilian world.[48] A *Los Angeles Times* report in 2012 modified that claim somewhat: "The Army surgeon general's office said no one without specific approval is allowed to go on deployment using psychotropic drugs, including antidepressants and stimulants, until they've been stabilized. Soldiers who need antipsychotic agents are not allowed to go to combat."[49] But there were limits. Military officials said in 2009 that "they [were] not using the drugs in order to send unstable warriors back to war."[50] Not all observers, however, accept these claims. "We have never medicated our troops to the extent we are doing now," a former military psychologist said in 2012. "And I don't believe the current increase in suicides and homicides in the military is a coincidence."[51]

Military psychopharmacology has never employed anabolic steroids as performance-enhancing drugs. The fantasy that the Nazis gave steroids to German troops during the Second World War has circulated for almost fifty years, and there is no evidence whatsoever to support it.[52] The Vietnam War took place during the early phase of the global anabolic steroid epidemic in elite sports, but there is little evidence that steroid use in Vietnam was anything other than episodic. The *Washington Times* reported in 1988 that "former Special Forces operatives also report receiving steroid injections before embarking on strenuous, deep-penetration assignments."[53] Nothing, however, indicates that military authorities endorsed such steroid use, assuming it happened.

But there is substantial evidence of steroid doping by American combat soldiers, including members of the special forces, in recent years, coinciding with the dramatic increase in steroid use by young men around the world.[54] Steroid use by military personnel, it should be pointed out, is a violation of the Uniform Code of Military Justice.[55]

STEROIDS IN THE US MILITARY: THE VIEW FROM THE RANKS

"What is the perception of AAS [anabolic-androgenic steroids] among the vast number of servicemen?" an anonymous website commentator asked on October 24, 2007. "Same brainwashing? I would assume that having a strong soldier would be a top priority." To which a like-minded poster added: "It's really a general expectation that the ideal Soldier is considerably stronger than the average person; many situations dictate the need for strength, lots of it." And how do high-ranking officers look at steroid use? According to the second poster, "most commanders won't honestly look at AAS with the same condemning eyes that they would, say heroin, barbiturates, etc."

The next day, however, a self-identified soldier stated: "Well I am currently in the military and let me tell you it is strongly frowned upon. I have actually talked to my commander about it if he ever thought about it considering he works out all the time. He was very ignorant [as] to the facts of [AAS] use." Ten days later, this message showed up: "As a former Marine I can tell you it varies with your command. There are some commands that look for it and frown upon it and then there are others where everyone is on them."[56] The online comments about the status of steroids in today's military world are numerous, but do not present a coherent story about what is going on in barracks and on battlefields where US troops are deployed.

We have, in fact, little hard data about the prevalence of AAS use among American military personnel, despite some substantial reporting on this issue.[57] In 1990, *Military Medicine* published an article reporting concern about unauthorized AAS use, a perception among commanders that steroid use was common among their soldiers, and the absence of an army policy to deal with it. Still, the authors confidently claimed that their small survey indicated only "a very small percentage of soldiers have used or are using AS," and that "there is currently no AS abuse problem among Army personnel."[58]

Today, however, official concern about AAS use by soldiers is out in the open. The US Army Public Health Command has declared that anabolic steroid use is illegal for "U.S. personnel deployed in a combat theater."[59] Nevertheless, anabolic steroid use by military personnel in and out of combat zones is well known and is reported to have increased in recent years.[60] Defense Department surveys found that steroid use by army personnel increased from 1.5 percent of troops in 2005 to 2.5 percent in 2008.[61] But such survey data, besides being of uncertain reliability, tell us nothing about how soldiers think and feel about these drugs and whether they should use them to survive the stresses and dangers of combat.

Online chat rooms are more revealing about the view from the ranks. Apart from the foolish or frivolous posts are a number of well-informed and insightful comments that can be compared with one another and with what we know from published sources. While the limitations of this material, such as the anonymity of the writers and the role of hearsay, are obvious, what these voices have to offer is clear to anyone who has done research in this area. All the important issues are here: What is the military's steroid policy? Does it make sense in light of what is required of soldiers on today's battlefield? How many of the troops are juicing? How many officers? How many of the special forces? Why is the enforcement of anti-AAS rules so inconsistent?

These chat rooms are a significant portal of entry into one of the gray zones in which anabolic steroid subcultures thrive around the world. They attract self-identified military personnel, as well as other interested parties, and in fact are the only real source of information about how enlisted soldiers think about anabolic steroids. Much of my confidence in the more substantial postings is based on what I know about American police officers' use of steroids and their motives for using them. A police department is a paramilitary culture that "employs a culture and protocols that closely approximate those of the armed forces."[62] Police and military organizations recruit from the same demographic. Many police departments actively recruit military veterans into their ranks, and many members of these action-oriented male subcultures share an interest in anabolic steroids. We know that much of the attraction to steroids within these groups is based on the perceived cosmetic benefits of having large, well-defined muscles. What we do not know is how many police officers and soldiers believe that bulking up is necessary to improve their chances of prevailing on the streets or on the battlefield.

Attempting to estimate the prevalence of steroid use among soldiers means weighing a great deal of hearsay along with a smaller number of credible reports. In a 2010 *New York Times* blog post that attracted comments well worth reading, the former army officer Tim Hsia wrote that "the use of steroids by soldiers when deployed is rumor."[63] This observation is contradicted by journalistic coverage and other sources. In a comment on Hsia's blog post, an Iraq War veteran who served with him discussed the availability and effects of steroids in combat zones: "Steroids and other pharmaceutical drugs can be easily acquired from the local national security forces that they [American troops] share these outposts with. Several of my subordinate leaders were using steroids (I discovered this after the fact), and quickly developed significant disciplinary problems. The NCOs were over-aggressive, irritable, and dealt poorly with stress. Not exactly a recipe for success in the COIN [counterinsurgency] fight." A 2007 posting states (spelling has been corrected):

> They still do PT [physical training] and all that. Roids just give them a boost. It seems not to be spoken of too often, it seems to be an underground thing but a good number still do it. Overseas, steroids are sold like candy. This doesn't pertain to just SEALS. It goes for most of the military. When you see a guy out in Iraq or Afghanistan gain like 20–30 pounds of muscle mass during his tour you would understand. I was also told by an [Army] Ranger friend of mine who is part of the 75th Ranger battalion out in Savannah, Georgia, that the higher ups encourage the use of legal steroids.[64]

This is an unconfirmed report. What a former NATO special forces soldier told me about the steroid use he saw in Afghanistan is not and is summarized later in this chapter.

In summary, online comments from self-identified military personnel depict a military drug culture that is as complex and incoherent as that of the larger society from which soldiers come. The enormous, $30 billion dietary supplements market has reproduced itself on military bases, and many soldiers rely on these products.[65] For example, a physician's assistant medical officer in Afghanistan called supplement use in 2010 "a huge issue on our base." As quoted previously, "At best," he wrote, "they are harmless and only waste soldiers' money, at worst they can cause kidney and liver failure."[66] Supercaffeinated drinks are everywhere now. According to the manufacturer of Rip It® Energy Fuel, which has tied its brand to support-the-troops messages, it "has been tested on the battlefield and is a favorite of our Troops."[67] On and off military bases, anabolic steroids play the role of the heavyweight performance enhancer that coexists with less potent but legal performance-enhancing drugs (PEDs).

STEROIDS IN THE US MILITARY: THE VIEW FROM THE TOP

Ambivalence toward anabolic-androgenic steroids (AAS) will always be found in social institutions based on the performances of action-oriented men such as soldiers, police officers, and athletes. The military establishment, law enforcement agencies, and sports federations are integral parts of a social and political order that remains committed to a prohibitionist policy regarding illicit performance-enhancing drugs. At the same time, a very large, though unknown, number of soldiers, police officers, and athletes use the drugs because they regard them as useful.

The ambivalence in an action-oriented subculture derives from a conflict between the traditional stigmatizing of illicit drugs and the strong temptation to use PEDs for what are seen as practical purposes. We should note that "practicality" is a problematic term here, since the psychophysiological effects of PEDs are easier to imagine than to confirm. Still, some of their effects are real, and many action-oriented men are determined to use them without regard to their licit or legal status.

The Department of the Army first expressed concern about unauthorized use of AAS in 1989. A memorandum prepared for the deputy chief of staff states: "Unit commanders perceive that . . . steroid use is commonplace with young soldiers, particularly in elite military units (Ranger and Special Forces)."[68] And although the US Army Public Health Command declared that anabolic steroid use is illegal for combat troops,[69] the illicit and unlawful use of anabolic steroids by military personnel in and out of combat zones is well known and is reported to have increased in recent years.[70] Official military policy is in line with general societal condemnation of steroid use not undertaken for what are designated as legitimate medical purposes. The Anabolic Steroids Control Act of 1990 established a legal and policy-making framework that is also official military policy regarding the use and abuse of these drugs.

US military commanders have declared repeatedly that steroid use is incompatible with military service. In 2010, for example, General Peter Chiarelli, the army's vice chief of staff, stated: "The use of steroids is a short-term gain for long-term problems that individuals are going to have, and we cannot tolerate them in any way, shape or form."[71]

Antisteroid statements from military sources emphasize the perceived practical disadvantages of steroid use rather than the moral stigma associated with athletic dopers. An exception to this rule was a semicoherent statement made by a special agent of the Naval Criminal Investigative Service (NCIS) in 2011: "Steroids are out there. They can be used for legitimate reasons and they can be used for personal reasons, like in sports and the military. Every medicine has a purpose, [but] doing it for cosmetic reasons is cheating"—a term that is normally applied to the world of sport. "'You could be an awesome Sailor, Soldier, Marine, or Airman, but the moment you use steroids, you're tainted,' she said. 'You ruined a 20-year career in a matter of minutes.'"[72] What is striking here is the notion of a taint that instantly transforms an exemplary fighter into a reject. Other military policy statements assert that steroid use is incompatible with combat effectiveness.

Perhaps the intent behind the NCIS special agent's statement is to associate steroid use, in the usual fashion, with character flaws that disqualify someone from military service. But this is a confusing commentary, in part because the "legitimate" use of steroids is not identified. What is more, the assertion that steroid use for "cosmetic" purposes is "cheating" suggests there may be other, perhaps military purposes for which the use of these drugs is allowable, although that cannot be what this commentator is trying to say. The idea that militarily effective steroid use would constitute "cheating" is illogical and originates in a false analogy between sports competitions and warfare.

A zero-tolerance policy for military steroid use has become official policy across much of the English-speaking world. In the United Kingdom, a military spokesman said: "The Armed Forces do not tolerate the taking of illegal drugs within their ranks, as it is incompatible with military service."[73] Brigadier John Donnelly, director of personnel services, stated in 2013: "Clearly in some parts of the Army there appears to be an increased use of steroids. We put out warnings on a regular basis reminding people about the dangers because they have significant physical and psychological side effects that are incompatible with military service. As drugs go, they are every bit as bad as recreational drugs."[74]

Senior Australian army commanders, concerned about an apparent increase in illegal drug use, warned soldiers in 2002 that the use of anabolic steroids was grounds for dismissal. A colonel serving as personnel operations director stated: "Involvement by members of the army with illegal drugs, including steroids, is not compatible with an effective army. Drug involvement leads to reduced performance, health impairment, presents a security risk and has the potential to endanger the safety of our soldiers."[75] The use of illegal drugs by officers, warrant officers, and noncommissioned officers indicated "severe shortcomings in personal leadership qualities."[76] A former Australian senior commander in the Middle East said in 2011 that steroids were dangerous in a combat environment because they could produce irrational aggression. "We need rational aggression," he said. "If soldiers become irrational and obsessive about their physique, it can be unhealthy and dangerous."[77]

It is also possible to embrace performance-enhancing substances while at the same time rejecting the use of anabolic steroids. In 1998 the commanders of Australia's special forces units—the Special Air Service Regiment, First Commando Regiment, and Fourth Battalion Royal Australian Regiment—adopted guidelines permitting the use of blood doping, creatine powder, caffeine, oral rehydration drinks, ephedrine, and the popular antinarcoleptic modafinil. The use of dietary supplements such as creatine is widespread among American military personnel, as we have seen.

How motivated are military commanders to suppress or eliminate steroid use by the soldiers under their command? There is a difference between commanders' zero-tolerance rhetoric and their ability or willingness to enforce it. The whistleblower who catalyzed a steroid bust at an Australian army barracks, provoking remarks about "personal leadership qualities" and "irrational aggression," claimed that the army had shown little interest in controlling the traffic in these drugs.[78]

US military personnel have offered similar observations. In 2010 a former US Army sergeant who had served for a year in Iraq confirmed that he had seen steroid use among his fellow soldiers that could not have been overlooked by anyone: "People got really big, really fast. There were some really extreme examples of people getting so huge that they weren't even able to clean themselves properly anymore, because their arms couldn't reach their back or anything like that." This cosmetic use of steroids was, according to the former sergeant, "generally an accepted form of drug abuse." Accepted by commanding officers, that is: "The chain of command saw that as soldiers trying to become better soldiers. They really looked the other way." Some officers may have seen a practical advantage in doing so: "If a captain sees his soldiers getting stronger at a quicker rate, that's not necessarily a bad thing."[79] The lack of interest among some commanders in going after steroid use is confirmed in anonymous online chat rooms where self-identified military personnel and others post their observations about military policy.

Looking the other way while receiving reports or rumors of steroid use in the ranks seems like a practical option in the absence of a coherent sense of what is going on. Take, for example, the story line from an army sergeant's 2010 commentary about why soldiers use the drugs. "The demand for steroids arose," according to the sergeant, "because the latest generation of body armor, and the need to carry around lots of ammo and water, meant troops were spending many hours running around, carrying lots of weight."[80] Tim Hsia, the Iraq War veteran and *New York Times* reporter, offered a similar account: "During my deployments in Iraq there were often rumors that certain soldiers were taking steroids because of their sudden increase in physical size. When the unit deployed these soldiers looked no different from the average soldier, but upon completion of the deployment they looked Rambo-esque. Some soldiers felt that others were getting away with steroid use because these soldiers were rarely seen in the gym and because drug testing through urinalysis was rarely done by units while deployed."[81] Soldiers were aware that the army seldom tested for steroids because of the high cost. As one journalist put it in 2013: "Despite being banned by the military, officials do little to thwart the use of steroids, largely because of cost concerns: Screenings run hundreds of dollars apiece."[82]

There are, then, at least three obstacles to controlling military steroid use: ambivalence about their military value, uncertainty about how many troops are using steroids, and the high cost of testing for them. An even more threatening breakdown of discipline regarding steroids occurs when high-ranking officers are assumed to be using the drugs that they are charged with eliminating from the ranks. An American soldier who was sentenced to five months in the brig "reported that many in his chain of command—including his first sergeant and his battalion's executive officer—used the drugs."[83]

Could a military command empowered by a society that stigmatizes anabolic steroids when used by athletes be tempted to administer these drugs to the troops? In fact, one former commander of the British forces in Afghanistan succumbed to this temptation and expressed this viewpoint in public as described below. Even the British officer who called steroids "incompatible with military service" and "every bit as bad as recreational drugs" offered his audience a reminder about the difficulties involved in controlling the kind of people who volunteer to go into combat: "But you can only go so far. We recruit risk takers. That is what being a soldier is about."[84]

Commanders who impose penalties on steroid users are thus in the awkward position of disciplining soldiers who are appreciated for their alpha-male qualities. That is why official condemnation of performance-enhancing substances can seem illogical, impractical, and even self-defeating. In 2009, for example, a former US Army captain argued that banning the sale of dietary supplements on American military bases would hurt the morale of the troops.[85] A year later, a journalist reported on the consequences of such an attitude: "While the use of steroids by soldiers when deployed is rumor, the use of supplements to become bigger, stronger and faster is a fact. When I had to conduct a health and welfare inspection, I was shocked by the profusion and variety of pills and powders I found in the rooms of soldiers. A few rooms could have been confused for mini-pharmacies."[86] According to a 2013 report: "The majority of deployed Marines use multiple dietary supplements and perceive a high benefit."[87] The motto of the Army Medical Corps, after all, is "conserve the fighting strength," and it has given massive amounts of antidepressants to combat troops in fulfillment of that mission.[88]

Commanders willing to tolerate "legal doping" on this scale may well be prepared to accept steroids if new circumstances were to arise. A former commander of the British forces in Afghanistan took the policy of toleration a step further when he offered an appreciation of steroid use by combat troops in September 2013: "There is a strong culture of physical fitness in the Army, and there has to be . . . and taking this kind of substance is part of that fitness culture in the same way it is with civilian fitness fanatics."[89] The fact that a high-ranking military commander was willing to publicly endorse steroid use by combat soldiers demonstrates the appeal of the functional rationale for military steroid use, which is accepted by an unknown number of soldiers. "It seems," an anonymous commentator wrote in 2010, "a growing number of infantry troops are using steroids, to help them build muscle mass, so that they can better handle the loads they have to carry in combat. For most of these troops, the additional muscle is seen as a matter of life and death."[90] In the absence of survey data, it remains unclear how many troops who use steroids do so for primarily cosmetic reasons, as opposed to those who genuinely believe that steroid use promotes their survival on the battlefield.

STEROIDS IN THE US MILITARY: THE SPECIAL FORCES

Fantasies about superwarriors are as old as the civilizations that first went to war against each other. Modern versions of these military "action figures" have often been imagined as soldiers who were transformed by performance-enhancing drugs. Fascination with their elite status translates easily into fantasies about their special access to powerful drugs. Imaginings of the drug-enhanced warrior include an element of wish fulfillment, as well. The myth of the Nazi steroid, which many still believe boosted the fighting abilities of Wehrmacht and SS troops, is the most common example of this sort of pharmacological magical thinking.[91] While many soldiers have used steroids for combat-related (as well as cosmetic) purposes, they have done so without official authorization from their commanding officers.

The US Special Operations Forces include the Navy SEALs, the Army Rangers, and the Army's Delta Force. Most of the comments that appear in online chat rooms and forums concern the Navy SEALs, whose image as the toughest and the hardiest of the elite forces has inspired many fantasies about their extraordinary fitness and competence and the ways in which they were achieved.

The romanticizing of special forces troops has become a staple of popular culture. This theme can be seen in films such as *Captain Phillips* (2013), in which Navy SEAL snipers rescue an American ship captain from Somali captors, and *Lone Survivor* (2013), in which four SEALs carry out a heroic but doomed counterinsurgency mission in the mountains of Afghanistan. The SOF call these men "warrior athletes" who possess an aura of invincibility that leaves mere athleticism far behind. And how will these men become supersoldiers? There is no mention of anabolic steroids or any other drugs. On the contrary, the anticlimactic announcement that follows the extolling of these "warrior athletes" is that their athletic superiority is built not on performance-enhancing substances, but on "good nutrition."[92]

The sparse published research on anabolic steroid use by special forces soldiers confirms the use of these drugs but not their prevalence. A 2012 study "found a surprisingly large number of androgen users (32 percent) among a small study population (16/50)." Even more striking is the 1999 finding that fully 64 percent of the candidates undergoing Ranger and SOF training were using dietary supplements, some of which may contain at least traces of anabolic steroids. That SOF troops were consuming supplements at a rate higher than that of the general military population "is concerning given the association between supplement and anabolic steroid use."[93]

Testimonies to the emotional intoxication steroids can provide on the battlefield make clear why some warfighters would want this kind of stimulation: "Guys talk about the rush the juice gives them when they go out on patrol. . . . I never liked firing my weapon before . . . but once I started juicing, I loved it. . . . Like I wanted nothing more than to split someone open. . . ." To some soldiers steroid use makes practical sense: "I'm not saying the Army condones it, but I also don't see them trying to stop it. . . . And why would they? They want the strongest and baddest Army, pretty sure they're going to look the other way."[94]

A NATO soldier who served in Afghanistan in 2003 told me about training with steroid-boosted American SOF troops who had impressive rope-climbing abilities but lacked endurance when it came to long treks through the rugged landscape of Afghanistan. Four Australian special forces soldiers were removed from Afghanistan in 2010 after being caught with or testing positive for steroids.[95] We do not see remarks about steroid use from self-identified SOF personnel in online military chat rooms. What we do see are speculations by outsiders about what elite SOF soldiers are like, whether they use steroids, and whether, if they do, it is an appropriate practice.

The constant focus of speculation about Navy SEALs is the question of how muscular they should be to operate with maximum effectiveness. This preoccupation with optimal muscle mass inevitably raises the related question whether steroids promote SEALs' survival in combat conditions. The popular association of extreme muscularity with strength and intimidation encourages most people to imagine that the superwarrior has a hypermuscular body type. An online commentator encountered this body type around the beginning of the Iraq War: "All of the Navy Seal units that I saw in Kuwait in 2003 were eating in the chow hall with everyone else. They had the muscularity size of those professional wrestlers you see on TV."[96] This observer may have had his own idea of what constitutes bulging muscles, or he may have happened on some of the most muscular men who had managed to survive the famously punishing ordeal of SEAL training.

A fighting force composed of SEAL or Ranger or Delta Force commandos who looked like bodybuilders would indicate widespread use of anabolic steroids by military men who were either breaking the law to obtain legally controlled substances or who were getting male hormone treatments from government doctors. What the evidence suggests, however, is that most special forces men are not hypermuscular and that it is a disadvantage in the field to carry extra muscle mass. "You think SEALs look like Rambo?" a journalist asked in 2010. "They don't—think more along the lines of Daniel Craig's James Bond. The average size of a SEAL is probably 5ft.-10, 175 pounds."[97]

This assessment recurs in online chat-room commentaries. "Steroid stallions were in style in the late 80's and early 90's," a former soldier wrote at ProfessionalSoldiers.com in 2010. "I don't remember seeing a single one make it through either Ranger school or SFAS [Special Forces Assessment and Selection]."[98] "One common misconception about special forces (probably due to unrealistic movies)," someone wrote in 2004, "is that most recruits are jacked up, huge, and ripped. Its just the opposite. Most of them are extremely thin, very lean, quick and mobile. I don't see how there is going to be any AAS that is going to allow you to maintain muscle mass when consuming very little food, running all day, and not sleeping."[99]

Another commenter in the thread added: "Big guys always struggle more than little guys. You see a few fit big guys around but generally the fittest are normal to small. One thing that struck me about the US Marines that were attached to our unit in Basra was how big they all were and how unfit they were in a running sense."[100] "Overall," said another, "I don't see the benefits of steroids making any major significant contribution to passing any military special operations selection courses from SEALs to Delta selection. Really, the most significant aspect as already mentioned is a mental toughness and physical toughness. The mental strength being more important of the two. The ability to 'endure' is going to be the significant aspect that makes or breaks."[101] And again: "All the SEALs I have known, with one notable exception, were typically 6' or under and trim but wiry as hell. It is a mental focus that gets you thru the training. Bulking up with muscles will work against you as you will require more oxygen and calories than the 'skinny' guy who is still on his feet. You're better off, in my opinion, investing in some mental focus training than in steroids if your goal is to get thru SEAL training."[102]

Chat-room comments from 2009 convey the same message about body types and the primacy of mental toughness. One self-identified former soldier who went through an extreme training regimen stated: "Ain't too many muscle bound fellas in special forces . . . They're just fit as a fiddle." Another man who apparently went through a similar training course wrote: "I have seen many great physical specimens cry like little babies with the mental stress you are going to be under. You don't need any extra hormones messing with your psyche."[103] And it is mental toughness that is mentioned over and over again: "It's all mental. They want people that know how to dig deep to take their bodies farther than they knew they could. . . . They want guys that will never give up."[104]

Speculation about the pharmacological enhancement of special forces operatives belongs to a tradition of fantasizing about extraordinary techniques for producing supersoldiers that has become entrenched in popular cultural forms such as films and comic books. As mentioned earlier, a Marvel Masterpieces ad for its

Captain America trading cards reads as follows: "In the darkest days of World War II, when a secret super-soldier serum transformed 90-pound weakling Steve Rogers into a physically perfect specimen of humanity, a legend was born—Captain America!"

The entertainment industry has played a major role in making anabolic steroid use—real or imagined—an integral part of the modern masculine ideal. The muscling up of actors playing superheroes in action films and television shows such as *Conan the Barbarian, Game of Thrones,* and *Thor* is driven by "comic book aesthetics" that will make many moviegoers "wonder whether actors use steroids to build their bodies." The military-steroid connection is exemplified by the fact that a former Navy SEAL was hired to pack muscle onto the Spartan army in the film *300.* In *Captain America: The First Avenger* (2011), "dozens of tiny needles inject the serum into Rogers' major muscle groups, and then he enters a pod where 'vita rays' stimulate his growth. On paper and on screen, the result is the same: Rogers emerges as a picture of physical perfection, a gleaming, rippling, flag-wearing, Nazi-killing machine."[105] Within the fantasy comic book world of hard-muscled masculinity, the pharmacological production of the warrior-savior is celebrated as a requirement of national security.

Steroids are integrated into the image of the American military despite its ban on the use of these drugs. A 2011 casting call for the television series *Wonder Woman* was reported to have been looking for "super-buff, worked-out, bodybuilder-type guys to play soldiers that appear to be on steroids."[106] There is nothing the military can do to prevent popular entertainment from promoting the image of the steroid-boosted fighting man whose special powers make him emblematic of the special forces soldier.

CONCLUSION

The leaders of our two social institutions that legally empower their members to kill have strikingly different attitudes toward anabolic steroid use. The military leadership has pursued a zero-tolerance policy they are unable to enforce. The great majority of police executives give lip service to a zero-tolerance policy they have no intention of enforcing. These opposing positions are indirectly reflected in the following account.

This story is about a white police officer who did not shoot a disorderly black man who was holding a gun and attempting to commit "suicide-by-cop." Stephen Mader, a twenty-five-year-old Marine Corps veteran, chose not to fire because: "For me, it wasn't enough to kind of take someone's life because they're holding a gun." Shortly thereafter, the drunken twenty-three-year-old was shot and killed by another officer who could not have known the suspect's gun was not loaded. Mader's police chief fired the ex-Marine for putting other officers' lives in danger.

One important difference between military and police cultures lies in their respective attitudes toward overall standards of discipline and expectations regarding individual self-control. "Around the country, police chiefs who've hired war veterans have commented on their maturity and self-control when facing danger," one reporter commented in December 2016. The police chief of a small town in Wisconsin, who is himself an Iraq veteran, says combat soldiers "have a better understanding of the rules of engagement and use of force than others might. They're used to seeing people holding guns, and they take the time to assess the real danger of the situation." As an academic psychologist put it: "Combat vets who've been exposed to extreme violence have a different 'threat threshold,' which means that they're in more control of their physiology, and they're not allowing this fight-or-flight response to drive them into action." The irony is that in Afghanistan, "the rules of engagement were sometimes stricter than use-of-force rules for civilian police in America." Marines in a combat zone were attempting to do the kind of "community policing" that is still in short supply in the United States.[1]

Military leaders have shown themselves to be much less tolerant of steroid use in the ranks than police chiefs are. During a conference at West Point in July 2015 I watched an Army officer become visibly angry at the idea that any man under his command would go into combat on steroids. In April of that year the Consortium of Health and Military Performance hosted a symposium on "Androgens, Anabolic Steroids, and Related Substances: What We Know and What We Need to Know." The conference report was published in *Military Medicine* in 2016.

Why is the performance-enhancement rationale for steroids unacceptable in the military? Because "the myriad effects on the emotional state of the warrior must be a concern for the SOF [Special Operations Forces] community as chronic use of AAS may be associated with depression, mania, hypomania, increased anxiety, irritability, extreme mood swings, high levels of aggression, and paranoia." What is more: "Androgen use without a prescription for a legitimate medical condition is illegal. Androgens are a Schedule III drug, which means they are substances or chemicals with potential for physical and psychological dependence. Military personnel who engage in illegal behaviors punishable under the Uniform Code of Military Justice put their careers at risk because they endanger 'unit security.'"[2]

The military leadership has thus promulgated a categorical and unambiguous anti-steroid policy. Soldiers' online comments suggest that, while lower-ranking officers' attitudes toward steroid use may differ, the message from the top of the command structure comes through loud and clear. That is why military-sponsored analyses of the steroid conundrum emphasize the potential risks rather than the potential benefits of steroid use on the battlefield.[3]

Compared with the US military, police departments are less disciplined and less stable professional environments. The Uniform Code of Military Justice has no analogue in police culture. The military can enforce a "community regulation of life-style" to a degree that no civilian or paramilitary (police) culture can.[4] While military bases tend to be isolated from civilian communities, police departments are embedded within them. Faced with the consequences of their integration into civilian society and the growing acceptance of testosterone use, police chiefs have decided that making a real effort to resist the testosterone tide is simply not worth the trouble.

This policy of acquiescence has been an open invitation to consequences such as excessive violence and the many local steroid scandals that have demoralized departments, created public mistrust of the police, and taken many offenders out of active service to the community for various periods of time. As police departments have acquired SWAT teams and massive amounts of military equipment, such as armored personnel carriers, military assault rifles, and submachine guns, they have not absorbed military-style discipline at the same time. The result has been the rise of "the militaristic, hyper-masculine 'cop,'" the "violent 'soldier' cop," and a "steroidal" policing style that, having accelerated during the drug wars of the 1980s and 1990s, has acquired a momentum of its own.[5] The police culture's unrelenting confrontation with the black population of the United States is the most ominous and destructive symptom of this "steroidal" policing style.

How might police steroid culture be eliminated? What could possibly catalyze such a deep transformation? In 2016 the former New York Police Commissioner William J. Bratton told potential agents of change that their cause was hopeless. "There are police reformers from outside the profession who think that changing police culture is a matter of passing regulations, establishing oversight bodies and more or less legislating a new order," he said. "It is not. Such oversight usually has only marginal impact. What changes police culture is leadership from within."[6]

The flaw in Bratton's model is that it optimistically assumes that "leadership from within" can transform a police culture that in many places is ruled by the "code of silence," police unions that refuse to engage in non-hostile dialogue with their critics, and in some cases police officials who refuse to acknowledge clear evidence of police misconduct. "The Police Department's disciplinary process is completely secretive," a lawyer for the American Civil Liberties Union said in 2017. "Right now, nobody knows what happens, and that makes police accountability impossible."[7]

A police leader unintimidated by the blue wall of silence and union threats to undo him could begin by focusing on tighter screening of those who are hired to be police officers. As one professor at the Cardozo School of Law put it, it is essential to "find the person who enjoys wielding power and weed him out."[8] What is more, there may be thousands of "gypsy cops" who "have drifted from police department to police department even after having been fired, forced to resign or convicted of a crime." There is no database of officers who have criminal convictions, but there are thousands of officers who have been stripped of their police authority.[9]

If William Bratton is right, and change can only come from within the police establishment, then a determined and unrelenting leadership that promulgates zero-tolerance policies is the only hope. It is a "major leadership question," says Walter Mack, a Marine combat veteran of Vietnam and an indefatigable former federal prosecutor who has worked to root out police corruption. "Cops are smart, they respond to good training, they respond to good leadership," he said. "Discipline is part of the enforcement mechanism, of seeing that your cops are functioning. You've got to make a decision: 'What is most important?' And make clear that there are certain things you're just not going to tolerate."[10]

ACKNOWLEDGMENTS

During twelve years of work on *Dopers in Uniform* I have been helped by many people who generously shared information and referred me to others who taught me things I needed to know. I want to thank Art Acevedo, Zach Arnold, Richard Auchus, M.D., Jesse Ausubel, Isaac Avilucea, Millard Baker, Stan Crowder, Tim Elfrink, James Ferstle, Shawn Fogarty, James Genovese, Gary Green, M.D., Joseph Gutman, M.D., Scott Henson, Kim Humphrey, Bianca Cain Johnson, Andreas Kimergård, Verner Møller, Mark Mueller, Tom Nolan, Harrison Pope, M.D., Jeff Proctor, Linda Robertson, Alan Tepperman, the Toronto Police Service Professional Standards Unit, and Charles E. Yesalis. My apologies to anyone whose name should appear in this list but does not.

I am greatly indebted to those at the University of Texas Press who committed to this project and have encouraged me from its inception, namely, Editor-in-Chief Robert Devens and Managing Editor Robert Kimzey. I am also grateful to Publicity and Communications Manager Colleen Ellis Devine for the time, effort, and imagination she has invested in promoting the book.

Among those to whom I have expressed my thanks above, I want to acknowledge the special (and indispensable) contribution of the sports journalist James Ferstle. For many years, Jim has compiled and sent to his colleagues a daily synopsis of news from around the world on the doping phenomenon in sport and in other social venues. It is impossible to overestimate the importance of Jim's contribution to my research on doping and to this book in particular. Without Jim's daily doping news feed, I would not have spotted the gradual increase in police doping reports that began around 2005. In this sense, it is Jim's professional generosity that made it possible to write this book.

This book also owes its existence to Drs. Jan and Terry Todd of the H. J. Lutcher Stark Center for Physical Culture and Sports at the University of Texas at Austin. At a relatively late point in our thirty-five years of friendship and colleagueship, Jan and Terry suggested that I transform my research on police steroid use into a book for the Terry and Jan Todd Series on Physical Culture and Sports at the University of Texas Press. Suffice it to say that it has been a privilege and a pleasure to do so. Serious research is an adventure akin to panning for gold. Accordingly, the research for *Dopers in Uniform* has taken me to dramatic and sometimes bizarre venues I would not have visited without the impetus of creating this book. My objective, here as elsewhere, has been to put together a portrait of how the world actually works.

Finally, I send heartfelt thanks to my wife, Louisa, for all of the encouragement and support she has given me over so many years of research and writing.

APPENDIX

An Iraq War Army Veteran on Steroid Use in Combat

SHAWN FOGARTY

Shawn Fogarty served in the US Army from 1999 to 2007 and was a military intelligence analyst with the First Cavalry Division in Baghdad from 2004 to 2005. Fogarty was honorably discharged with the rank of Staff Sergeant, enrolled at the University of Texas at Austin, and graduated in 2013 with a major in American Studies. The author came to know Fogarty as a student taking his course on performance-enhancing drugs. Readers will note that the following portrait of the soldier's steroid dilemma, written before this book existed, confirms the judgment of most of the military personnel quoted in chapter five. What combat soldiers need is mental toughness, not abnormal muscle mass; a calm and reliable state of mind, not hormone-driven volatility.

I spent eight years in the military as an intelligence analyst, seven years on active duty and one year in the Texas National Guard. Most of my time was spent at Fort Hood, Texas, but I was also stationed in Korea and did a deployment to Iraq. I worked in a mechanized infantry division, a cavalry division, and a strategic command. My experiences put me in contact with a wide range of occupational specialties and different types of people. Being well rounded, I was highly successful and quickly made my way up the ranks, going from private to staff sergeant in only four years.

Some soldiers will tell you that steroids allowed them to survive on the battlefield, that if it were not for steroids they would not have accomplished their mission. They may believe that to be true, but they are wrong. The army prepares you, through its physical fitness program, to be able to withstand the physical demands of being a soldier. Steroids are more harmful than helpful.

Soldiers are often asked to carry heavy loads over long distances. They may be forced to carry large, bulky weapons or lift heavy objects. Strength is an important asset for a soldier. But it isn't just muscular strength; mental toughness is another kind of strength. One of the most important lessons for successful soldiers is to learn that you can push through pain and fatigue; if you ignore your body telling you to stop, you can continue. Determination, discipline, reliability, courage, and intelligence are also desirable traits, more so than even physical strength. Soldiers exercise every morning and must be able to pass a physical fitness test. They are motivated to score high, and are rewarded for doing so. Promotions are based on physical fitness scores, so there is an incentive to perform well.

Most units go through an obstacle course or a confidence course designed to build skill in traversing challenging landscapes and obstacles. They can include rope climbing and river crossings. Units can require road marches with weighted rucksacks, ensuring their personnel are capable of completing missions that may require them to haul gear by foot over long distances. "The army fitness program more than prepares you for whatever you might be asked to do," says former army staff sergeant Brad Richards. "Being strong is definitely important, but there was never a time when I wished I was on or had taken steroids to be stronger." Knowing that you can complete difficult tasks is more important than actually doing them. It gives you the confidence to try any task that could be handed down, and the belief that you will accomplish it. Thousands of soldiers can complete these tasks without the aid of steroids. The determination to keep moving when your legs are screaming at you to stop is what gets you out of a bad situation. Being reliable allows your teammates to trust you when you tell them you won't let them fall. Knowing what to do when everything seems to go badly keeps you calm and gives you the resolve to finish and get out alive.

Being big and bulky is a disadvantage for the modern soldier. Elite forces are generally lean, which allows their bodies to maximize endurance and strength. A model soldier can cover two miles in thirteen minutes and has the strength to perform eighty push-ups in two minutes, and eighty sit-ups just as fast. Put tactically, it can mean hauling gear for six miles at a jogger's pace and then being able to climb fences and ropes or pull a trailer by hand. Big, bulky soldiers may have trouble covering long distances and maintaining a high level of stamina. There is no need to be superhumanly strong.

It is a cliché that in war you can throw the plans out the window once the first bullet flies. That isn't entirely true, but it outlines the idea that you have to think on your feet and be flexible in stressful situations. Take the highly publicized raid on Osama bin Laden as an example. The SEAL team that performed the raid in Pakistan dealt with trouble before they even had boots on the ground: one of their helicopters crash-landed. That didn't stop them. They quickly got back on their original plan and raided the compound room by room. In the dark of night, they had to quickly differentiate threats from nonthreats (men from women and children, mostly) while keeping an eye out for booby traps. They needed clear heads in order to think and react quickly, knowing that a bad decision could result in the loss of life for an innocent person or a teammate. That is what it is like at the elite-forces level.

One of the things that always bothered me in Iraq was not being able to tell who was a threat and who wasn't. The bad guys didn't wear black hats—they blended in. The guy who fired mortars and rockets at you last night could be the same one trying to sell you an advance copy of *Troy* on DVD out in the market. Some guys with AKs are there to protect buildings and overpasses in one region, while in another a guy with an AK on an overpass is a threat. It is important to be able to quickly assess a situation to determine whether action is needed and what type of response is warranted.

Now, let's assume someone in one of these situations is on steroids. Would he be able to make the same sound and decisive judgments? Steroids increase aggressive behavior in users. What would be the impact of steroid-fueled aggression on someone equipped and capable of taking someone's life? Being overly aggressive might cause them to make a mistake. No amount of physical strength is going to help you to make a better decision. Strength won't let you be more accurate on a gun. Strength won't help you solve problems within a region.

It can be argued that being strong creates a persona, that it intimidates. While intimidation has its use in the armed forces, it is generally something that is avoided by individual soldiers. Tanks are intimidating. Fast, stealthy, quiet soldiers armed to the teeth are intimidating. There isn't a need to pile on. A brigade in Iraq placed the following notice right at the gate as you exited the secure area: Be Polite, Be Professional, Be Prepared to Kill. The three Ps they called it. Adhering to the three Ps was important because we were trying to change the hearts and minds of the citizens. We wanted them to trust us, and we wanted to gain their confidence so that they would help us find and remove the insurgents. Acting aggressive and pushy wasn't going to help the situation. It was a difficult line to straddle, being on high alert yet friendly, but it was a way to create a feeling of teamwork.

I knew a few people rumored to be on steroids during my time in the army, and I firmly believe they just wanted to be big. They didn't use steroids because they thought it would help them in a battle or save their lives. They used it to look big or get girls or get their name on the 300-pound bench board in the gym. People who want to use steroids will use them and come up with a reason later. I have read the reports of persons in the military who argue for the use of steroids, and I just don't buy the reasons. I have been there, and I never encountered even a moment when I could see a benefit for someone to be on steroids. It is infinitely more important to have a clear mind than to need to be so strong that only steroids can get you there. Steroids don't provide instant muscles; you have to work out to get it to work. The working out is enough to do the job; the steroids aren't needed.

I think the use of steroids in the military is a little blown out of proportion by civilians and the media. I don't necessarily mean in the number of users, but in the reason for use. In eight years of service, I only once suspected someone might be using steroids, and I ended up changing my stance on that after talking with him. Any soldier worth his weight will tell you that you don't need steroids to stay alive. One perk of being in the army is the top-flight gyms. The weight rooms are world class: spacious, full of equipment, clean, music filled, comfortable. They attract people who want to get big.

Some of the best soldiers I worked with were short, little, skinny guys who were mentally tough, smart, and willing to push themselves to get to the end. They weren't guys with the bodies of MMA fighters or professional linebackers. They were proficient with their weapon and knew what to do in dicey situations by thinking clearly. I spoke with four army veterans about enhancements. Each one said that they were all for the use of enhancements in the military, except for steroids. They cited the need to think clearly and quickly, and the ability to have endurance and stamina, as reasons not to use steroids, as well as the long-term health effects. Steroids cause death and serious problems. Plenty of soldiers came back from Iraq with drinking problems stemming from the psychological effect of war. The widespread use of steroids would only have increased those numbers. It would be a different story if steroids allowed soldiers to return home instead of dying in battle, but that is not the case. Quick decision making and determination are more valuable attributes than extreme physical strength. As Brad Richards says, "It isn't worth the side effects of steroids just to be a little stronger. Even a lot stronger. You don't need it."

NOTES

PREFACE

1. Philip Matthew Stinson, "Police Crime: The Criminal Behavior of Sworn Law Enforcement Officers," *Sociology Compass* 9 (2015): 6.

2. Conor Friedersdorf, "Police Have a Much Bigger Domestic-Abuse Problem than the NFL Does," *Atlantic*, September 19, 2014.

INTRODUCTION

1. Angie Cannon, "Steroid-Using Police Causing Brutality Fears," *Miami Herald*, May 18, 1987.

2. "Ex-Newtown Cop Gets 16 Months in Steroid Arrest," *Newtown (CT) News-Times*, August 25, 2016, newstimes.com/local/article/Ex-Newtown-cop-facing-sentencing-in-steroid-arrest-9183611.php.

3. Alcohol abuse and dependency has been an ongoing problem in the law enforcement community. Because drinking has been an acceptable way for officers to cope with the stressors of their work, problems with alcohol frequently go undetected. Repeated exposure to trauma, suicide, domestic violence, and mental health crises takes its toll on even the most highly resilient officer. Repeated exposure to these types of stressors often produces frustration, depression, anger, and other emotions, which officers are taught to suppress. Alcohol, because it is legal and acceptable, is frequently used as a means to escape or blow off steam, in what is known to law enforcement personnel as "choir practice." See Elizabeth A. Willman, "Alcohol Use among Law Enforcement," *Journal of Law Enforcement* 2, no. 3 (2012), jghcs.info/index.php/l/article/view/150/147 (subscription required);

see also James Genovese, "Alcoholism among Law Enforcement Personnel: Its Unique Challenges," n.d., Milestone Group LLC, milestonegroupnj.com/?page_id=348, and Genovese, "Suffering in Silence: Cops and Booze," September 16, 2012, Milestone Group LLC, milestonegroupnj.com/?p=194.

4. "Police Chiefs Discuss a Tough Issue: Alcohol and Drug Abuse by Officers," *Subject to Debate: A Newsletter of the Police Executive Research Forum* 26, no. 5 (September–October 2012): 2.

5. National Center for Women and Policing, "Police Family Violence Fact Sheet," womenandpolicing.com/violencefs.asp; Conor Friedersdorf, "Police Have a Much Bigger Domestic-Abuse Problem than the NFL Does," *Atlantic*, September 19, 2014; Ira W. Hutchison, "The Influence of Alcohol and Drugs on Women's Utilization of the Police for Domestic Violence," final report submitted to the National Institute of Justice, June 1999, ncjrs.gov/pdffiles1/nij/grants/179277.pdf.

6. "Treatment and Redemption," *Police: The Law Enforcement Magazine*, June 18, 2013, policemag.com/channel/careers-training/articles/2013/06/treatment-and-redemption.aspx.

7. *Subject to Debate*, "Police Chiefs Discuss a Tough Issue," 1.

8. Genovese, "Alcoholism among Law Enforcement Personnel."

9. Cannon, "Steroid-Using Police."

10. The video of the killing of James Boyd is available at youtube.com/watch?v=6tpAZObNZfI, uploaded March 25, 2014.

11. "Two Former Albuquerque Officers Are on Trial in the Killing of a Homeless Man," *New York Times*, September 19, 2016.

12. "Jury Begins Deliberating in Sandy, Perez Murder Trial," KRQE NEWS 13, October 7, 2016, krqe.com/2016/10/06/closing-arguments-expected-thursday-in-sandy-perez-trial.

13. See, for example, "Murder Charges Sought for Albuquerque Cops Who Shot Homeless Man Dead on Video," *Huffington Post*, June 23, 2015, huffingtonpost.com/2015/06/23/murder-albuquerque-cops-shoot-homeless-man_n_7647552.html; "Court to Decide on Evidence in Sandy, Perez Trial," KRQE NEWS 13, July 12, 2016; "Judge Throws Out Voluntary Manslaughter Charges in Sandy, Perez Trial," KRQE NEWS 13, September 28, 2016. An exception to this rule is a statement by Stephen Torres, the father of a schizophrenic man named Christopher Torres, who was shot in the back three times by an APD officer in April 2011: "Once we started doing the research, I mean, you get to a point where after a while you don't want to do it any more because you don't want to hear any more about what's been going on. I mean the problems our police department has been having over the last 20 to 30 years with insurance fraud and prostitution and drugs within the police department, abuse of steroids." See Fault Lines, "Shot in the Back: Police Violence in Albuquerque," AlJazeera.com, April 16, 2016, aljazeera.com/indepth/features/2016/04/shot-police-violence-albuquerque-160412094651720.html.

14. "Albuquerque Police Violated Civil Rights, Justice Department Finds," *Wall Street Journal*, April 10, 2014.

15. Rachel Aviv, "Your Son Is Deceased," *New Yorker*, February 2, 2015.

16. "Police OK'd to Test for Steroids," *Albuquerque Journal*, October 31, 2007.

17. "Albuquerque Police to Be Tested for Steroids," *Campus Safety Magazine*, November 8, 2007.

18. "Update: Steroid Use Subject of APD Probe," *Albuquerque Journal*, December 21, 2012.

19. "Albuquerque Police Launch Officer Steroid Probe," *Roswell (NM) Daily Record*, December 19, 2012.

20. "Albuquerque Police Officers Probably Use Steroids," MedInform.org, December 27, 2012, medinform.org/albuquerque-police-officers-probably-use-steroids.php.

21. "Albuquerque Police to Undergo Random Steroid Testing," Associated Press, June 6, 2015.

22. "Steroid-Use Claims Go Back Years," *Albuquerque Journal*, January 7, 2013.

23. Brad Hall, personal communication with the author, October 8, 2016.

24. "Ex-Detective Says He Regrets 'Lunatic' Remark before Killing," Associated Press, October 5, 2016.

25. "APD's Tragic 'Game Changer': Keith Sandy," *Albuquerque Journal*, February 7, 2015.

26. See, for example, Robert Hoffman and Thomas Collingwood, *Fit for Duty*, 3rd ed. (Urbana-Champaign, IL: Human Kinetics, 2015), 256.

27. Catherine Gallagher, Edward R. Maguire, Stephen D. Mastrofski, and Michael D, Reisig, "The Public Image of the Police: Final Report to the International Association of Chiefs of Police by the Administration of Justice Program George Mason University," October 2, 2001, iacp.org/The-Public-Image-of-the-Police.

28. "'Cops' Moves from Fox to Spike," *Police: The Law Enforcement Magazine*, May 6, 2013, policemag.com/channel/patrol/news/2013/05/06/civil-rights-groups-lament-racial-stereotypes-in-cops.aspx.

29. Alyssa Eisenberg, "How Police Censorship Shaped Hollywood," *Washington Post*, October 24, 2016.

30. Alyssa Eisenberg, "In Pop Culture, There Are No Bad Police Shootings," *Washington Post*, October 26, 2016.

31. *"Cries Unheard: The Donna Yaklich Story,"* *Wikipedia*, en.wikipedia.org/wiki/Cries_Unheard:_The_Donna_Yaklich_Story.

32. For example, an alcoholic officer in an episode of *Blue Bloods* has put in an honorable career and is headed into retirement. The exceptions include *Southland* and *True Detective*, which portray police officers struggling with drug and alcohol addiction.

CHAPTER ONE: WHAT WE KNOW ABOUT COPS ON STEROIDS

1. Craig B. Futterman, "Use of Statistical Evidence to Address Police Supervisory and Disciplinary Practices: The Chicago Police Department's Broken System," *DePaul Journal for Social Justice* 1, no. 2 (2007): 265.

2. "Chicago Rarely Penalizes Officers for Complaints, Data Shows," *New York Times*, November 19, 2015.

3. "Chicago's Mayor Demands Sweeping Police Reform," *New York Times*, December 9, 2015.

4. "Despite Anger, Chicago Mayor's Event Goes On," *New York Times*, January 16, 2016.

5. "A Florida Police Killing, like Many, Disputed and Little Noticed," *New York Times*, May 31, 2015.

6. "Lack of Videos Hampers Inquiries into Houston Police Shootings," *New York Times*, February 23, 2016. nytimes.com/2016/02/24/us/lack-of-videos-hampers-inquiries-into-houston-police-shootings.html?_r=0.

7. James Pinkerton, "Unarmed and Dangerous," *Houston Chronicle*, houstonchronicle.com/local/investigations/item/Bulletproof-Part-1-Unarmed-and-Dangerous-24419.php.

8. Emily DePrang, "Crimes Unpunished," *Texas Observer*, July 10, 2013.

9. Emily DePrang, "The Horror Every Day: Police Brutality in Houston Goes Unpunished," *Texas Observer*, September 4, 2013.

10. David J. Krajicek, "Cop 'Roid Rage: Are Steroids behind the Worst Police Abuses?" Alternet, August 19, 2015, alternet.org/civil-liberties/cop-roid-rage-are-steroids-behind-worst-police-abuses.

11. "Expert: Data sketchy on steroid use by police," *Richmond Times-Dispatch*, June 6, 2005.

12. "Elite Users of Steroids Rarely Face Criminal Prosecution," *Wall Street Journal*, December 14, 2004.

13. Amy Brittain and Mark Mueller, "N.J. Doctor supplied steroids to hundreds of law enforcement officers, firefighters," *Newark Star-Ledger*, December 12, 2010.

14. Examples of such newspapers include the following: the *Newark Star-Ledger, Richmond Times-Dispatch, Roanoke Times, Salt Lake City Tribune, Deseret News, Orlando Sentinel, New Hampshire Union Leader, Broward–Palm Beach New Times, New York Daily News, Memphis Commercial Appeal, Oregonian,* Augusta (GA) *Chronicle,* Scottsboro (AL) *Daily Sentinel, Palm Beach Post, Arizona Republic,* and Casper (WY) *Star-Tribune.*

15. See, for example, "UK-M Bodybuilding Forum," uk-muscle.co.uk and "Welcome to MuscleTalk," muscletalk.co.uk.

16. Quoted in Brent E. Turvey and Stan Crowder, *Anabolic Steroid Abuse in Public Safety Personnel: A Forensic Manual* (New York: Elsevier, 2015): 30.

17. *Subject to Debate*, "Police Chiefs Discuss a Tough Issue," 4.

18. "Pittsburgh Police Discipline in Question," *Pittsburgh Post-Gazette*, March 20, 2013.

19. "Phoenix Police Terminate Random Steroids Testing," *Arizona Republic*, July 8, 2015, azcentral.com/story/news/local/phoenix/2015/07/09/phoenix-police-terminate-random-steroids-testing/29897401.

20. Brent E. Turvey and Stan Crowder, *Anabolic Steroid Abuse in Public Safety Personnel: A Forensic Manual* (New York: Elsevier, 2015), 106, 110, 107, 109.

21. Ibid., 111, 109, 110, 116.

22. Cannon, "Steroid-Using Police."

23. Charles Swanson and Larry Gaines, "Abuse of Anabolic Steroids, *FBI Law Enforcement Bulletin*, August: 19, 1991.

24. Stephen Hudak, "Steroids: A Threat to Police Officers," *Cleveland Plain Dealer*, July 25, 2003.

25. *Steroid Abuse by Law Enforcement Personnel: A Guide for Understanding the Dangers of Anabolic Steroids* (Washington, DC: US Department of Justice, Drug Enforcement Administration, Office of Diversion Control, 2004); hereafter cited as DEA, *Steroid Abuse by Law Enforcement Personnel*.

26. Kim R. Humphrey et al., "Anabolic Steroid Use and Abuse by Police Officers: Policy and Prevention," *Police Chief*, June 2008, iacpmag.wp.matrixdev.net/anabolic-steroid-use-and-abuse-by-police-officers-policy-prevention (subscription required).

27. "Steroids Don't Turn Officers into Hotshots," *Boston Herald*, July 2, 2009.

28. "Police Target Performance Drug Use," *Australian*, August 1, 2005.

29. Angie Cannon, "Steroid-Using Police Causing Brutality Fears," *Miami Herald*, May 18, 1987.

30. Ibid.

31. Doug Gillon, "Questions for House—'Explosion' in Numbers Abusing Steroids," *Glasgow Herald*, April 15, 1996.

32. "Elite Soldiers Face Charges as 'Police Uncover Drug Use,'" *Sydney Morning Herald*, July 24, 2002.

33. Mark Dunn, "Three Groups Pinpointed as Steroid Users," *Australia Herald Sun*, July 18, 2003.

34. "Cops Accused of Using Steroids to Bulk Up and Give Themselves an Edge," Associated Press, February 4, 2005.

35. DEA, *Steroid Abuse by Law Enforcement Personnel*.

36. Sabrina Rubin Erdely, "Juicers in Blue," *Men's Health*, October 2005.

37. John M. Wills, "Are You Juiced? Big, Strong, and Stupid," Officer.com, July 2007.

38. Sean McGrew, "Amen Brotha . . . Maybe OT . . . I Don't Know Anymore," comment on the *Trailer Sailor* website, December 12, 2008, forum.trailersailor.com/post.php?id=668750.

39. "N.J. to Investigate Illegal Steroid Use by Law Enforcement Officers," *Newark Star-Ledger*, December 15, 2010.

40. "Muscle Needed to Clean Up Cop Steroid Scandal," *Newark Star-Ledger*, December 15, 2010.

41. Quoted in "When the Police Go Military," *New York Times*, December 3, 2011.

42. DBentonSmith, comment on the subreddit /r/Politics, reddit.com/r/politics/comments/1htgcn/steroid_drug_abuse_by_police_linked_to_roid_rage.

43. Ibid.

44. Turvey and Crowder, *Anabolic Steroid Abuse*, 95.

45. Ibid.

46. Bob Norman, "The Underworld of Steroids and Cops in Broward," *New Times Broward–Palm Beach*, April 4, 2009, browardpalmbeach.com/news/the-underworld-of-steroids-and-cops-in-broward-6460259.

47. "News from the San Joaquin Valley," Associated Press, May 4, 2006.

48. "Walker County Deputies Suspended for Using Steroids; Four Deputies Could Be Fired," May 20, 2003.

49. "Pursue Steroids Probe," editorial, *Palm Beach Post*, December 31, 2005; Norman, "Underworld of Steroids."

50. Lisa Rosetta, "Cleared in Shooting: Family Claimed He Was under the Influence," *Salt Lake Tribune*, August 4, 2006, archive.sltrib.com/article.php?id=4135010&itype=NGPSID.

51. "Too Easy on Rogue Cops," editorial, *Boston Globe*, July 9, 2009.

52. Karl B. Hille, "Ariz. Police Steroid Use Poses Concerns," *Washington Examiner*, August 23, 2008; *Arizona Republic*, "Phoenix Police Terminate Testing."

53. Kevin Krause and Selwyn Crawford, "Arlington Officer Accused of Buying Steroids and Helping Supplier Spot Police Surveillance," *Dallas Morning News*, June 12, 2013, dallasnews.com/news/crime/headlines/20130612-arlington-officer-accused-of-buying-steroids-and-helping-supplier-spot-police-surveillance.ece.

54. Michele McPhee, "Busted," *Boston Magazine*, April 2008, bostonmagazine.com/2008/03/cleaning-up-the-boston-police-department.

55. Bianca Cain Johnson, "Police and Steroids: Hard to Control, Hard to Prove," *Augusta (GA) Chronicle*, November 1, 2014, chronicle.augusta.com/news/crime-courts/2014-11-01/police-and-steroids-hard-control-hard-prove.

56. Erdely, "Juicers in Blue."

57. Kate Howard, "Probe of Police Steroid Use Hits Tenn.," *Tennessean*, April 5, 2008.

58. Ibid.

59. Susan Donaldson James, "Police Juice Up on Steroids to Get 'Edge' on Criminals," ABCNews.com, October 18, 2007.

60. Brian Stimson, "Steroids and Law Enforcement: The Elephant in the Room," *Skanner News* (Portland, OR), March 22, 2010.

61. The states are Alabama, Arizona, Arkansas, California, Colorado, Connecticut, Florida, Georgia, Hawai'i, Illinois, Indiana, Kentucky, Louisiana, Maryland, Massachusetts, Michigan, Minnesota, Mississippi, Montana, Nevada, New Hampshire, New Jersey, New Mexico, Minnesota, New York, North Carolina, Ohio, Oklahoma, Oregon, Pennsylvania, Tennessee, Texas, Utah, Virginia, Washington State, West Virginia, and Wyoming.

62. Kristina Davis, "Police Chiefs Fight Steroid-Abuse Trend," *San Diego Union-Tribune*, November 12, 2008, legacy.sandiegouniontribune.com/news/metro/20081112-9999-1m12steroids.html.

63. Gary Gaffney, "Feds Say Juiced Police Problem Getting Bigger," *Steroid Nation*, March 17, 2008, grg51.typepad.com/steroid_nation/2008/03.

64. Turvey and Crowder, *Anabolic Steroid Abuse*, 35.

65. Charlie Gillis, "When the Police Are on the Juice," *Maclean's*, June 4, 2008.

66. Ibid.

67. Turvey and Crowder, *Anabolic Steroid Abuse*, 110, 111.

68. Ibid., 116.

69. "Undermining Police Accountability: No Wonder Opponents Label AB 2067 the 'Rogue Officers' Bill of Rights,'" editorial, *Los Angeles Times*, February 20, 1992, articles.latimes.com/1992-02-20/local/me-3316_1_law-enforcement-officers.

70. Gerald L. Britt, "Rogue Officers Dishonor Police Departments' Good Work," *Dallas Morning News*, September 3, 2014, dallasnews.com/opinion/latest-columns/20140902-rogue-officers-dishonor-police-departments-good-work.ece.

71. "Bratton Says New York Police Dept. Must Dismiss Bad Officers," *New York Times*, October 2, 2014.

72. Rick Garcia, "Footage Reveals Covert LAPD Unit Designed To Weed Out Department's 'Bad Apples,'" CBS Los Angeles, November 3, 2014, losangeles.cbslocal.com/2014/11/03/footage-reveals-covert-lapd-unit-designed-to-weed-out-departments-bad-apples.

73. Hannah Osborne, "Police ''Roid Rage': Widespread Corruption Linked to Steroid Abuse and Gym Use," *International Business Times*, January 23, 2013, ibtimes.co.uk/police-corruption-steriod-abuse-gyms-forming-relationships-427009.

74. "BPD Puts Squeeze on Juicing Cops," *Boston Herald*, July 3, 2009, bostonherald.com/news_opinion/local_coverage/2009/07/bpd_puts_squeeze_juicing_cops.

75. Personal communication to the author, July 7, 2015.

76. "Disgraced Police Officers Jailed after Steroids Plot," *St. Helens (UK) Star*, November 22, 2011.

77. "Spokane Police Officers Investigated for Steroids," *Spokane Review*, October 4, 2014.

78. Marc Lallanilla, "Big Guns: When Cops Use Steroids," ABCNews.com, May 24, 2005, abcnews.go.com/Health/US/story?id=775659&page=1#.T85UaGB9n4c.

79. Louie Rosella, "Chief Launches Probe into Steroid Use," *Brampton (ON) Guardian*, January 29, 2008, bramptonguardian.com/news-story/3153307-chief-launches-probe-into-steroid-use.

80. "Prison Guard Who Violated Prisoner's Rights Indicted for Steroids," *New Hampshire Union Leader*, June 15, 2010.

81. "Ex-Phoenix officer Arrested in Robberies Had Tested Positive for Steroids," *Arizona Republic*, December 13, 2010; "Guilty Verdicts for Former Police Officer-Turned Bank Robber," press release, Federal Bureau of Investigation, Phoenix Division, February 2, 2012, fbi.gov/phoenix/press-releases/2012/guilty-verdicts-for-former-police-officer-turned-bank-robber.

82. "Court records: Drugged-Up Cop Disclosed Informant," *Lancaster (OH) Eagle-Gazette*, November 22, 2011, lancastereaglegazette.com/article/AB/201 11121/NEWS010702/111220305/Records-Cop-disclosed-informant.

83. Brandi Kruse, "Head of King County SWAT Retires amid 'Corruption' Scandal," July 7, 2014, MyNorthwest.com, mynorthwest.com/11/2561109/Head-of-King-County-SWAT-retires-amid-corruption-scandal; Lynsi Burton, "King Co. Sheriff's Deputy Charged with Prostituting Wife, Theft, Dealing Steroids," June 19, 2014, *Seattle Post-Intelligencer*, seattlepi.com/local/article/King-Co-Sheriff-s-deputy-arrested-for-promoting-5564880.php.

84. Erdely, "Juicers in Blue."

85. Fia Klötz et al., "Criminality among Individuals Testing Positive for the Presence of Anabolic Androgenic Steroids," *Archives of General Psychiatry* 63 (2006): 1274–1279.

86. See, for example, the case of Dr. James Shortt of South Carolina, in John Hoberman, "Sports Physicians and Doping: Medical Ethics and Elite Performance," in *The Social Organization of Sports Medicine: Critical Socio-Cultural Perspectives*, ed. Dominic Malcolm and Parissa Safai (New York: Routledge, 2012), 256.

87. Klötz et al., "Criminality among Individuals."

88. "Brooklyn Pharmacy Owner at Center of Steroid Scandal Kills Self, Cops," *New York Daily News*, January 29, 2008; "Strong at Any Cost: Five Deaths in 19 Months Linked to Steroids, Lowen's pharmacy," *Newark Star-Ledger*, December 12, 2010.

89. "Cops Turn Eye to Mob after Steroid-Scandal Pharmacy Owner Kills Himself," *New York Daily News*, January 30, 2008.

90. "In Bay Ridge, Shock Over a Pharmacy Owner's Death," *New York Times*, February 1, 2008.

91. *New York Daily News*, "Cops Turn Eye to Mob."

92. Sean Gardiner, "A Shot Reputation," *Village Voice*, January 29, 2008.

93. "Strong at Any Cost: What Led to His Death? Mystery Surrounds JC Police Captain's Apparent Suicide," *Newark Star-Ledger*, June 16, 2008.

94. "Final Determination in the Matter of Amy Brittain, Complainant," Docket No.: AP 2010–0770, Pennsylvania Office of Open Records, 2.

95. "Preliminary report: Death of Steroids Dealer David Jacobs a Suicide," *New York Daily News*, June 6, 2008.

96. "Police Say Steroids Dealer Shot Himself," *New York Times*, June 7, 2008.

97. Ibid.

98. "Convicted Steroids Dealer Who Gave Names to NFL Found Dead," ESPN. com, June 6, 2008, sports.espn.go.com/nfl/news/story?id=3427526.

99. "Plano Steroid Dealer Says He's Ready to Name Names of Police Officers Who Got Steroids from His Network," *Grits for Breakfast* (blog), May 27, 2008, gritsforbreakfast.blogspot.com/2008/05/plano-steroid-dealer-says-he-sold-to. html.

100. "Steroid Dealer Had Five Times Allowed Amount of Steroids in His System," August 5, 2008, KSDK.com (St. Louis, MO), archive.ksdk.com/news/article /151530/3/Steroid-Dealer-Had-Five-Times-Allowed-Amount-of-Steroids-in-His-System (page no longer available).

101. "Steroid Dealer David Jacobs Death Ruled a Suicide," *Dallas Morning News*, June 7, 2008.

102. "Why Only Athletes and Bodybuilders? Plano Steroid Prosecutions Ignore Alleged Police Doping," *Grits for Breakfast*, September 7, 2008.

103. Krause and Crawford, "Arlington Officer Accused of Buying Steroids"; Kevin Krause, "Authorities Say 11 Arrested after Dallas-Based Steroid Ring Is Broken Up," *Dallas Morning News*, July 6, 2014.

104. Tawnell D. Hobbs, "Dallas ISD Investigation into Alleged Illegal Steroid Use in Its Police Department Finds Wrongdoing," *Dallas Morning News*, October 8, 2014.

105. Timothy J. Flanagan and Michael S. Vaughn, "Public Opinion about Police Abuse of Force," in *Police Violence: Understanding and Controlling Police Abuse of Force*, ed. William A. Geller (New Haven, CT: Yale University Press, 1996), 117.

106. Bonnie Kristian, "Seven Reasons Police Brutality Is Systemic, Not Anecdotal," *American Conservative*, July 2, 2014, theamericanconservative.com/ seven-reasons-police-brutality-is-systematic-not-anecdotal.

107. Wayne Barrett, "Ray Kelly's Lonely War," *Daily Beast*, November 7, 2011, thedailybeast.com/articles/2011/11/07/wayne-barrett-is-ray-kelly-to-blame-for-nypd-s-troubles.html.

108. "Use of Force," Office of Justice Programs, Bureau of Justice Statistics, 2011, bjs.gov/index.cfm?ty=tp&tid=703.

109. Cannon, "Steroid-Using Police"; "Seven Charged with Thefts along River; Miami Police Drug Trial Nearing Close," *Los Angeles Times*, January 7, 1987.

110. "When Cops Go Bad," *Frontline*, PBS, October 16, 1990, pbs.org/wgbh/ pages/frontline/shows/drugs/archive/copsgobad.html.

111. Leonard Levitt, *NYPD Confidential: Power and Corruption in the Country's Greatest Police Force* (New York: St. Martin's, 2009), 78–95.

112. Kristian, "Seven Reasons Police Brutality."

113. Rachel Aviv, "Your Son Is Deceased," *New Yorker*, February 2, 2015; Nick Pinto, "When Cops Break Bad: Inside a Police Force Gone Wild," *Rolling Stone*, January 29, 2015, rollingstone.com/culture/features/when-cops-break-bad-albuquerque-police-force-gone-wild-20150129.

114. Cindy Carcamo, "Justice Department Orders Reforms, Monitor for Albuquerque Police," *Los Angeles Times*, October 31, 2014, latimes.com/nation/la-na-albuquerque-police-20141031-story.html.

115. Matt Sledge and Saki Knafo, "Why Bad New York Cops Can Get Away With Abuse," *Huffington Post*, July 31, 2014, huffingtonpost.com/2014/07/30/nypd-accountability_n_5630665.html.

116. Harriet Van Horne, quoted in J. W. Sterling, "Changes in Role Concepts of Police Officers during Recruit Training: A Progress Report, 1969," 31 (mimeographed), cited in Robert W. Balch, "The Police Personality: Fact or Fiction," *Journal of Criminal Law and Criminology* 63 (1972): 107.

117. Balch, "Police Personality," 106.

118. Hans Toch, "The Violence-Prone Police Officer," in *Police Violence: Understanding and Controlling Police Abuse of Force*, ed. William A. Geller (New Haven, CT: Yale University Press, 1996), 95, 95, 111.

119. Victor E. Kappeler, Richard D. Sluder, and Geoffrey P. Alpert, *Forces of Deviance: Understanding the Dark Side of Policing*, 2nd. ed. (Prospect Heights, IL: Waveland, 1998), 141.

120. "NYPD Scandals Obscure the Decency of the Majority, Cops Say," *Daily Beast*, November 11, 2011.

121. Laurence Miller, "The Dorner Case: When Cops Turn Rogue and How to Prevent It," PoliceOne.com, February 14, 2013, policeone.com/health-fitness/articles/6120461-The-Dorner-case-When-cops-turn-rogue-and-how-to-prevent-it.

122. Jerome Skolnick, "Code Blue," *American Prospect*, December 19, 2001.

123. Kappeler, Sluder, and Alpert, *Forces of Deviance*, 135, 138.

124. "Assaulted by Police," Unprofessional Standards Department, May 8, 2014, upsd.co.uk/assaulted-by-police.

125. Leonard Levitt, "NYPD Confidential: Controversial Chief to Retire," August 11, 2014, AM New York, amny.com/opinion/columnists/leonard-levitt/nypd-confidential-controversial-chief-to-retire-1.9029639.

126. Greg Donaldson, "Captain Midnight," *New York Magazine*, April 30, 2001, nymag.com/nymag/features/4624.

127. Graham Rayman, "Deputy Chief Michael Marino in Stop-and-Frisk Trial: 'Do Your Job or Suffer the Consequences,'" *Village Voice*, March 25, 2013.

128. "NYPD Big Michael Marino Found Guilty of Using Steroid during Departmental Trial," *New York Daily News*, September 8, 2010, nydailynews.com/new-york/nypd-big-michael-marino-found-guilty-steroid-departmental-trial-article-1.440127.

129. Graham Rayman, "NYPD Tapes Fallout: Precinct Commander and Deputy Chief under Investigation," *Village Voice*, August 23, 2010; "Judge Calls for Punishment of Police Official," *New York Times*, September 7, 2010; "An Officer Had Backup: Secret Tapes," *New York Times*, March 13, 2012.

130. Victoria Bekiempis, "Judge Awards $1.1M to Pay Fees for Lawyers of NYPD Whistleblower Adrian Schoolcraft," *New York Daily News*, September 9, 2016, nydailynews.com/new-york/lawyers-nypd-whistleblower-awarded-1-1m-fees-article-1.2784086.

131. Kappeler, Sluder, and Alpert, *Forces of Deviance*, 104.

132. Toch, "Violence-Prone Police Officer," 110.

133. Craig Horowitz, "An Officer and an Atrocity," *New York*, n.d., nymag.com/nymetro/news/crimelaw/features/1265/index5.html.

134. Miller, "The Dorner Case."

135. Amy Brittain and Mark Mueller, "N.J. Doctor Supplied Steroids to Hundreds of Law Enforcement Officers, Firefighters," *Newark Star-Ledger*, December 12, 2010.

136. Jonathan Eiseman, "NJ to Probe Cops and Firefighters for Steroid Abuse," NBCNewYork.com, December 15, 2010, nbcnewyork.com/news/local/New-Jersey-to-Investigate-Cops-and-Firefighters-for-Steriod-Abuse-111924564.html.

137. *Newark Star-Ledger*, "Muscle Needed."

138. "McKeon Calls for Attorney General Investigation into Police Steroid Abuse," press release, Assembly Democrats, December 13, 2010, assemblydems.com/Article.asp?ArticleID=3437.

139. "Cops on Steroids Hard to Spot," NorthJersey.com, December 14, 2010.

140. Amy Brittain and Mark Mueller, "N.J. to Investigate Illegal Steroid Use by Law Enforcement Officers," *Newark Star-Ledger*, December 15, 2010, nj.com/news/index.ssf/2010/12/nj_attorney_gen_dow_forms_pane.html.

141. Amy Brittain and Mark Mueller, "N.J. Taxpayers Get Bill for Millions in Steroid, Growth Hormone Prescriptions for Cops, Firefighters," *Newark Star-Ledger*, December 12, 2010, nj.com/news/index.ssf/2010/12/nj_taxpayers_fund_millions_in.html.

142. Amy Brittain and Mark Mueller, "Booming Anti-Aging Business Relies on Risky Mix of Steroids, Growth Hormone," *Newark Star-Ledger*, December 12, 2010, nj.com/news/index.ssf/2010/12/booming_anti-aging_business_re.html.

143. "Attorney General Announces Strict Reforms to Curtail Improper Steroid Use among Law Enforcement in New Jersey," press release, Office of the Attorney General, July 7, 2011, nj.gov/oag/newsreleases11/pr20110707c.html.

144. Ibid.

145. Ibid.

146. Kyle J. D. Mulrooney and Katinka van de Ven, "'Muscle Profiling': Anti-doping policy and deviant leisure," *Deviant Leisure*, January 21, 2015, deviant leisure.wordpress.com/2015/01/21/muscle-profiling-anti-doping-policy-and-deviant-leisure.

147. Ibid.

148. See, for example, Brian Corrigan, "Anabolic Steroids and the Mind," *Medical Journal of Australia* 165 (1996): 223.

149. Brittain and Mueller, "N.J. Doctor Supplied Steroids."

150. Brittain and Mueller, "N.J. Taxpayers Get Bill."

CHAPTER TWO: POLICE CHIEFS AND THE STEROID DILEMMA

1. "Former South Bend police officer to be sentenced for dealing steroids," WNDU (South Bend, IN), March 10, 2010, wndu.com/home/headlines/8721 1487.html.

2. Tom Moor, "Officer Charged in Domestic Dispute," *South Bend (IN) Tribune*, July 27, 2006, articles.southbendtribune.com/2006-07-27/news/26987487_1_criminal-charges-mischief-and-disorderly-conduct-domestic-dispute; "Former South Bend Cop Arrested in Edwardsburg Drug Raid," *Elkhart (IN) Truth*, October 22, 2009.

3. "Officer Fired, Accused of Lying," *Broward County (FL) Sun-Sentinel*, April 19, 2003.

4. Brendan J. Lyons, "Ex-Cop Admits Steroid Charges," *Albany Times-Union*, January 19, 2011, timesunion.com/local/article/Ex-cop-admits-steroids-charges-964524.php.

5. Michael O'Keeffe, "Ex-Cop Faces Steroid Charges," *New York Daily News*, November 16, 2007, nydailynews.com/sports/more-sports/ex-cop-faces-steroid-charges-article-1.259947#ixzz1xFHYcNIo.

6. Spencer S. Hsu, "Four FBI Employees Accused of Using Steroids," *Washington Post*, September 16, 2010, washingtonpost.com/wp-dyn/content/article/2010/09/15/AR2010091506374.html.

7. "Steroids: A Threat to Police Officers," *Cleveland Plain Dealer*, July 25, 2003.

8. "Stories on Jersey City Doctor Who Trafficked Steroids to Law Enforcement Officers Have Shut Down at Least One Company's 'Fountain of Youth' Ads," *Newark Star-Ledger*, December 23, 2010.

9. Dennis Welch, "Sheriff's Office Fires Back on Steroids Issue," *East Valley (AZ) Tribune*, February 10, 2008, eastvalleytribune.com/news/article_f77fd87a-8478-5700-a595-790e74025f4d.html.

10. Millard Baker, "Arizona to Restrict Medical Use of Anabolic Steroids by Police Officers," MESO-Rx Steroids, March 22, 2008, thinksteroids.com/news/arizona-to-restrict-medical-use-of-anabolic-steroids-by-police-officers.

11. "Officer Investigated for Allegedly Ordering Steroids," *Rocky Mountain News*, January 1, 2003.

12. Ibid.

13. "15 Broward County Deputies Taken Off Patrol during Steroids Inquiry," *Palm Beach Post*, February 26, 2009.

14. Bob Norman, "Plantation's Police Chief Breaks Records Laws to Cover for Cops on Steroids," *New Times Broward–Palm Beach*, March 24, 2009, broward-palmbeach.com/2009-03-26/news/plantation-s-police-chief-breaks-records-laws-to-cover-for-cops-on-steroids.

15. Peter Franceschina, "Scott Rothstein Gets 50 Years," *Broward County (FL) Sun-Sentinel*, June 9, 2010, articles.sun-sentinel.com/2010-06-09/news/fl-roth stein-sentence-20100608_1_scott-rothstein-rothstein-s-parents-ponzi-scheme.

16. "Scott Rothstein's Buddy 'Meatballs' Applies to Be Fort Lauderdale Cop," *New Times Broward–Palm Beach*, June 13, 2011.

17. "West Palm Beach Police Officers Face Steroid Testing, Disciplinary Action," *Broward County (FL) Sun-Sentinel*, December 20, 2005.

18. Katie Colaneri, "Hoboken Officials React to Reports of 'a Dozen or More' Cops Filling Illegal Prescriptions," *Jersey Journal*, December 13, 2010, nj.com/hobokennow/index.ssf/2010/12/hoboken_officials_react_to_rep.html.

19. "3 Officers Face Inquiry," *Broward County (FL) Sun-Sentinel*, October 14, 2005.

20. "Police Union, Officials Clash in Steroid Scandal," *Palm Beach Post*, December 20, 2005.

21. Sean Gardiner, "Cops on Steroids," *Village Voice*, December 11, 2007, villagevoice.com/2007-12-11/news/cops-on-steroids.

22. "N.Y., N.Y. Doctor Is Sentenced to 5-Year Probation for Role in Steroid, Human Growth Hormone Sales," *Newark Star-Ledger*, May 12, 2010, nj.com/news/index.ssf/2010/05/nj_ny_doctor_is_sentenced_to_5.html.

23. Kramer vs. City of Jersey City, Civil Action No. 09–3767 (PGS), US District Court for the District of New Jersey, June 3, 2010, casetext.com/case/kramer-v-city-of-jersey-city.

24. Ron Zeitlinger, "Appeals Court Agrees: Rights of Jersey City Cops Who Tested for Steroids Not Violated," *Jersey Journal*, March 31, 2014, nj.com/hudson/index.ssf/2014/03/appeals_court_agrees_rights_of_jersey_city_cops_who_tested_for_steroids_not_violated.html.

25. "Jersey City Police Chief Wins Court battle over Steroid Testing," *Newark Star-Ledger*, December 23, 2011.

26. "Canby Cop Bought Steroids on the Job, FBI Says," *Oregonian*, November 15, 2008; Maxine Bernstein, "Canby Police Chief Resigns," *Oregonian*, April 14, 2009, oregonlive.com/news/index.ssf/2009/04/canby_police_chief_resigns.html.

27. Maxine Bernstein, "Canby Steroid Supplier's Cooperation with FBI Spreads Investigation to Other Law Enforcement Agencies, including Portland,"

Oregonian, May 3, 2010, oregonlive.com/clackamascounty/index.ssf/2010/05/canby_steroid_suppliers_cooper.html.

28. Bianca Cain Johnson, "Police and Steroids: Hard to Control, Hard to Prove," *Augusta (GA) Chronicle,* November 1, 2014, chronicle.augusta.com/news/crime-courts/2014-11-01/police-and-steroids-hard-control-hard-prove.

29. Rex Hall Jr., "Kalamazoo Police Sergeant Resigns amid Steroid-Use Allegations," *Kalamazoo Gazette,* May 5, 2010, mlive.com/news/kalamazoo/index.ssf/2010/05/kalamazoo_police_sergeant_resi.html.

30. "Incident Involving Officers Not Prosecutable," *Scottsboro (AL) Daily Sentinel,* December 1, 2011.

31. Kerry Burke and Alison Gendar, "Bay Ridge Parkway Gym Targeted in Steroid Investigation," *New York Daily News,* October 29, 2007, nydailynews.com/news/bay-ridge-parkway-gym-targeted-steroid-investigation-article-1.229787#ixzz1ww8LboGb.

32. Alison Gendar, "PBA Boss Patrick Lynch Charges Favoritism after Deputy Chief Cleared in Steroid Case," *New York Daily News,* October 22, 2007, nycpba.org/archive/nydn/07/nydn-071022-marino.html.

33. Gardiner, "Cops on Steroids."

34. "Internal Research Clears BSO Deputies in Steroid Investigation," *Broward County (FL) Sun-Sentinel,* December 21, 2005.

35. "Steroid Use Shakes Up Police Force," *Broward County (FL) Sun-Sentinel,* December 20, 2005.

36. "Investigation Links Police with Steroids," *Broward County (FL) Sun-Sentinel,* March 17, 2006.

37. "Report: Police Didn't Illegally Buy Steroids from Deerfield Pharmacy," *Palm Beach Post,* March 16, 2005.

38. "Investigation Links Police with Steroids," *Broward County (FL) Sun-Sentinel,* March 17, 2006.

39. Amy Brittain and Mark Mueller, "N.J. Taxpayers Get Bill for Millions in Steroid, Growth Hormone Prescriptions for Cops, Firefighters," *Newark Star-Ledger,* December 13, 2010, nj.com/news/index.ssf/2010/12/nj_taxpayers_fund_millions_in.html.

40. Ibid.

41. "Officer Trampus Gaspard (L) & Keith Richard (R)," May 24, 2006, policecrime.proboards.com/thread/3099/officer-trampus-gaspard-richard-picture.

42. Donna Rossi, "Cop Fired for Steroids Wins Badge Back," KPHO.com (Phoenix, AZ), March 11, 2010, kpho.com/story/14780591/cop-fired-for-steroids-wins-badge-back-3-11-2010.

43. "Phoenix Officer Gets 30-Day Suspension in Steroid Case," *Arizona Republic,* July 12, 2010.

44. "Report: Police didn't illegally buy steroids from Deerfield pharmacy," *Palm Beach Post,* March 16, 2006.

45. Stephen McLamb, "Scottsboro Mayor Confirms Illegal Steroid Abuse among Officers," WAFF.com (Huntsville, AL), December 20, 2011, waff.com/story/16105675/scottsboro-mayor-confirms-illegal-steroid-abuse.

46. "Officer Daniel Zehrer's Punishment for Positive Steroid Test Is Delayed Pension," *New York Daily News*, October 8, 2010.

47. Lynn Turner, "Former Paw Paw Police Officer Robert Kusmack Sentenced to Year of Probation for Steroids Possession," *Kalamazoo Gazette*, April 18, 2011, mlive.com/news/kalamazoo/index.ssf/2011/04/former_paw_paw_police_officer_3.html.

48. "Former Trooper Gets Probation," *Casper (WY) Star-Tribune*, December 30, 2009.

49. "Former Narcotics Top Cop Gets Probation in Drug Case," *Memphis Commercial Appeal*, January 26, 2010.

50. "Corrections Officer Sentenced for Selling Steroids to Police Informant," WKTV (Utica, NY), July 10, 2010, ironmagazine.com/2010/corrections-officer-sentenced-for-selling-steroids-to-police-informant.

51. Levi Pulkkinen, "No Prison for Ex-ICE Agent Who Imported Steroids," *Seattle Post-Intelligencer*, October 31, 2010, seattlepi.com/local/article/No-prison-for-ex-ICE-agent-who-imported-steroids-778207.php.

52. "Former Jefferson County Deputy Gets Probation For Steroids," CBS Denver, April 17, 2014, denver.cbslocal.com/2014/04/17/jefferson-county-deputy-gets-probation-for-steroids.

53. Veronica Slaght, "Clinton Township Police Officer Trains for National Powerlifting Competition," *Newark Star-Ledger*, July 13, 2009, nj.com/news/local/index.ssf/2009/07/clinton_cop_pulls_more_than_hi.html.

54. "Clinton Township Police Officer and Champion Powerlifter Charged with Steroid Possession," *Lehigh Valley (PA) Express-Times* April 6, 2012, lehighvalleylive.com/hunterdon-county/express-times/index.ssf/2012/04/clinton_township_police_office_1.html.

55. Ibid.

56. Norman, "Plantation's Police Chief."

57. Warren Richey, "How Scott Rothstein Rode $1.2 Billion Ponzi Scheme to Wealth and Power," *Christian Science Monitor*, January 27, 20120. csmonitor.com/USA/2010/0127/How-Scott-Rothstein-rode-1.2-billion-Ponzi-scheme-to-wealth-and-power.

58. Sabrina Rubin Erdely, "Juicers in Blue," *Men's Health*, October 2005, menshealth.com/health/scandals-cops-and-steroids.

59. "Suffolk Says Drug Ring Involving Police Officers Was Informal but Lucrative," *New York Times*, September 20, 2002, nytimes.com/2002/09/20/nyregion/suffolk-says-drug-ring-involving-police-officers-was-informal-but-lucrative.html.

60. "Probe of Police Steroid Use Hits Tenn.," April 10, 2008, bikernews.org/wtn/print.php?news.4790.

61. "Cop busted with steroids," December 30, 2004, http://anabolicminds.com/forum/general-chat/23088-cop-busted-steroids.html.

62. Trisha Estabrooks, "Edmonton Police Chief Says More Officers Admit to Steroid Use," CBC.com, May 22, 2015, cbc.ca/news/canada/edmonton/edmonton-police-chief-says-more-officers-admit-to-steroid-use-1.3083993.

63. Dan Oakes, "Steroid-Abusing Australian Soldiers Sent Home in Disgrace," *Sydney Morning Herald*, June 8, 2010, smh.com.au/world/steroidabusing-australian-soldiers-sent-home-in-disgrace-20100607-xquy.html.

64. Jon Ungoed-Thomas, "Police Taking Steroids to Counter Thugs," *London Sunday Times*, December 6, 1998.

65. Erdely, "Juicers in Blue."

66. Susan Donaldson James, "Police Juice Up on Steroids to Get 'Edge' on Criminals," ABCNews.com, October 18, 2007, abcnews.go.com/US/story?id=3745740.

67. Michael Ferraresi, "Phoenix Officer Fighting Steroid-Use Case," *Arizona Republic*, January 13, 2010, azcentral.com/news/articles/20100113steroids0113.html.

68. Pamela Kulbarsh, "Never Too Buff," Officer.com, January 12, 2011, officer.com/article/10227643/never-too-buff.

69. Karen Voyles, "Details in Prison Steroid Ring Arise," *Gainesville (FL) Sun*, August 12, 2005.

70. NuclearDruid, "'Dopers in Uniform' Comes to Phoenix," The Mental Militia, July 24, 2007, secure.thementalmilitia.com/forums/index.php?topic=14835.0.

71. Charlie Gillis, "When the Police Are on the Juice," *Maclean's*, June 16, 2008, 42–43.

72. Paul Kelso, "One Million Britons May Use Steroids Regularly," Sky News, January 7, 2015, news.sky.com/story/1403431/one-million-britons-may-use-steroids-regularly.

73. Gillis, "When the Police."

74. "Police Chiefs Discuss a Tough Issue: Alcohol and Drug Abuse by Officers," *Subject to Debate: A Newsletter of the Police Executive Research Forum* (September–October 2012): 4.

75. Ibid., 2.

76. Tanya Eiserer, "They Drink When They're Blue: Stress, Peer Pressure Contribute to Police's Alcohol Culture," *Dallas Morning News*, November 8, 2012, dallasnews.com/investigations/headlines/20120115-they-drink-when-theyre-blue-stress-peer-pressure-contribute-to-polices-alcohol-culture.ece.

77. Davey, Jeremy, Patricia Obst, and Mary Sheehan, "It Goes with the Job: Officers' Insights into the Impact of Stress and Culture within the Policing Occupation," *Drugs: Education, Prevention, and Policy* 8 (2001): 147.

78. Elizabeth A. Willman, "Alcohol Use among Law Enforcement," *Journal of Law Enforcement* 2 (2012): 1.

79. "Denver Police Chief Orders Review of Alcohol Abuse Reports in Ranks," *Denver Post*, June 1, 2014.

80. Willman, "Alcohol Use among Law Enforcement," 12; James Genovese, "Alcoholism among Law Enforcement Personnel: Its Unique Challenges," Milestone Group, LLC, n.d., milestonegroupnj.com/?page_id=348.

81. *Subject to Debate*, "Police Chiefs Discuss a Tough Issue," 2.

82. Ibid., 3.

83. Ibid., 1.

84. J. Martin, "Former Philadelphia Officer Gidelson Gets Four Years for Selling Steroids," January 9, 2013, articles.philly.com/2013-01-09/news/36218731_1_drug-dealer-keith-gidelson-diamond (payment required).

85. "Philly Police Det. Indicted in Operating Steroid Distribution Ring," *Law Officer*, April 28, 2011, lawofficer.com/archive/philly-police-det-indicted-in-operating-steroid-distribution-ring.

86. Gina Lombroso and Cesare Lombroso, *Criminal Man, According to the Classification of Cesare Lombroso* (Montclair, NJ: Patterson Smith, 1972; orig. pub. 1876), 46.

87. Carol Burke, *Camp All-American, Hanoi Jane, and the High-and-Tight* (Boston, Beacon, 2004), 92.

88. National Gang Intelligence Center, *(U) Gang-Related Activity in the US Armed Forces Increasing*, January 12, 2007, 17, 20, unclassified report, narcosphere. narconews.com/userfiles/70/ngic_gangs.pdf.

89. Nick Ralston, "Police Told: No More Tattoos on Face and Neck," *Sydney Morning Herald*, December 2, 2013, smh.com.au/nsw/police-told-no-more-tattoos-on-face-and-neck-20131201-2yjua.html.

90. Steven M. Cox, William P. McCamey, and Gene L. Scaramella, "Recruitment and Selection of Police Officers," in *Introduction to Policing*, 2nd ed. (Thousand Oaks, CA: Sage, 2013), 68; sagepub.com/upm-data/53256_ch_4.pdf.

91. "Ban on Tattoos, Grills for Broward County Deputies," *Miami Herald*, January 31, 2011.

92. Ibid.

93. "Honolulu Police Department Tattoo Ban Follows National Trend, but to What End?," *Huffington Post*, November 2, 2013, huffingtonpost.com/2013/11/02/honolulu-police—tattoo-ban_n_4206377.html.

94. James William Gibson, *Warrior Dreams: Violence and Manhood in Post-Vietnam America* (New York: Hill & Wang, 1994), 115.

95. Chris Greenwood, "Ink Addicts Need Not Apply: Met Police Bans Recruits with 'Thuggish' Visible Tattoos and Orders Existing Officers to Submit for Inspection," *Daily Mail*, October 16, 2012, dailymail.co.uk/news/article-2218787/Met-Police-BANS-recruits-thuggish-visible-tattoos.html.

96. "Anti-Tattoo Policy for NSW Police," *Australian*, December 2, 2013, theaustralian.com.au/news/latest-news/anti-tattoo-policy-for-nsw-police/story-fn3dxiwe-1226773072824.

97. *Huffington Post*, "Honolulu Police Department."

98. "Tattoo Policy Notice for Police Applicants," City of Great Falls, MT, n.d., greatfallsmt.net/police/tattoo-policy-notice-police-applicants.

99. "Tattoo Policy: Notice for Police Applicants," City of McKinney, TX, n.d., mckinneytexas.org/Faq.aspx?QID=611.

100. "Denver Police Department Considers Tattoo Cover Up," CBS Denver, April 10, 2014, denver.cbslocal.com/2014/04/10/denver-police-department-considers-tattoo-cover-up.

101. Naomi Martin, "New NOPD Tattoo Ban Could Affect Morale and Recruitment, Unions Warn," *New Orleans Times-Picayune*, July 3, 2013, nola.com/crime/index.ssf/2013/07/nopd_tattoo_ban.html.

102. Juliana Keeping, "Oklahoma City Police Force Policy Banning Tattoos Eliminates Qualified Applicants, Union Head Says," *Oklahoman*, December 11, 2013, newsok.com/oklahoma-city-police-force-policy-banning-tattoos-eliminates-qualified-applicants-union-head-says/article/3913597.

103. "Appearance Directive—No Grillz," March 15, 2011, officerresource.com/forums/showthread.php?t=45097.

104. Sara Castellanos, "For Aurora Police Officers Ink Is Out," *Aurora (CO) Sentinel*, August 1, 2010, available from the Fraternal Order of Police, fop.net/NewsArticle.aspx?news_article_id=2601.

105. "PoliceLink's Law Enforcement Tattoo Showcase," PoliceLink: The Nation's Law Enforcement Community, n.d., policelink.monster.com/training/articles/155435-policelinks-law-enforcement-tattoo-showcase?page=2.

106. "Connecticut State Police Policy on Tattoos, Social Media a Step Backward," editorial, *New Haven Register*, September 9, 2013, nhregister.com/opinion/20130909/editorial-connecticut-state-police-policy-on-tattoos-social-media-a-step-backward&template=printart.

107. "Police Workers Punished for Racist Web Posts on West Indian Parade," *New York Times*, August 22, 2012.

108. Daniel Genis, "An Ex-Con's Guide to Prison Weightlifting," Deadspin, May 6, 2014, fittish.deadspin.com/an-ex-cons-guide-to-prison-weightlifting-1571930353.

109. James, "Police Juice Up."

110. Alan Tepperman, "We Will Not Pump You Up: Punishment and Prison Weightlifting in the 1990s," academia.edu/552799/We_Will_NOT_Pump_You_Up_Punishment_and_Prison_Weightlifting_in_the_1990s.

111. Norman Silvester, "Cons Pull Out of Prison Strongman Contest over Fears They'll Be Busted for Taking Steroids," *Daily Record*, April 28, 2013, dailyrecord.co.uk/news/scottish-news/cons-pull-out-prison-strongman-1858129.

112. Leonard Levitt, *NYPD Confidential: Power and Corruption in the Country's Greatest Police Force* (New York: St. Martin's, 2009), 266.

113. "Improving Your Command Presence," Law Officer, April 1, 2011 lawofficer.com/article/tactics-and-weapons/improving-your-command-presenc.

114. John Bennett, "How Command Presence Affects Your Survival," PoliceOne.com, October 7, 2010, policeone.com/close-quarters-combat/articles/2748139-How-command-presence-affects-your-survival.

115. Ibid.

116. Ron Richards, "Command Presence: Feeding Your Own Self Confidence," WithTheCommand.com, May 2004, withthecommand.com/2004-May/PA-Richards-commandpresence.html.

117. Mark W. Clark, "Treatment and Redemption," *Police: The Law Enforcement Magazine*, June 18, 2013, policemag.com/channel/careers-training/articles/2013/06/treatment-and-redemption.aspx.

118. James Genovese, "Alcoholism among Law Enforcement Personnel: Its Unique Challenges," Milestone Group LLC, July 22, 2010, milestonegroupnj.com/?page_id=348.

119. Amy Brittain and Mark Mueller, "N.J. Doctor Supplied Steroids to Hundreds of Law Enforcement Officers, Firefighters," *Newark Star-Ledger*, December 12, 2010.

120. See thomas.loc.gov/cgi-bin/query/z?c101:H.R.4658.IH: (1990); "Rules—2005," US Department of Justice, Drug Enforcement Administration, Diversion Control Division, November 23, 2005, deadiversion.usdoj.gov/fed_regs/rules/2005/fr1216.htm; Larry K. Houck, "Designer Anabolic Steroid Control Act of 2012 Introduced," *FDA Blog*, July 26, 2012, fdalawblog.net/fda_law_blog_hyman_phelps/2012/07/designer-anabolic-steroid-control-act-of-2012-introduced-would-bulk-up-federal-anabolic-steroid-cont.html.

121. Kramer et al. v. City of Jersey City et al., No. 10-2963, US Court of Appeals for the Third Circuit, submitted November 15, 2011, opinion filed December 20, 2011, www2.ca3.uscourts.gov/opinarch/102963np.pdf. This opinion was reaffirmed in 2014 in the case Nicholas Kramer and Brian McGovern v. City of Jersey City et al., Docket no. A–3373–12T4, Superior Court of New Jersey, Appellate Division, decided March 28, 2014, caselaw.findlaw.com/nj-superior-court-appellate-division/1661813.html

122. Houck, "Designer Anabolic Steroid Control Act."

123. Simon J. Midgley, Nick Heather, and John B. Davies, "Levels of Aggression among a Group of Anabolic-Androgenic Steroid Users," *Medicine, Science and the Law* 41 (2001): 314.

124. "Police on Steroids: An Emerging Problem," *Richmond Times-Dispatch*, June 6, 2005.

125. Neil Harvey, "Ex-Deputy Receives Maximum Sentences," *Roanoke Times*, May 8, 2013, roanoke.com/news/crime/franklin_county/ex-deputy-receives-

maximum-sentences/article_2a4dc463-d7eb-5b6d-98eb-ed367dc71946.html.

126. Melissa Powell, "Jonathan Agee Pleads No Contest in Christianburg over Officer's Wounding," *Roanoke Times*, January 22, 2013, roanoke.com/webmin/news/jonathan-agee-pleads-no-contest-in-christiansburg-over-officer-s/article_0a658c0b-c6dd-5481-8148-6abd1568957b.html.

127. Harvey, "Ex-Deputy Receives Maximum Sentences."

128. Harrison G. Pope Jr. and David L. Katz, "Homicide and Near-Suicide by Anabolic Steroid Users," *Journal of Clinical Psychiatry* 51 (January 1990): 30; see also Harrison G. Pope and David L. Katz, "Psychiatric Effects of Exogenous Anabolic-Androgenic Steroids," in *Psychoneuroendocrinology: The Scientific Basis of Clinical Practice* (Washington, DC: American Psychiatric Press, 2003): 331–358.

129. Commonwealth v. Jonathan Agee, videotaped deposition of Harrison G. Pope, MD, MPH.

130. "Former Deputy Jonathan Agee Gets 3 Life Sentences," *Roanoke Times*, May 8, 2013.

131. Pat Reavy, "'Roids,' Ex-Officer Linked," *Salt Lake City Deseret News*, August 3, 2006, deseretnews.com/article/640199588/Roids-ex-officer-linked.html?pg=all.

132. Lisa Rosetta, "Cleared in Shooting: Family Claimed He Was under the Influence," *Salt Lake City Tribune*, August 4, 2006.

133. Dave Seglins and John Nicol, "Steroid Allegations within Niagara Police Go Back Years," CBC, September 10, 2012, cbc.ca/news/canada/steroid-allegations-within-niagara-police-go-back-years-1.1160507: "CBC News has obtained more than 100 pages of emails that appear to belong to one Niagara Regional Police officer who served for years on the elite Emergency Task Unit (ETU). While it is impossible to verify with certainty who wrote them, the CBC has taken steps to check their authenticity and has no reason to doubt they are genuine. The emails detail what appear to be a string of illegal purchases of thousands of dollars worth of anabolic steroids from multiple illegal labs and distributors, including purchases from a lab that was busted in Quebec."

134. Ibid.

135. Brittain and Mueller, "N.J. Doctor Supplied Steroids."

136. Brittain and Mueller, "N.J. Taxpayers Get Bill."

137. Kim R. Humphrey et al., "Anabolic Steroid Use and Abuse by Police Officers: Policy and Prevention," *Police Chief*, June 2008, iacpmag.wp.matrixdev.net/anabolic-steroid-use-and-abuse-by-police-officers-policy-prevention (subscription required).

138. "Omission of Steroids From Police Drug Testing Surprises Officers," *Los Angeles Times*, August 8, 1991.

139. "News from the San Joaquin Valley," Associated Press, May 4, 2006.

CHAPTER THREE: POLICE UNIONS AND STEROIDS

1. "After Shootings, Police Union Chief in New War," *New York Times*, December 24, 2014.

2. "The Badge and the Swastika," *Willamette (OR) Week*, October 1, 2003; "The Cop Who Liked Nazis," *Willamette (OR) Week*, February 11, 2004.

3. "Asleep at the Wheel at City Hall: Editorial Agenda 2014," *Oregonian*, July 29, 2014.

4. "Portland Wants Random Drug Testing of Officers," Associated Press, October 2, 2010; "Portland Police Union Fights Drug Testing," KATU News (Portland, OR), October 4, 2010.

5. "Court Upholds Hair-Drug Tests for NYPD," NBC New York, December 17, 2009.

6. "Do the Police Need More Drug Tests?," editorial, *Oregonian*, November 1, 2010.

7. "Cicilline Retreats on Drug Testing at Providence Police Dept.," *Providence Journal*, March 15, 2010.

8. Maxine Bernstein, "Portland Police Bureau Plans to Move Ahead with Random Drug-Testing This Year, and Include Exam for Steroids," *Oregonian*, January 1, 2012, oregonlive.com/portland/index.ssf/2012/01/portland_police_bureau_plans_t.html.

9. Maxine Bernstein, "Portland Police Contract Includes Random Drug Testing, but Delays Testing for Steroids," *Oregonian*, March 3, 2013, oregonlive.com/portland/index.ssf/2011/02/portland_police_contract_inclu.html.

10. Maxine Bernstein, "Portland Police Union's Tentative Contract Protects Officers Who Take Supplements Containing Steroids," *Oregonian*, November 20, 2013, oregonlive.com/portland/index.ssf/2013/11/portland_police_tentative_cont.html.

11. A. J. Perez, "Cops' Use of Illegal Steroids a 'Big Problem,'" AOL News, December 26, 2010.

12. "DOC to Randomly Test Workers for Steroids, Other Drugs," Associated Press, May 9, 2006.

13. "Police Unions Wrong to Block Drug Testing," Port Huron, Michigan *Times Herald*, June 13, 2003.

14. AP, "DOC to Randomly Test Workers."

15. "Philly Police Det. Indicted in Operating Steroid Distribution Ring," Law Officer, April 28, 2011, lawofficer.com/archive/philly-police-det-indicted-in-operating-steroid-distribution-ring.

16. "Bratton Says New York Police Dept. Must Dismiss Bad Officers," *New York Times*, October 2, 2014.

17. "Undermining Police Accountability: No Wonder Opponents Label AB 2067 the 'Rogue Officers' Bill of Rights,'" editorial, *Los Angeles Times*, February 20, 1992, articles.latimes.com/1992-02-20/local/me-3316_1_law-enforcement-officers.

18. Patrick Lynch, "Cop-Bashers' Bogus 'Bad Apples' Bull," *New York Post*, October 5, 2014.

19. "Don't Shoot," *Economist*, December 13, 2014, 28.

20. Melody Gutierrez and Kim Minugh, "California Police Unions Fight Discipline of Officers under Prosecutors' Lists," *Sacramento Bee*, September 12, 2013, inlandpolitics.com/blog/2013/09/12/sacbee-california-police-unions-fight-discipline-of-officers-under-prosecutors-lists.

21. Carl B. Klockars et al., "The Measurement of Police Integrity," *National Institute of Justice: Research in Brief*, May 2000, ncjrs.gov/pdffiles1/nij/181465.pdf.

22. Hannah Osborne, "Police 'Roid Rage: Widespread Corruption Linked to Steroid Abuse and Gym Use," *International Business Times*, January 23, 2013, ibtimes.co.uk/police-corruption-steriod-abuse-gyms-forming-relationships-427009.

23. Paul Kelso, "One Million Britons May Use Steroids Regularly," Sky News, January 7, 2015, news.sky.com/story/1403431/one-million-britons-may-use-steroids-regularly.

24. Klockars et al., "Measurement of Police Integrity."

25. Dick Lehr, *The Fence: A Police Cover-Up along Boston's Racial Divide* (New York: HarperCollins, 2010), 100.

26. "N.Y.C. Police Maligned Paradegoers on Facebook," *New York Times*, December 5, 2011, nytimes.com/2011/12/06/nyregion/on-facebook-nypd-officers-malign-west-indian-paradegoers.html?pagewanted=all&_r=0.

27. "Legislation Would Make New Officers Live in City," *New York Times*, December 11, 2011, nytimes.com/2011/12/12/nyregion/bill-would-make-new-nyc-officers-live-in-city.html.

28. Klockars et al., "Measurement of Police Integrity," 2.

29. Jerome H. Skolnick and James J. Fyfe, *Above the Law: Police and the Excessive Use of Force* (New York: Free Press, 1993): 92, quoted in Lehr, *The Fence*, 198.

30. Dick Lehr, *The Fence: A Police Cover-Up Along Boston's Racial Divide* (New York: HarperCollins, 2010): 349, 350.

31. Quoted in Lehr, *The Fence*, 277.

32. Quoted in ibid., 76.

33. "Experts Say N.Y. Police Department Isn't Policing Itself," *New York Times*, November 2, 2011.

34. Wayne Barrett, "Ray Kelly's Lonely War," *Daily Beast*, November 7, 2011, thedailybeast.com/articles/2011/11/07/wayne-barrett-is-ray-kelly-to-blame-for-nypd-s-troubles.html.

35. Michael Coakley, "Drug Tests of Cops Are Cutting Edge of Controversial Trend," *Chicago Tribune*, May 4, 1986, articles.chicagotribune.com/1986-05-04/news/8602010136_1_4th-amendment-testing-illegal-substances.

36. Ibid.

37. Robert G. Remis, "Drug-Impaired Police Officers/Firefighters and the Reasonable Suspicion Standard: Whose Turn Is It to Give Condolences to the

Innocent Victim's Family?" *Akron Law Review* 22, no. 4 (1989): 678, 677, uakron. edu/dotAsset/4bf667c9-a682-4e97-8881-59740f8ba00d.pdf.

38. Quoted in ibid., 682.

39. "Police Officer Drug Tests Rare during Alleged Steroid Scandal," CBS DFW, July 29, 2013, dfw.cbslocal.com/2013/07/29/during-steroid-scandal-few-arlington-police-officers-faced-drug-tests.

40. "Police, Firefighters Face Different Steroid Standards," August 15, 2007, cited in bibliography of Brent E. Turvey and Stan Crowder, *Anabolic Steroid Abuse in Public Safety Personnel: A Forensic Manual.*

41. Andrew J. Harvey, "Drug Abuse and Testing in Law Enforcement: No Easy Answers," *FBI Law Enforcement Bulletin* 60, no. 6 (June 1991): 12–15, ncjrs.gov/pdffiles1/Digitization/130305NCJRS.pdf.

42. *New Jersey Law Enforcement Drug Testing Manual,* New Jersey Division of Criminal Justice, July 15, 2001, 4, nj.gov/oag/dcj/njpdresources/pdfs/drug-testing-manual-v4.pdf.

43. Lisa J. Huriash, "Police Balking at Testing for Drugs," *Broward County (FL) Sun-Sentinel,* March 9, 2009, articles.sun-sentinel.com/2009-03-09/news/0903090070_1_drug-test-test-results-reasonable-suspicion.

44. Harvey, "Drug Abuse and Testing," 6.

45. "To Some Cops, 'Roids Trump Reason," April 29, 2011, articles.philly.com/2011-04-29/news/29487560_1_steroids-ring-police-officers-law-enforcement-agencies (payment required).

46. "Muscle Man Jailed after Cops Suspect Steroids," *The Local* (Sweden), August 7, 2014, thelocal.se/20140807/police-ransack-house-of-unusually-large-man.

47. Kim R. Humphrey et al., "Anabolic Steroid Use and Abuse by Police Officers: Policy and Prevention," *Police Chief,* June 2008, iacpmag.wp.matrixdev.net/anabolic-steroid-use-and-abuse-by-police-officers-policy-prevention (subscription required).

48. "Miami Police Could Start Steroid Testing Cops Next Month," *Miami New Times,* October 21, 2014.

49. Tim Elfrink, *Miami New Times,* personal communication, September 28, 2015.

50. "Police Union's Endorsement of Trump Carries an Asterisk," Market-Watch, September 20, 2016, marketwatch.com/story/police-unions-endorsement-of-trump-carries-an-asterisk-2016-09-20; Jason Hopkins, "Can Trump Snag Fraternal Order of Police Endorsement?" Townhall, August 5, 2016, townhall.com/tipsheet/jasonhopkins/2016/08/05/can-trump-snag-fraternal-order-of-police-endorsement-n2202305.

51. "The Nation's Largest Police Union Endorses Donald Trump," National Public Radio, September 18, 2016, npr.org/2016/09/18/494451660/the-nations-largest-police-union-endorses-donald-trump.

52. Alice Speri, "Police Unions Reject Charges of Bias, Find a Hero in Donald Trump," *The Intercept*, October 9, 2016, theintercept.com/2016/10/09/police-unions-reject-charges-of-bias-find-a-hero-in-donald-trump.

53. Steven Greenhut, "Police Union Intimidates City Council," Reason.com, October 26, 2012, reason.com/archives/2012/10/26/police-union-intimidates-california-city.

54. Steven Greenhut, "How Union Power Corrupts Police Departments," Union Watch, September 3, 2012, unionwatch.org/how-union-power-corrupts-police-departments.

55. "Officers Rally and Dinkins Is Their Target," *New York Times*, September 17, 1992, nytimes.com/1992/09/17/nyregion/officers-rally-and-dinkins-is-their-target.html; see also "Strong Words for a Police Riot," *New York Times*, September 30, 1992.

56. "PBA Rally Will Be Met with Strength," *New York Daily News*, December 21, 2000.

57. Russ Baker, "The Rogue Police Union," *Village Voice*, December 7, 1993.

58. Fred Grimm, "Police Unions Negotiations Can Get Down, Dirty," *Miami Herald*, March 24, 2014, rondelord.com/2014/03/27/fred-grimm-police-unions-negotiations-can-get-down-dirty.

59. "Can They Police Themselves?," *New York Times*, November 6, 2011.

60. Barrett, "Ray Kelly's Lonely War"; Douglas Montero, "16 Cops Arraigned in NYPD Tix-Fix Scandal," *New York Post*, October 28, 2011, nypost.com/2011/10/28/16-cops-arraigned-in-nypd-tix-fix-scandal; see also Joe Bruno, "Are New York City DA's outside of the Bronx Ignoring Ticket Fixing Scandal?," *Joe Bruno on the Mob* (blog), October 31, 2011, joebrunoonthemob.wordpress.com/tag/nypd-ticket-fixing-scandal.

61. Gutierrez and Minugh, "California Police Unions."

62. Nadia Prupis, "NYC Police Union Chief Defends NYPD's Killing of Eric Garner," Common Dreams, August 6, 2014, commondreams.org/news/2014/08/06/nyc-police-union-chief-defends-nypds-killing-eric-garner.

63. Nicole Bode, Mathew Katz, and Trevor Kapp, "Eric Garner Was Not Put in a Chokehold, Police Unions Say," DNAinfo, August 5, 2014, dnainfo.com/new-york/20140805/civic-center/eric-garner-was-not-put-chokehold-police-unions-say.

64. "NYC Police Union Blasts Mayor, Urges Democrats to Snub Convention Bid," Reuters, July 3, 2014.

65. Anthony Cormier and Matthew Doig, "Special Report: Unions Protect Problem Officers," *Sarasota (FL) Herald Tribune*, December 1, 2011, heraldtribune.com/article/20111206/article/111209976.

66. Kristian Foden-Vencil, "Portland Police Chief Wants Body Cameras, Union Not So Sure," OPB (Oregon Public Broadcasting), September 11, 2013, opb.org/news/article/portland-police-chief-wants-body-cameras-union-not-so-sure.

67. Douglas Hanks, "Police Union Tries to Block Camera Plan for Miami-Dade Officers," *Miami Herald*, August 22, 2014, miamiherald.com/2014/08/22/4304006/police-union-tries-to-block-camera.html.

68. Joe Schoenmann, "Police Union Threatens Legal Action over Metro's Decision to Test Body-Mounted Cameras," *Las Vegas Sun*, May 7, 2012, lasvegassun.com/news/2012/may/07/police-union-threatens-legal-action-over-metros-de.

69. Tony Farrar, "Self-Awareness to Being Watched and Socially-Desirable Behavior: A Field Experiment on the Effect of Body-Worn Cameras on Police Use of Force," Police Foundation, March 2013, 8–9, policefoundation.org/publication/self-awareness-to-being-watched-and-socially-desirable-behavior-a-field-experiment-on-the-effect-of-body-worn-cameras-on-police-use-of-force.

70. "New York Police Officers to Test Body-Worn Cameras," Associated Press, September 4, 2014, available from the *Daily Mail*, dailymail.co.uk/wires/ap/article-2744319/New-York-police-officers-test-body-worn-cameras.html.

71. Randy Rider, "Roid Rage—No Good Reason," Officer.com, August 8, 2012, officer.com/article/10756939/roid-rage-no-good-reason.

72. Perez, "Cops' Use of Illegal Steroids."

73. Maxine Bernstein, "City Won't Allow Fitness Premium Pay for Portland Police in Their Next Contract unless a Physical Fitness Test Is Given," *Oregonian*, February 1, 2012, oregonlive.com/portland/index.ssf/2012/02/city_wont_allow_fitness_premiu.html.

74. "Killeen Police Fitness Test Deemed Illegal," KXXV.com (Waco-Killeen-Temple, TX), February 10, 2010, kxxv.com/story/11965803/killeen-police-fitness-test-deemed-illegal.

75. "Jeffersonville, Police Union Physical Fitness Dispute Settled," Louisville Metro Police Department, December 19, 2011, lmpd.com/news/story.php?sid=929.

CHAPTER FOUR: THE GYM CULTURE, WHERE MUSCULAR COPS MEET

1. Liz Goff and Susan Cleary, "Queens Drug Sting," *Western Ontario Gazette*, September 12, 2007, qgazette.com/news/2007-09-12/Features/Queens_Drug_Sting.html.

2. Ibid.

3. "Numerous Figures Linked to Steroid Ring Had Ties to Denver Gym," *Denver Post*, July 3, 2005.

4. Jordan Baker, "Generation V Buff, but Not So Pretty after Dark," *Sydney Morning Herald*, September 1, 2011, huntervalleynews.net.au/story/934933/generation-v-buff-but-not-so-pretty-after-dark.

5. "The Steroid Subculture Expands," philly.com, November 13, 1988, articles.philly.com/1988-11-13/news/26248280_1_steroid-users-dianabol-anavar (payment required).

6. "Personal Trainers and Steroids" (discussion thread), 2002–20004, MindandMuscle.com, mindandmuscle.net/forum/5368-personal-trainers-steroids.

7. Paul Goldstein, "Anabolic Steroids: An Ethnographic Approach," in *Anabolic Steroid Abuse*, ed. Geralinie C. Lin and Lynda Erinoff (Rockville, MD: National Institute on Drug Abuse, 1990), 74–96.

8. Ibid.

9. Nick Sas, "Concerns of Drug Abuse at the Gym," *West Australian*, November 12, 2011, au.news.yahoo.com/wa/a/11608978/concerns-of-drug-abuse-at-the-gym/#page1.

10. Alex Fynes-Clinton, "Steroid Use Is All the Rage as Drug Seizures Soar," *Queensland Sunday Mail*, April 1, 2012, couriermail.com.au/news/queensland/steroid-use-is-all-the-rage/story-e6freoof-1226315536131.

11. Baker, "Generation V Buff."

12. Mark Morri, "Outlaw Bikie Gangs Move In to NSW," *Australia Daily Telegraph*, April 5, 2011, dailytelegraph.com.au/outlaw-bikie-gangs-move-in-to-nsw/news-story/46abc2c076d3029ee29cfa663a8b3a8c?sv=42f7c1a3206b3a8c6d211174242bf6dd.

13. Millard Baker, "Whistleblower Leads to Australia Crackdown on Steroids in the Military," Steroids.Info, March 27, 2011, steroids.info/2011/03/27/whistleblower-leads-to-australia-crackdown-on-steroids-in-the-military.

14. "Police Department to Start Routinely Testing Officers for Steroid Use," *New York Times*, April 10, 2008.

15. Kerry Burke and Alison Gendar, "Bay Ridge Parkway Gym Targeted in Steroid Investigation," *New York Daily News*, October 20, 2007, nydailynews.com/news/bay-ridge-parkway-gym-targeted-steroid-investigation-article-1.229787#ixzz1ww8LboGb.

16. John Wills, "Are You Juiced?," Officer.com, June 4, 2007, officer.com/article/10249768/are-you-juiced?page=2.

17. Philip J. Sweitzer, "Drug Law Enforcement in Crisis: Cops on Steroids," *De Paul Journal of Sports Law and Contemporary Problems* 193 (Fall 2004): 195, 198, 209, 209.

18. Ibid., 195–196.

19. Angie Cannon, "Steroid-Using Police Cause Brutality Fears," *Miami Herald*, May 18, 1987.

20. Sweitzer, "Drug Law Enforcement," 209–210, 226.

21. "Officer Charged with Drug Possession," *Denver Post*, April 13, 2003; "Denver Cop's Home Raided," *Denver Post*, January 1, 2003.

22. "Police Family Violence Fact Sheet," National Center for Women and Policing, n.d., womenandpolicing.com/violencefs.asp.

23. Brendan J. Lyons, "Ex-Cop Admits Steroid Charges," *Albany Times-Union*, January 19, 2011, timesunion.com/local/article/Ex-cop-admits-steroids-charges-964524.php; Hal Habib, "Ex-Cop Arrested for Distribution of Steroids,"

Palm Beach Post, November 15, 2007, forums.steroid.com/news/321237-ex-cop-arrested-distribution-steroids.html; Anthony Forgione obituary, *Newsday*, June 22, 2013, legacy.com/obituaries/newsday/obituary.aspx?pid=165461788.

24. "Bodybuilding Officer Is an Unlikely Suspect," *New York Times*, June 6, 1996, nytimes.com/1996/06/06/nyregion/bodybuilding-officer-is-an-unlikely-suspect.html?pagewanted=all&src=pm.

25. "An Ex-Officer Is Convicted in a Beating," *New York Times*, February 24, 1999, nytimes.com/1999/02/24/nyregion/an-ex-officer-is-convicted-in-a-beating.html; "Ex-Officer Gets 8 Years in Race-Tinged Beating at L.I. Nightclub," *New York Times*, April 20, 1999, nytimes.com/1999/04/20/nyregion/ex-officer-gets-8-years-in-race-tinged-beating-at-li-nightclub.html.

26. "Atlanta's Police 'Gang' Unravels with Nightclub Owner's Slaying," *New York Times*, May 20, 1993; "6 Police Officers Linked to Atlanta-Area Crime Ring," *Orlando Sentinel*, March 7, 1993, articles.orlandosentinel.com/1993-03-07/news/9303060396_1_clayton-county-crime-ring-police-officers.

27. Sweitzer, "Drug Law Enforcement," 209–210, 198, 209, 227.

28. "Army Trainers in Steroids Probe," *Australia Herald Sun*, March 29, 2011.

29. Spencer Ackerman, "Army Commandos Look to Wield the Power of Thor," Wired.com, July 15, 2011.

30. Spencer Ackerman, "The Petraeus Workout," *American Prospect*, September 4, 2007, prospect.org/article/petraeus-workout.

31. Danielle Burton, "10 Things You Didn't Know About David Petraeus," *US News & World Report*, March 7, 2008, usnews.com/news/national/articles/2008/03/27/10-things-you-didnt-know-about-david-petraeus.

32. Jflt_jnyg, "Military-Steroids in Iraq," T Nation, June 29, 2006, tnation.t-nation.com/free_online_forum/sports_training_performance_bodybuilding_gear/militarysteroids_in_iraq?pageNo=0.

33. "Joint Base Lewis-McChord Rocked by Scandal," *Stars and Stripes*, December 27, 2010.

34. Ibid.; "Steroid Use on Rise in the Army," *The Seattle Times*, November 20, 2010; "Army Faces Growing Steroid Use Problem," *McClatchy DC Bureau*, November 22, 2010.

35. Peter Finn and Carol D. Leonnig, "Afghan Shootings Refocus Attention on Fort Lewis-McChord," *Washington Post*, March 13, 2012, washingtonpost.com/world/national-security/afghan-shootings-refocus-attention-on-fort-lewis-mc-chord/2012/03/13/gIQApTNYAS_story.html.

36. Barbara Starr, "Lawyer: Special Ops Troops Gave Accused Killer Alcohol, Steroids," CNN.com, May 30, 2013, cnn.com/2013/05/30/us/soldier-afghan-killings-plea.

37. "A 'Kill Team' of American Soldiers in Afghanistan," WBUR (Boston), March 12, 2012, hereandnow.wbur.org/2012/03/12/kill-team.

38. "Murder Count Gone, but More Charges for Bales," *Army Times*, June 3, 2012.

39. Patricia Murphy, "Steroid Problems in the Military," KUOW.org (Puget Sound, WA), November 22, 2010, www2.kuow.org/program.php?id=21869.

40. James Dao, "A Focus on the Effects of Dietary Supplements among Troops in War Zones," *New York Times*, September 7, 2009.

41. Tim Hsia, "The Performance-Enhanced Military," *New York Times*, May 7, 2010, atwar.blogs.nytimes.com/2010/05/07/the-performance-enhanced-military/?_php=true&_type=blogs&_r=0.

42. N. M. Cassler et al., "Patterns and Perceptions of Supplement Use by U.S. Marines Deployed to Afghanistan," *Military Medicine* 178 (June 2013): 659–64.

43. "Infantry: Yet Another Illegal Battlefield Drug," StrategyPage.com, December 1, 2010, strategypage.com/htmw/htinf/articles/20101201.aspx.

44. Joe Shute, "Is Body-Building Bad for Soldiers' Health?," *Telegraph*, October 25, 2013, telegraph.co.uk/news/uknews/defence/10404822/Is-body-building-bad-for-soldiers-health.html.

45. Francis Horton, "Bodybuilding a Stronger Soldier," US Army, June 3, 2010, army.mil/article/40282/Bodybuilding_a_stronger_Soldier.

46. Mary Rose, "Bodybuilding Soldiers Compete in Iraq," *Killeen (TX) Daily Herald*, August 15, 2012, m.kdhnews.com/archive/bodybuilding-soldiers-compete-in-iraq/article_78c01e65-3606-5c84-bf89-7fcee095c5f3.html?mode=jqm.

47. Shute, "Is Body-Building Bad?"

48. Mark Nicol, "Twice as Many Soldiers Caught on Drugs in Body-Building Fad: 590 Failed Drug Tests This Year," *Mail on Sunday*, December 7, 2013, dailymail.co.uk/news/article-2520066/Twice-soldiers-caught-drugs-body-building-fad-590-failed-drug-tests-year.html.

49. "Hundreds Fail UK Military Drug Tests," *Yorkshire Post*, December 29, 2011.

50. Millard Baker, "Americans and Bodybuilding Subculture Blamed for Bringing Steroids to British Army," Steroid.com, n.d., steroid.com/blog/Americans-and-Bodybuilding-Subculture-Blamed-for-Bringing-Steroids-to-British-Army.php.

51. Disclosure: the author has published essays on Millard Baker's website.

52. Tom Coghlan and Deborah Haynes, "Troops Surrender to Illegal Drugs amid Bodybuilding Craze," *Times*, September 23, 2013, thetimes.co.uk/tto/news/uk/defence/article3876155.ece.

53. "Steroid Ring Found in Italy; Some Said to Go to US Troops," Associated Press, August 2, 2005.

54. Jeremy Scahill, *Blackwater: The Rise of the World's Most Powerful Mercenary Army* (New York: Nation Books, 2007), 135.

55. "The Media and the PMC," *Eeben Barlow's Military and Security Blog*, April

10, 2009, eebenbarlowsmilitaryandsecurityblog.blogspot.com/2009/04/media-and-pmc.html.

56. Ernesto Londono and Saad al-Izzi, "In Iraq, Muscle Is a Growth Industry: Security Needs Give Bodybuilding a Lift," *Washington Post*, Foreign Service, June 10, 2008.

57. Terri Judd, "Steroids, Drink and Paranoia: The Murky World of the Private Security Contractor," *Independent*, September 1, 2009, independent.co.uk/news/world/middle-east/steroids-drink-and-paranoia-the-murky-world-of-the-private-security-contractor-1779885.html.

58. Matt, "Medical: Steroid Use and Security Contracting, Is It Worth It?," *Feral Jundi* (blog), September 1, 2009, feraljundi.com/933/medical-steroid-use-and-security-contracting-is-it-worth-it.

59. Spencer S. Hsu and Victoria St. Martin, "Four Blackwater Guards Sentenced in Iraq Shootings of 31 Unarmed Civilians," *Washington Post*, April 3, 2015, washingtonpost.com/local/crime/four-blackwater-guards-sentenced-in-iraq-shootings-of-31-unarmed-civilians/2015/04/13/55b777e0-dee4-11e4-be40-566e2653afe5_story.html.

60. Scahill, *Blackwater*, 39.

61. Jeremy Scahill, "US Businessman: Blackwater Paid Me to Buy Steroids and Weapons on Black Market for its Shooters," *Nation*, September 23, 2010, thenation.com/article/us-businessman-blackwater-paid-me-buy-steroids-and-weapons-black-market-its-shooters.

62. William Saletan, "American Unexceptionalism," Slate, June 30, 2014, slate.com/articles/news_and_politics/frame_game/2014/06/blackwater_shows_there_s_nothing_special_in_the_nature_of_americans.html.

63. Scahill, *Blackwater*, 164, 143.

64. Saletan, "American Unexceptionalism."

65. Carol Burke, *Camp All-American, Hanoi Jane, and the High-and-Tight* (Boston, Beacon, 2004), 92–93.

66. Ibid., 91–92.

67. "5 Roided Out Body Building Movies," Screen Junkies, n.d., screenjunkies.com/movies/movie-lists/5-roided-out-body-building-movies.

68. "Muscle summer—The Men of 'Captain America,' 'Thor' and 'Conan,'" Hero Complex, May 28, 2011, herocomplex.latimes.com/movies/muscle-summer-the-men-of-captain-america-thor-and-conan; see also Millard Baker, "Steroids in 'Captain America,' 'Thor' and 'Conan the Barbarian,'" Steroids. Info, August 12, 2011, steroids.info/2011/08/12/steroids-in-captain-america-thor-and-conan-the-barbarian.

69. Zach Gottlieb, "Jersey Shore Juice Heads: More Than a Fad?," Science Line, February 19, 2010, scienceline.org/2010/02/jersey-shore-juice-heads-more-than-a-fad; see also "Betting the Situation Will Not Get Lost in Translation,"

New York Times, March 23, 2010, query.nytimes.com/gst/fullpage.html?res= 9506E0DD143BF930A15750C0A9669D8B63.

70. Rich Piepho, "Is the Situation on Steroids? Is Ronnie on Steroids?," Wet Paint, August 10, 2010, wetpaint.com/is-the-situation-on-steroids-is-ronnie-on-steroids-692908.

71. "Mary J. Blige Named in Steroid Report," *New York Daily News*, January 14, 2008.

72. Piepho, "Is the Situation on Steroids?"

73. Nathan S., "Does Hip-Hop Have a Steroids Problem?," DJ Booth, February 3, 2010, djbooth.net/index/news/entry/hip-hop-steroids-problem.

74. Paul Stokes, "James Murphy: I Took Steroids to Record LCD Soundsystem's 'This Is Happening,'" NME, May 25, 2010, nme.com/news/music/lcd-soundsystem-28-1296040.

75. Kate Lunau, "Giving Testosterone a Workout," *Maclean's*, September 14, 2012, www2.macleans.ca/2011/09/14/giving-testosterone-a-workout.

76. Penny Crowley, "Twinkle NOT wrinkle," Independent.ie, August 27, 2011, independent.ie/lifestyle/independent-woman/celebrity-news-gossip/twinkle-not-wrinkle-2859418.html.

77. James Nye, "How Many Hollywood Stars Rely on Steroids to Get Their Buff Bodies?," *Daily Mail*, October 22, 2013, dailymail.co.uk/news/article-2400714/How-Hollywood-stars-rely-steroids-buff-bodies-Up-20-percent-leading-men-using-PEDs-claims-new-report.html.

78. A. O. Scott, "Hey, Brooklyn, Where'd You Get Those Muscles?," *New York Times*, July 21, 2011.

79. Richard Davenport-Hines, *The Pursuit of Oblivion: A Global History of Narcotics* (New York: Norton, 2002), 13.

80. "10 Questions," *Time*, August 25, 2014.

81. Dick Cavett, "Boxing the Black Dog," *Time*, August 25, 2014.

82. Gene Lees, *Cats of Any Color: Jazz, Black and White* (New York: Da Capo, 2001), 103.

83. Harris Stratyner, "A Myth about Alcohol, Drugs, and Creativity," *Psychology Today*, July 26, 2010.

84. Logan Hill, "Building a Bigger Action Hero," *Men's Journal*, May 2014.

85. "MMA Fans" (discussion thread), Police Link, policelink.monster.com/topics/5124-mma-fans/posts.

86. "Patrol Officers & MMA Fighters" (discussion thread), Officer.com, forum.officer.com/forum/officers-and-law-enforcement-professionals-only/the-squad-room/non-lethal/182034-patrol-officers-mma-fighters.

87. Amaury Murgado, "MMA Is Not the Biggest Threat," *Police*, October 5, 2010, policemag.com/channel/patrol/articles/2010/10/mma-is-not-the-biggest-threat.aspx.

88. "Patrol Officers & MMA Fighters."

89. Mike Fish, "MMA Testosterone Exemptions High," ESPN.com, February 25, 2014, espn.go.com/espn/otl/story/_/id/10500652/therapeutic-use-exemptions-testosterone-mma-outpace-other-sports-lines-finds.

90. "UFC Prez Dana White Changes Tune on Drugs in 'Combat Sports,'" Associated Press, January 28, 2014.

91. Ibid.

92. "Dana Said," Fightlinker, March 29, 2012, fightlinker.com/dana-said.

93. "Dana White Is Gonna 'Come Down on This Thing,'" Fightlinker, April 23, 2012, fightlinker.com/dana-white-promises-to-come-down-on-cheating.

94. "WADA Gets Aggro about Shitty Testing," Fightlinker, May 5, 2011, fightlinker.com/wada-gets-aggro-about-shitty-testing.

95. Fish, "MMA Testosterone Exemptions."

96. AP, "UFC Prez Dana White."

97. Fish, "MMA Testosterone Exemptions."

98. Ibid.

99. Tim Elfrink, "Biogenesis Just Hints at Florida's Anti-Aging Catastrophe," *Miami New Times*, December 19, 2013.

100. Zach Arnold, "A Crash Course on Testosterone, Hypogonadism, and Doping," Boxing Insider, May 10, 2012, boxinginsider.com/columns/a-crash-course-on-testosterone-hypgonadism-and-doping.

101. Ibid.

102. Ibid.

103. Ibid.

104. Iain Kidd, "Testosterone Replacement Therapy Facts," SB Nation, May 13, 2013, bloodyelbow.com/2013/5/13/4326732/testosterone-replacement-therapy-facts.

105. Zach Arnold, "UFC's Current Stance on the Testosterone Issue: Not Much of a Plan," Fight Opinion, March 28, 2012, fightopinion.com/2012/03/28/ufc-plan-testosterone.

106. Jonathan Snowden, "The Dangerous Hyperbole Surrounding Testosterone Replacement Therapy," Bleacher Report, March 30, 2012, bleacherreport.com/articles/1125664-the-dangerous-hyperbole-surrounding-testosterone-replacement-therapy.

107. Arnold, "UFC's Current Stance."

108. Ben Fowlkes, "In MMA's War on Drugs, Some Experts Say We're Not Fighting the Right Battles," MMA Fighting, February 17, 2012, mmafighting.com/2012/2/17/2804766/in-mmas-war-on-drugs-some-experts-say-were-not-fighting-the-right.

109. See, for example, John Hoberman, "Sports Physicians and the Doping Crisis in Elite Sport," *Clinical Journal of Sportmedicine* 12 (2002): 203–208;

Hoberman, "Sports Physicians and Doping: Medical Ethics and Elite Performance," in *The Social Organization of Sports Medicine: Critical Socio-Cultural Perspectives*, ed. Dominic Malcolm and Parissa Safai (New York: Routledge, 2012), 247–264.

110. Arnold, "Crash Course on Testosterone."

111. Sabe De, "The Truty on TRT—Testosterone Replacement Therapy under Fire," FightMD.com, April 19, 2014, fightmd.com/my-blog/trt.

112. Harrison G. Pope et al, "Anabolic Steroid Users' Attitudes toward Physicians," *Addiction* 99 (September 21004): 1189–1194.

113. Tom Ngo, "UFC Owner Takes Firm Stance against TRT, Wants Random Drug Testing," 5th Round, July 21, 2011, 5thround.com/82638/lorenzo-fertitta-takes-firm-stance-against-trt-pushes-for-random-drug-testing.

114. Trent Reinsmith, "Dana White: 'Nobody Knows What the F—— They are Talking about When It Comes to TRT and the Testing," SB Nation, June 2, 2014, bloodyelbow.com/2014/6/2/5770854/dana-white-nobody-knows-what-the-f-they-are-talking-about-when-it-comes-to-trt-vitor-belfort.

115. Personal communication to the author, July 13, 2014.

116. Cyrus D. Rahnema et al., "Anabolic Steroid–Induced Hypogonadism: Diagnosis and Treatment," *Fertility and Sterility* 101 (May 2014): 1273.

117. Robert M. Coward et al., "Anabolic Steroid Induced Hypogonadism in Young Men," *Journal of Urology* 190 (December 2013): 2201.

118. Mike Chiappetta, "PEDs in MMA: Amid TRT Controversy, a Hidden Danger," MMA Fighting, March 23, 2012, mmafighting.com/news/2012/3/23/2893917/peds-in-mma-amid-trt-controversy-a-hidden-danger.

119. Ibid.

120. Jonathan Snowden, "Is MMA Too Violent? One Reporter Says Enough Is Enough," SB Nation, September 28, 2010, bloodyelbow.com/2010/9/28/1716896/is-mma-too-violent-one-reporter-says-enough-is-enough.

121. Fish, "MMA Testosterone Exemptions High."

122. "History," Hells Angels Motorcycle Club World, affa.hells-angels.com/hamc-history; "Hells Angels," *Wikipedia*, en.wikipedia.org/wiki/Hells_Angels.

123. "Bandidos Motorcycle Club," *Wikipedia*, en.wikipedia.org/wiki/Bandidos_Motorcycle_Club.

124. James F. Quinn, "Angels, Bandidos, Outlaws, and Pagans: The Evolution of Organized Crime among the Big Four 1% Motorcycle Clubs," *Deviant Behavior* 22 (2001): 388.

125. "(U) OMGs and the Military 2010 Update: ATF Intelligence Report," US Department of Justice, Bureau of Alcohol, Tobacco, Firearms and Explosives, Office of Strategic Intelligence and Information, 2010, 3, docplayer.net/3692939-Atf-u-omgs-and-the-military-2010-update-atf-intelligence-report.html.

126. Ibid.

127. Ibid., 34, 35.

128. Ibid., 2.

129. Ibid., 6.

130. Ibid., 9, 32.

131. Ibid., 10.

132. Ibid., 20.

133. Ibid., 25.

134. Ibid., 19.

135. Ibid., 18.

136. Lisa Riordan Seville and Hannah Rappleye, "Lines Blur between Cops and Bikers across the Country," NBC News, October 9, 2013, nbcnews.com/news/other/lines-blur-between-cops-bikers-across-country-f8C11364142.

137. Zusha Elinson, "Police Biker Clubs Draw Scrutiny in Wake of Bar Brawl," *Wall Street Journal*, July 22, 2013, wsj.com/articles/SB10001424127887323836504578553523684965066.

138. "Police Clubs and Biker Gangs Blur Lines, Drawing Concern," Associated Press, June 7, 2015.

139. "The Iron Order Is Made Up of Law Enforcement Riders," *US News & World Report*, February 2, 2016.

140. See "Blue Knights, International LEMC," blueknights.org; "The Iron Order Is Made Up of Law Enforcement Officers," usnews.com, February 2, 2016; "Police Clubs and Biker Gangs Blur Lines, Drawing Concern," Associated Press, June 7, 2015.

141. "Choir Boys is a brotherhood of retired or active duty law enforcement officers. Our membership is 100% law enforcement and we are not a 1% [outlaw] club." Choir Boys Law Enforcement Motorcycle Club, cuffsrun.com/about-us.

142. "Our common purpose is a strong brotherhood and a love for the road. We place our values above all else: Honesty, Integrity, Loyalty, and Duty. We require these qualities in ourselves and those we associate with." Blue Reapers MC, bluereapersmc.com/index.html.

143. Iron Circle Law Enforcement Motorcycle Club, ironcirclelemc.org.

144. Blue Breed LEMC, shane6727.wixsite.com/new-breed/music.

145. Blue Thunder Law Enforcement Motorcycle Club, bluethunderlemc.org.

146. Police report, prescottads.com/Courier-pdf-doc/Iron-Brotherhood-DPS-1.pdf, 125.

147. Bill Rankin, "Feds Suspect Corrupt Leak in Motorcycle Gang Investigation," *Atlanta Journal Constitution*, October 11, 2012, bikersofamerica.blogspot.com/2012/10/feds-suspect-corrupt-leak-in-motorcycle.html.

148. Marty Gallagher, "Lee Moran," Starting Strength, September 20, 2013, startingstrength.com/index.php/site/article/lee_moran#.VIYAaF6TSzA.

149. "Guilty Plea for Pagans President in Shooting Steven Mondevergine Was Charged with Opening Fire During an Argument," June 19, 2001, articles.philly.

com/2001-06-19/news/25325198_1_pagans-plea-hearing-motorcycle-gang (payment required).

150. Mark Morri, "105 Bikie Chapters hit NSW," *Australia Daily Telegraph*, April 4, 2011, heraldsun.com.au/ipad/bikie-chapters-hit-nsw/news-story/21a046 35ac97e595a7db4e12e5d7eab2.

151. "Vicious Lawless Association Disestablishment Bill 2013," Parliament of Queensland, legislation.qld.gov.au/Bills/54PDF/2013/VicLawAssDisB13.pdf; Greg Barns, "Queensland's 'War' on Bikie Gangs Goes Too Far," ABC (Australian Broadcasting Corporation) News, October 15, 2013, abc.net.au/news/2013-10-16/barns-queensland-bikie-laws/5025742; Anne Cappellano, "Are you a Vicious Lawless Associate?," Independent Australia, December 13, 2014, independentaustralia.net/politics/politics-display/are-you-a-vicious-lawless-associate,5876.

152. "Tattoo Parlours Bill 2013," Parliament of Queensland, legislation.qld.gov.au/Bills/54PDF/2013/TattooParloursB13.pdf.

153. "Bikie Crackdown: Gangs Could Be Banned from Security and Gym Jobs," Australian Associated Press, October 15, 2013, theguardian.com/world/2013/oct/16/bikie-crackdown-we-will-crush-them-says-queensland-attorney-general-jarrod-beijie-says.

154. Bev Lacey, "Former Cop Says Bikie Gangs Are Fleeing QLD Laws," Northern Star, January 24, 2014, northernstar.com.au/news/bikie-gangs-flee-laws/2148758.

155. Liz Davies and Eamonn Duff, "Steroid Seizures Linked to Bikie Gangs on the Rise," *Sydney Morning Herald*, May 28, 2012, smh.com.au/national/steroid-seizures-linked-to-bikie-gangs-on-the-rise-20120527-1zd65.html; "Motorcycle Gangs Use and Sell Steroids," MedInform.org, June 12, 2012, medinform.org/motorcycle-gangs-use-and-sell-steroids.php.

156. Dan Oakes, "Steroid Possession Joins List of Charges against Hells Angel 'Skitzo' Hewat," *Australia Age*, May 19, 2013, theage.com.au/victoria/steroid-possession-joins-list-of-charges-against-hells-angel-skitzo-hewat-20130518-2jtlm.html.

157. Carly Crawford, "Bikie Shootings, Drugs in Sport and Often Caught Up in It Is Gym Owner and Cleanskin Tony Doherty," *Australia Herald Sun*, March 22, 2013, heraldsun.com.au/news/law-order/bikie-shootings-drugs-in-sport-and-often-caught-up-in-it-is-gym-owner-and-cleanskin-tony-doherty/story-fnat79vb-1226607996413.

158. "Raids Link Police with Organised Crime," Australian Broadcasting Corporation, September 10, 2013, abc.net.au/7.30/content/2013/s3865770.htm.

159. *Drugs in Sport: Second Report of the Senate Standing Committee on Environment, Recreation and the Arts*, Parliament of the Commonwealth of Australia (Canberra: Australian Government Publishing Service, May 1990), 357, trove.nla.gov.au/work/5850956?selectedversion=NBD8162043.

160. Ibid., 367.

161. Ian Burrell, "Police Officers Moonlight as Nightclub Bouncers," *Independent*, February 23, 1999, independent.co.uk/news/police-officers-moonlight-as-nightclub-bouncers-1072667.html.

CHAPTER FIVE: STEROIDS IN THE MILITARY

1. Quoted in David B. Kopell and Paul M. Blackman, "Can Soldiers Be Peace Officers? The Waco Disaster and the Militarization of American Law Enforcement," *Akron Law Review* 30 (1997): 619–659.

2. Philip J. Sweitzer, "Drug Law Enforcement in Crisis: Cops on Steroids," *De Paul Journal of Sports Law and Contemporary Problems* 193 (Fall 2004): 193.

3. Ibid., 198, 209.

4. Quoted in Kopell and Blackman, "Can Soldiers Be Peace Officers?"

5. Peter B. Kraska and Louis J. Cubellis, "Militarizing Mayberry and Beyond: Making Sense of American Paramilitary Policing," *Justice Quarterly* 14 (December 1997): 609.

6. Frank R. Cooper, "'Who's the Man?': Masculinities Studies, Terry Stops, and Police Training," 2009, Suffolk University Law School Faculty Publications 57, http://lsr.nellco.org/suffolk_fp/57.

7. John C. Ricke, "From Military to Police: Are You Ready?," Police Link, n.d. policelink.monster.com/benefits/articles/136068-from-military-to-police-are-you-ready.

8. James Ploskonka, "Veterans Are Eligible for Assistance to Train for Careers in Criminal Justice," December 21, 2011, cleveland.com/employment/plain-dealer/index.ssf/2011/12/veterans_are_eligible_for_assistance_to_train_for_careers_in_criminal_justice.html.

9. "Military Experience," Philadelphia Police Department, n.d., phillypolice.com/careers/military-experience.

10. "Military Veteran?," DiscoverPolicing. org, n.d., discoverpolicing.org/find_your_career/?fa=military_veterans.

11. "By the Numbers: Women in the U.S. Military," CNN.com, January 24, 2013, cnn.com/2013/01/24/us/military-women-glance.

12. "Equality Denied: The Status of Women in Policing, 1999," Feminist Majority Foundation, womenandpolicing.org/final_1999statusreport.htm.

13. Ibid. Here is a recruiting text that does not distinguish between male and female military veterans: "Police recruiters are looking for physically and mentally fit candidates with good decision-making abilities, common sense, and well-defined morals who can respect a paramilitary chain of command. So the men and women leaving active-duty military jobs would seem to be a perfect fit for police careers" (Mark Clark, "Military Vets Joining Law Enforcement," *Police*, January 14, 2014, policemag.com/channel/careers-training/articles/2014/01/military-vets-joining-law-enforcement.aspx).

14. Clark, "Military Vets Joining Law Enforcement."

15. Patricia A. Deuster et al., *The Special Operations Forces Nutrition Guide* (2012), 1, navyseals.com/wp-content/uploads/2012/12/special-operations-nutrition-guide.pdf.

16. "Improving Your Command Presence," Law Officer, April 1, 2011, lawofficer.com/article/tactics-and-weapons/improving-your-command-presenc.

17. Alice Su, "A Dispatch From the Counterterrorism Olympics," *Atlantic*, May 13, 2014.

18. Deuster et al., *Special Operations Forces Nutrition Guide*, 212.

19. Ibid., 1.

20. "SWAT," *Wikipedia*, en.wikipedia.org/wiki/SWAT.

21. See fbijobs.gov.

22. Kopell and Blackman, "Can Soldiers Be Peace Officers?"

23. Will Brink, "Rethinking SWAT Training," *Police*, June 13, 2013, policemag.com/channel/swat/articles/2013/06/rethinking-swat-training.aspx.

24. Peter B. Kraska and Victor E. Kappeler, "Militarizing American Police: The Rise and Normalization of Paramilitary Units," *Social Problems* 44 (February 1997): 12.

25. Karan R. Singh, "Treading the Thin Blue Line: Military Special-Operations-Trained Police SWAT Teams and the Constitution," *William and Mary Bill of Rights Journal* 9 (2001): 674.

26. Kraska and Cubellis, "Militarizing Mayberry."

27. Peter B. Kraska, "Militarization and Policing: Its Relevance to 21st Century Police," *Policing* (2007): 1–13.

28. Sweitzer, "Drug Law Enforcement," 228.

29. Lynn A. Tovar, "Vicarious Traumatization and Spirituality in Law Enforcement," *FBI Law Enforcement Bulletin*, July 2011, leb.fbi.gov/2011/july/vicarious-traumatization-and-spirituality-in-law-enforcement.

30. "Number of Police Officers Killed By Gunfire Fell 14 Percent in 2015, Study Says," NPR, December 29, 2015, npr.org/sections/thetwo-way/2015/12/29/461402091/number-of-police-officers-killed-by-gunfire-fell-14-percent-in-2015-study-says. According to the FBI, there were 698,460 law enforcement officers in the United States in 2011 (fbi.gov/about-us/cjis/ucr/crime-in-the-u.s/2011/crime-in-the-u.s.-2011/tables/table_74_full-time_law_enforcement_employees_by_population_group_percent_male_and_female_2011.xls).

31. Ryan C. W. Hall et al., "Psychiatric Complications of Anabolic Steroid Abuse," *Psychosomatics* 46 (July–August 2005): 288, 286, 287.

32. See *On the Front Lines: Police Stress and Family Well-Being: Hearing before the Select Committee on Children, Youth, and Families House of Representatives*, 102nd Cong., 1st sess., May 20, 1991, testimony of Leanor Boulin Johnson, 32–48 (Washington DC: Government Printing Office, 1991); P. H. Neidig, H. E. Russell, and A. F. Seng, "Interspousal Aggression in Law Enforcement Families: A

Preliminary Investigation," *Police Studies* 15, no. 1 (1992): 30–38; M. Straus and R. Gelles, *Physical Violence in American Families: Risk Factors and Adaptations to Violence in 8,145 Families* (New Brunswick, NJ: Transaction, 1990); P. H. Neidig, A. F. Seng, and H. E. Russell, "Interspousal Aggression in Law Enforcement Personnel Attending the FOP Biennial Conference," *National FOP Journal*, Fall–Winter 1992, 25–28, cited in "Police Family Violence Fact Sheet," National Center for Women and Policing, womenandpolicing.org/violenceFS.asp.

33. Karen Houppert, "Base Crimes," *Mother Jones*, July–August 2005, motherjones.com/politics/2005/07/base-crimes. According to Jon Elliston and Catherine Lutz: "One Army-funded study, however, found in 1998 that reports of 'severe aggression' against spouses ran more than three times higher among Army families than among civilian ones" ("Hidden Casualties: An Epidemic of Domestic Violence When Troops Return from War," *Southern Exposure* 31, no. 1 [Spring 2003], southernstudies.org/sites/default/files/HiddenCasualties.pdf).

34. Wayman C. Mullins and Michael J. McMains, "Impact of Traumatic Stress on Domestic Violence in Policing," in *Domestic Violence by Law Enforcement Officers*, ed. Donald C. Sheehan (Washington, DC: US Department of Justice, Federal Bureau of Investigation, 2000), 257–268, webapp1.dlib.indiana.edu/virtual_disk_library/index.cgi/4951188/FID707/DVBPO/IOT.pdf.

35. Policemen's Benevolent Ass'n of N.J., Local 318 v. Washington Twp. (Gloucester County), 850 F.2d 133, 141 (3d Cir. 1988).

36. Mark Thompson, "America's Medicated Army," *Time*, February 9, 2009.

37. Lukasz Kamienski, *Shooting Up: A Short History of Drugs and War* (New York: Oxford University Press, 2016), 188, 189, 121, 189.

38. Melody Petersen, "U.S. Military: Heavily Armed and Medicated," NBC News, May 19, 2009, nbcnews.com/id/30748260/ns/health-health_care/t/us-military-heavily-armed-medicated.

39. Quoted in Kamienski, *Shooting Up*, 190.

40. Kamienski, *Shooting Up*, 5, 28.

41. Kim Murphy, "Soldiers at War in a Fog of Psychotropic Drugs," *Seattle Times*, April 10, 2012, seattletimes.com/nation-world/soldiers-at-war-in-fog-of-psychotropic-drugs.

42. Jamie Reno, "'Medicating Our Troops Into Oblivion': Prescription Drugs Said to Be Endangering U.S. Soldiers," *International Business Times*, April 19, 2014, ibtimes.com/medicating-our-troops-oblivion-prescription-drugs-said-be-endangering-us-soldiers-1572217.

43. Kelley Vlahos, "The Military's Prescription Drug Addiction," *American Conservative*, October 3, 2013, theamericanconservative.com/articles/the-militarys-prescription-drug-addiction.

44. Quoted in Murphy, "Soldiers at War."

45. Catharine L. Annas and George J. Annas, "Enhancing the Fighting Force: Medical Research on American Soldiers," *Journal of Contemporary Health Law*

and Policy 25 (Spring 2009): 5, sevenhorizons.org/docs/AnnasEnhancingFightingforce.pdf; emphasis in the original.

46. Quoted in ibid., 7.

47. Thompson, "America's Medicated Army."

48. Petersen, "Heavily Armed and Medicated."

49. Murphy, "Soldiers at War."

50. Ibid.

51. Ibid.

52. Marcel Reinold and John Hoberman, "The Myth of the Nazi Steroid," *International Journal of the History of Sport* (2014): 1–13, dx.doi.org/10.1080/09523367.2014.884563.

53. Susan Katz Keating, "Flying on Amphetamines Is No Departure from Tradition," *Washington Times*, August 22, 1988.

54. See, for example, Ben Wilson, "Big Read: Britain's Steroid Epidemic," *Men's Health*, July 14, 2016, menshealth.co.uk/building-muscle/big-read-britains-steroid-epidemic.

55. Department of Defense, "Instruction: Military Personnel Drug Abuse Testing Program," September 13, 2012, dtic.mil/whs/directives/corres/pdf/101001p.pdf.

56. "Steroids and the Military" (discussion thread), 2007, http://tnation.t-nation.com/free_online_forum/sports_training_performance_bodybuilding_gear/steroids_and_the_military.

57. See, for example, Tim Hsia, "The Performance-Enhanced Military," *New York Times*, May 7, 2010; Patricia Murphy, "Steroid Problems in the Military," KUOW.org (Puget Sound, WA), November 22, 2010, www2.kuow.org/program.php?id=21869 ; "Steroid Use on Rise in the Army," *Seattle Times*, November 20, 2010; National Naval Medical Center, "Anabolic Steroids: The Good, the Bad, the Ugly," March 17, 2011; "Joint Base Lewis-McChord Rocked by Scandal," *Stars and Stripes*, May 17, 2011; "Murder Count Gone, but More Charges for Bales," *Army Times*, June 3, 2012; "Military Doctor: Almost Half of Testosterone-Boosting Supplements May Have Illegal Steroids," *Military Times*, July 19, 2013.

58. Michael S. Bahrke and John S. O'Connor, "Anabolic-Androgenic Steroid Use by Soldiers: The U.S. Army Steroid Testing Policy," *Military Medicine* 155 (November 1990): 573–574.

59. US Army Public Health Command, "Anabolic Steroids," n.d., phc.amedd.army.mil/topics/healthyliving/asm/Pages/SteroidAbuse.aspx.

60. *Seattle Times*, "Steroid Use on Rise."

61. Ibid.

62. Philadelphia Police Department, "Military Experience," phillypolice.com/careers/military-experience.

63. Hsia, "Performance-Enhanced Military"

64. "A Question of Navy Seals Nutrition," March–April 2007, militaryphotos. net/forums/archive/index.php/t-108326.html. The 1st Battalion, 75th Ranger Regiment is based at Hunter Army Airfield in Georgia.

65. D. Lariviere, "Nutritional Supplements Flexing Muscles as Growth Industry," Forbes.com, April 4, 2013, forbes.com/sites/davidlariviere/2013/04/18/nutritional-supplements-flexing-their-muscles-as-growth-industry.

66. Hsia, "Performance-Enhanced Military."

67. "Military Support," Rip It Energy Fuel, ripitenergy.com/#military-support.

68. Bahrke and O'Connor, "Anabolic-Androgenic Steroid Use."

69. US Army Public Health Command, "Anabolic Steroids."

70. Seattle Times, "Steroid Use on Rise."

71. Ibid.

72. National Naval Medical Center, "Anabolic Steroids."

73. Bob Preece, "Hundreds Fail UK Military Drug Tests," Yorkshire Post, December 29, 2011, yorkshirepost.co.uk/news/main-topics/general-news/hundreds-fail-uk-military-drug-tests-1-4099770.

74. Joe Shute, "Is Body-Building Bad for Soldiers' Health?," Telegraph, October 25, 2013, telegraph.co.uk/news/uknews/defence/10404822/Is-body-building-bad-for-soldiers-health.html.

75. Andrew Webster, "Soldiers Found to Be Using Steroids," Australia Age, July 21, 2002, theage.com.au/articles/2002/07/20/1026898930028.html.

76. Craig Skehan, "Elite Soldiers Face Charges as 'Police Uncover Drug Use,'" Sydney Morning Herald, July 24, 2002, smh.com.au/articles/2002/07/23/1027332379814.html.

77. "Army Trainers in Steroids Probe," Australia Herald Sun, March 29, 2011.

78. Ibid.

79. Murphy, "Steroid Problems in the Military"; Seattle Times, "Steroid Use on Rise."

80. "Infantry: Yet Another Illegal Battlefield Drug," Strategy Page, December 1, 2010, strategypage.com/htmw/htinf/articles/20101201.aspx.

81. Hsia, "Performance-Enhanced Military."

82. Katie Drummond, "This Is Your Military on Drugs," New Republic, February 5, 2013, newrepublic.com/article/112269.

83. Army Times, "Murder Count Gone."

84. Telegraph, "Is Body-Building Bad?"

85. James Dao, "A Focus on the Effects of Dietary Supplements among Troops in War Zones," New York Times, September 7, 2009.

86. Hsia, "Performance-Enhanced Military."

87. N. M. Cassler et al., "Patterns and Perceptions of Supplement Use by U.S. Marines Deployed to Afghanistan," Military Medicine 178 (June 2013): 659–664.

88. "America's Medicated Army," Time (June 5, 2008).

89. Ben Farmer, "18 Soldiers Face Sack after Army Doping Test," *Telegraph*, September 17, 2013, telegraph.co.uk/news/uknews/defence/10315125/18-soldiers-face-sack-after-Army-doping-test.html.

90. Strategy Page, "Another Illegal Battlefield Drug."

91. Reinold and Hoberman, "Myth of the Nazi Steroid."

92. Deuster et al., *Special Operations Forces Nutrition Guide.*

93. Melissa L. Givens, Patricia A. Deuster, and Brian R. Kupchak, "CHAMP Symposium on Androgens, Anabolic Steroids, and Related Substances: What We Know and What We Need to Know," *Military Medicine* 181 (July 2016): 680.

94. Jacob Bucher, "Soldiering With Substance: Substance and Steroid Use Among Military Personnel," *Journal of Drug Education* 42 (2012): 284, 286.

95. Dan Oakes, "Steroid-Abusing Australian Soldiers Sent Home in Disgrace," *Sydney Morning Herald*, June 8, 2010, smh.com.au/world/steroidabusing-australian-soldiers-sent-home-in-disgrace-20100607-xquy.html. According to an article in the *San Diego Union-Tribune*, eight SEALs tested positive for "illegal drug use" in 2004; the drugs involved were not identified ("U.S. Being Forced to Transfer Some Units," June 19, 2004).

96. "A Question of Navy Seals Nutrition."

97. Chris Jansing, "A Typical SEAL? Think 007, Not Rambo," NBC News, January 29, 2010.

98. "Steroids" (discussion thread), Professional Soldiers, February 18, 2010, professionalsoldiers.com/forums/showthread.php?t=27708.

99. Archaic, "Navy SEALs Hypothetical" (discussion thread), T Nation, March 2004, tnation.t-nation.com/free_online_forum/sports_training_performance_bodybuilding_gear/navy_seals_hypothetical_q.

100. Ibid.

101. Ibid.

102. Ibid.

103. "Special Forces Prep" (discussion thread), iSteroids.com, September 2009, forums.isteroids.com/anabolic-steroids-questions-answers/76053-special-forces-prep.html.

104. Archaic, "Navy SEALs Hypothetical."

105. "Muscle summer—the men of 'Captain America,' 'Thor' and 'Conan,'" Hero Complex, May 28, 2011, herocomplex.latimes.com/movies/muscle-summer-the-men-of-captain-america-thor-and-conan.

106. Patrick Hruby, "Big Hollywood: Steroids Find Their Role in Entertainment Industry," *Washington Times*, August 24, 2011, washingtontimes.com/news/2011/aug/24/peds-find-their-role-in-hollywood/?page=all.

CONCLUSION

1. Martin Kaste, "Military-Trained Police May Be Less Hasty To Shoot, But That Got This Vet Fired," National Public Radio, December 8, 2016.

2. Melissa L. Givens, Patricia A. Deuster, and Brian R. Kupchak, "CHAMP Symposium on Androgens, Anabolic Steroids, and Related Substances: What We Know and What We Need to Know," *Military Medicine* 181 (July 2016).

3. See, for example, 2nd Lt. Billy-Joe Liane, USAF MSC and MAJ Charles Magee, MC USA, "Guerilla Warfare on the Pancreas? A Case of Acute Pancreatitis From a Supplement Known to Contain Anabolic-Androgenic Steroids," *Military Medicine* 181 (2016): e1395–e1397. "As more about the risks associated with PED [performance enhancing-drug] use is understood, emerging screening strategies need to be evaluated and considered for high-risk populations. Due to the frequency of product adulteration, pathophysiologic mechanisms cannot be elucidated or determined without quantitative analysis of PEDs and other supplements. Educating physicians to further the science through supplement analysis may have an important role in advancing the science, and addressing the risk for future warfighters and athletes." [e1397]

4. See, for example, Joseph M. Rothberg et al., "Life and Death in the U.S. Army," *JAMA*, November 7, 1990: 2241–2244. "The sharp reduction in death among black men to the level where rates of death by homicide do not differ between white and black soldiers suggests that the control of violence by community regulation of life-style is possible and might confer considerable mortality reduction in nonmilitary populations." [2244]

5. Philip J. Sweitzer, "Drug Law Enforcement in Crisis: Cops on Steroids," *De Paul Journal of Sports Law and Contemporary Problems* 193 (Fall 2004): 193.

6. William J. Bratton, "How to Reform the Police From Within," *New York Times*, September 16, 2016.

7. "Two Suits Have One Aim On Disciplinary Records," *New York Times*, February 1, 2017.

8. Ken Auletta, "Fixing Broken Windows," *The New Yorker*, September 7, 2015, 44.

9. "Cast-Out Police Officers Are Often Hired in Other Cities," *New York Times*, September 10, 2016.

10. "Bratton Tries a Community Policing Approach, on the New York Police," *New York Times*, September 20, 2015.

INDEX

crime associated with steroid use, 44–47, 73, 114. *See also individual crimes*

Dailey, Daniel, 85
Dallas Police Department, 51
danger of police work, 3, 12, 43, 56, 164
Davis, Edward F., 27, 40
Dawe, Ralph, 83
de Blasio, Bill, 146–147
DeFazio, Edward, 64–65
Department of Justice, US, 7, 8, 9, 54
depression, 100, 189, 198, 219, 240
Designer Anabolic Steroid Control Act of 2012, 115, 116
Designer Anabolic Steroid Control Act of 2014, 115
dietary supplements: military's use of, 167–168, 216, 227–228, 230–231, 233; police officers' use of, 127, 128; special operations forces' use of, 235
Dinkins, David, 143
Dirty Thirty cops, 53
district attorneys, 85. *See also* police officers: prosecutors' relationship with; punishment, police: by prosecution; *and individual attorneys*
divorce, 21, 56, 61, 219
Dolphin gym, 158
domestic violence: and alcohol abuse, 3, 100; and the military, 219–220; by police officers, x, xi, 3, 23, 56, 69, 100, 120, 219; and post-traumatic stress disorder, 220; and steroid use, x, xi, 23
Dorner, Christopher, 53
Dow, Paula, 63–64, 66–69
Dragnet, 13
Drishti, Ed, 78
drug dealers, 76, 83; in gyms, 10, 19, 22, 154–155
Drug Enforcement Administration (DEA), 24, 29, 35, 65, 116
drug testing; in Albuquerque Police Department, 7–8; city authorities'

support of, 125; cost of, 24, 64, 161, 232; court rulings about, 80; effectiveness of, 2, 32; and excessive force, use of, 68; frequency of, x, 2, 17; in the military, 232; and mixed martial arts, 186; police chiefs' policies of, 2, 7–8, 16–17, 23, 80; police unions' attitude toward, 2, 16–17, 23, 24, 123, 127, 129; in Portland Police Department, 125–129; random, 23, 32, 88–89, 135, 136–137; and "reasonable suspicion" requirement, 17, 37, 80, 128, 135–141. *See also* punishment, police; steroids, anabolic; *and individual police departments*
drunk driving (DWI), 1, 4, 100
Duffee, Todd, 189

Emanuel, Rahm, 16
England. *See* United Kingdom
Evans, Mike, 92
excessive force. *See* police brutality

fatigue, 74, 79–80, 189
FBI Law Enforcement Bulletin, 26, 218
Federal Bureau of Investigation (FBI), 8, 17, 35, 217; steroid use in, 74
films. *See* police officers: film and television portrayal of; steroids, anabolic: film and television portrayal of
firefighters, 22, 23–25, 28, 30, 35, 81, 159
First Amendment, 146
Flohr, Troy, 74
Florida Police Benevolent Association (FPBA), 129
Foley, Tom 72, 92
Food and Drug Administration, 17, 35, 188
Forgione, Anthony, 73, 162–163
Fourth Amendment, 136
Fraternal Order of Police (FOP), 17, 129–130; and Miami police riots, 144–145; and physical fitness testing,

Lenahan, John T., 63

Lombroso, Cesare, 102, 104

Los Angeles Police Department, 58, 61

Los Angeles Times, 40

Louima, Abner, 54

Lovvorn v. City of Chattanooga, Tenn. (1988), 137

Lowen's Compounding Pharmacy, 48–49, 79, 83, 158

Lowry, Howard, 174

"low T." *See* hypogonadism

Lucente, Richard, 79

Lynch, Patrick, 83, 124, 145, 146

Macik, Tony, 73

male bonding, 55, 164, 175, 200, 203, 217

Mancini, Frank, 35–36

marijuana, 136, 221

Marino, Michael, 58–60

masculinity: in police forces, 14, 56, 100, 212–214, 241; popular culture ideal of, 238; steroids as means of increasing, 106

Massey, Larry, 77

McGinn, Randi, 6

McGuire, Leo, 64

McKeon, John, 64

media. *See* police officers: news media portrayal of; police officers: film and television portrayal of; steroids, anabolic: news media coverage of

medical fraud: and death of patient, 47; and legitimate doctor-patient relationships, 65–66, 75, 85; in New Jersey, 67, 68–69; in steroid prescribing, 22, 24, 44, 74, 193–194, 198. *See also* insurance fraud; New Jersey steroid scandals

Merced County, CA, 33

mercenaries. *See* private security contractors

Miami-Dade Police Department (MDPD), 140–141, 148

Miami Herald, 1, 26, 28

Miami police union, 136

Miami River Cops, 1, 5, 26, 53

military: and discipline, 175–176, 232, 239–240; drug use, attitude toward, 93, 165–167, 240; and functional view of steroid use, 167–168, 216, 228, 233, 240; inconsistent steroid policy enforcement in, 166–167, 225, 231–233; and mental toughness, 237, 240, 245–246; and obstacles to controlling steroid use, 232; official policy of, toward steroids, 216, 228–229, 230, 239, 241; perception of private contractors, 175; and physical fitness, 236–237, 245–246; and practical disadvantages of steroid use, 229, 240; prevalence of steroid use among, 226–227, 228; psychotropic drug use in, 220–224; recruitment from, into police force, 31, 213–215; and role of steroids in combat, 236–237; and soldiers' view of steroid use, 166–167, 224–227, 248–249; suicides and homicides in, 224; and tattoos, 103–104, 176; warrior model of, 216–217; and weightlifting, 164–171. *See also* Special Operations Forces (SOF)

Military Medicine, 225

Milwaukee Police Department, 99

mixed martial arts (MMA): compared to traditional sports, 198–199; doping problem in, 186–190; and head trauma, 191, 197–198; justifications for testosterone replacement therapy in, 190–192, 195–198; police officers' use of methods, 185–186; and therapeutic use exemptions, 188–192, 196–197

Mollen Commission, 53

motorcycle clubs, police. *See* law enforcement motorcycle clubs (LEMCs) motorcycle gangs, 114; in Australia, 156–157, 206–207; and discipline, 175–176; and gym culture, 107, 206–207; hostility of, toward police, 201–202; and military connection, 199–201; outlaw identities in, 199–201; police attraction to culture of, 202–206; pop-cultural romanticizing of, 205–206; steroid use by, 106, 156–157, 207. *See also* "action-oriented" males; law enforcement motorcycle clubs (LEMCs); *and individual gangs/clubs*

Mueller, Mark, 70
muscle profiling, 68, 112, 140
muscularity, advantages and disadvantages of, ix, 3, 4, 44, 97–98, 212. *See also* bodybuilding

nandrolone, 88, 121
National Football League (NFL), 50
National Latino Police Officers Association, 142
Navy SEALS, 217, 234, 235–237
Nazis, steroid use of, 224, 234
Newark Star-Ledger, 30, 61, 70, 120
New Jersey COPS, 75
New Jersey Law Enforcement Drug Testing Manual (2001), 139
New Jersey steroid scandals, 22, 30, 61–62; and proposed reforms, 67–69; state officials' response to, 62–67; and violence correlation, 120–121. *See also individual departments*
New York City Police Department (NYPD): and "bad apples" theory, 52, 130–131; and corruption complaints, 134–135; "cowboy culture" of, 57; officer endangerment in, 12; and racism, 110, 130; and random drug testing, 89. *See also individual officers*
New York Times, 16, 18
Nisour Square massacre, 173–174, 175

O'Donnell, Eugene, 55
online chat rooms, 225–226
Oregonian, 125–126
Ousa, Bounmy, 35
outlaw motorcycle gangs (OMGs). *See* motorcycle gangs
Oxycontin (oxycodone), 3, 98

Palmatier, John J., 105
Palm Beach, FL, 89
Patrolmen's Benevolent Association (PBA), 123–124, 143–146
peer pressure, 69, 96, 126, 137
Perez, Dominique, 6
performance- and image-enhancing drugs (PIEDs), 27, 228. *See also* steroids, anabolic
Petraeus, David, 165–166
pharmacies, 70, 72. *See also individual pharmacies*
Phoenix Police Department, 23–24, 35, 45, 88, 95, 138
physicians: bodybuilding, 156; competence of prescribing, 192–195; medical authority of, 189–190. *See also* medical fraud
Pittsburgh Police Department, 23
Plantation, FL, police union, 139
police brutality: damage done by, 43; vs. defensible tactics, 132–133; definition of, 57; and fatal shootings, 6–7, 16; justification of, by police unions, 146–149; portrayal of, by police departments, 52, 55–57; portrayal of, by victims, 52–53; public concern about, 10; punishment for, xi, 15–17, 21; and steroids, public link to, 1. *See also* African Americans
Police Chief magazine, 27, 121, 140
police chiefs/commanders: defense of steroid use among officers, 76–77; and drug testing, 2, 7–8, 16–17, 23, 80; and emotional toll of policing,

56, 101; and enforcement of steroid regulations, x–xi, 2, 15, 23; non-steroid drug use, response to, 100–101; and public relations around steroids, 32; steroid use, indifference toward, 20–21, 23, 81–84, 241; and tattoos, 108–109. *See also* punishment; *individual chiefs; and individual police departments*

police officers: character defects/mental health problems of, 44–47, 100, 121, 162, 215; chiefs, relationship with, 101, 103, 134, 161–162; dehumanization of, 55; and discipline, 175–176, 239–240, 241, 242; discussion of problem officers among, 60–61; film and television portrayal of, 10–13, 21; fitness competition among, 149–150; generational conflicts among, 103–105; gender equity in, 214–215; as heroes, 21, 43, 52, 90–94; militarization of, 211–215; news media portrayal of, 5, 18, 21, 132, 158; paramilitary style of, 54–55, 93, 213, 217–218; physical transformation of, 29–31; proportion of, using steroids, x, 2–3, 19, 25, 27, 37–41, 135; prosecutors' relationship with, 17, 21, 42, 66, 87–88; public attitude toward, 10–11, 19, 20–21, 52, 119, 132; recruitment of, 31, 213–215; socially advantaged citizens' reliance on, 52; stereotypes of, 131–135; urban vs. rural, 2–3, 38. *See also* "bad apples" theory; police chiefs; police unions; "cop's cop," the; "rogue cop," the; *and individual departments*

police riots, 143–144

police unions: and code of silence, 134; conflicts of, with political leaders, 146–147; and defense of officers, 77–78, 86, 126; and drug testing, 2, 16–17, 23, 24, 123, 127, 129;

emotional toll of policing, attitude toward, 56; and fitness standards, 149–151; and police intimidation, 142–145; political endorsements of, 141–142, 147; political power of, 123–124, 141; public relations of, 129; resistance of, to police regulation, 145–149; and surveillance of police behavior, 146–149; and tattoo restrictions, 108; as threat to civil order, 124. *See also individual unions*

Pope, Dr. Harrison G., 24, 37, 114, 118, 194

popular culture. *See* comic-book heroes; steroids, anabolic: film and television portrayal of

Portland, OR, 81

Portland Police Association (PPA), 125, 127–128, 148, 150

Portland Police Bureau, 124–129

post-traumatic stress disorder (PTSD), 100, 218, 220

PowerMedica, 35, 84, 85

prescriptions. *See* medical fraud; physicians; steroids, anabolic: felony use of

privacy, 79–80, 86, 101

private security contractors, 14, 106, 171–175, 201

Providence Police Department, 127

psychotherapy, 4, 101

psychotropic drugs, 220–224

"Public Image of the Police, The" (IACP), 10, 13

Pumping Iron, 28

punishment, police, 82–89; disgrace and dishonor as, 91–94; how to reform, 21, 241–242; inconsistency/infrequency of, 1–2, 15–18; juries' role in, 10; and medical/physiological alibis, 76–77, 116–118, 127; police in-house procedures, 93, 122; probation as, 89–90; by prosecution, x–xi, 17–18, 21, 65–67, 86–90, 91;

and self-reporting, 69, 100; unions' resistance to, 146–147; zero-tolerance policies, 1, 32, 88, 93, 177. *See also individual police departments*

Purdie, Constable Geoff, 119–120

racism, 10, 105, 110, 130, 133. *See also* African Americans

Ramsey, Charles, x, 23

Reece, Stephen, 92

Repeat Offenders Project (ROP), 9

"rogue cop," the, 21, 131; definition of, 52–61. *See also* "bad apples" theory; police brutality

"roid rage," 69; connection of, to other criminal acts, 47, 48; and domestic violence, 23; as misleading diagnosis, 48, 61; portrayal of, in government, 115–116; portrayal of, in legal system, 115–120; portrayal of, in media and folklore, 19, 61, 116, 119. *See also* steroids, anabolic; police brutality

Rossi, John, 48–49

Roundtree, Richard, 36

Sanders, Gene, 29, 37, 38–39

Sandy, Keith, 6, 9

Santa Clara County, CA, 122

Santiago, Joseph, 69, 86–87

Santucci, Steven, 2

Schoolcraft, Adrian, 59

Schroeder, Larry, 84–85

Schultz, Ray, 7, 8, 9

Schwarzenegger, Arnold, 28, 71, 161

Scotland, 28

Scottsboro, AL, 89

Second World War, 221, 222

secrecy, police: catch-22 caused by, 60; about drug and alcohol abuse, 100; about steroid use, ix–x, 13, 20, 31–33, 53, 242

Sewell, Dr. James, 38

sexual assault, 4

Shinnick, Edward, 49–50

side effects, x, 29–31, 196

60 Minutes, 25–26

Skolnick, Jerome, 57

Smith, Albert, 19

soldiers. *See* military

Special Operations Forces (SOF), 215–216, 217, 247; romanticizing of, 234; steroid use among, 235. *See also* Army Rangers; Navy Seals; special weapons and tactics (SWAT) teams

special weapons and tactics (SWAT) teams, 82, 84, 163, 186, 217–218

sports leagues and federations, 177, 188. *See also individual leagues*

sports supplements. *See* dietary supplements

Stallone, Sylvester, 178, 180–181

stanozolol, 87, 121

state and federal agencies, 34–36. *See also individual agencies*

stereotypes. *See* police officers: stereotypes of

Steroid Abuse by Law Enforcement Personnel (DEA), 26

"steroidal" policing style, x, 114, 241. *See also* "roid rage"

steroids, anabolic: and "anti-aging" therapy, 2, 22, 71–72, 78, 156; athletes' use of, 18, 20, 37, 50, 92, 135, 177, 184; celebrities' immunity to punishment for, 179–185; and childhood abuse of users, 220; cosmetic use of, 44, 160, 211, 226, 229, 231, 233, 248; emotional intoxication of use, 235; entertainment industry, use in, 157, 176–179; felony use of, x, 9, 15, 18, 19; film and television portrayal of, 178–179, 237–238; functional rationale for using, 28–29, 52, 89–90, 94–98, 167–168, 233; as marker of character flaw/deviance, 44–47, 100, 121, 162, 215, 220; medically legitimate uses of, 72–73, 77, 86; military's use of (*see* military); news media coverage of, 18,

20, 26, 32, 116, 171; police officers' use of (*see* police officers); propaganda about effects of, 71, 179; public awareness of, 20–21, 28, 32, 161; public's use of, 5, 71, 157; "quasi-legal" methods of obtaining, 75, 78, 180; and sexual enhancement, 74, 156; side effects of, x, 29–31, 196; societal effects of, 156–157; underestimation of use of, 24, 27, 37–40; use of, as "cheating," 93, 180, 188, 229–230; and violence correlation, 114–122, 219–220. *See also* bodybuilding; drug dealers; medical fraud; testosterone

stress: among police officers, 3, 21, 43, 56, 100, 101; and steroid use, 218–220

suicide, 3, 48–51, 100, 224

Sweden, 68, 140

Sweitzer, Philip J., 159–160, 162, 163–164, 212, 218

Tasers. *See* weapons

tattoos: chiefs' response to, 102–103, 108–109; and conformity, 105; and gangs, 103; generational conflict over, 103, 104–105; and the military, 103–104; police restrictions on, 106–108; relationship of, to steroid use, 102–109; and self-expression, 109–110; as sign of rebellion, 102, 105–106, 109–110

television. *See* police officers: film and television portrayal of; steroids, anabolic: film and television portrayal of

testing. *See* drug testing

testosterone: legal use of, 22, 24, 32, 44, 115; prevalence of, 2, 25; and stress, 218. *See also* medical fraud; steroids, anabolic; testosterone replacement therapy (TRT)

testosterone replacement therapy (TRT), 44, 75, 187–190; and competence of prescribing physicians, 192–195;

justifications for prescribing in mixed martial arts, 190–192, 195–198; in other professional athletes, 188–189; pharmaceutical companies' advertising for, 190. *See also* hypogonadism; medical fraud; physicians; steroids, anabolic

Texas Rangers, 35

Thomas, Kelly, 142

ticket fixing, 145

Tillman, Cedric, 88, 89

Tirey, Mark, 34

Trenton Police Department, 69, 86–88

Turner, Daryl, 127

Trump, Donald J., 141–142

Tweedy, Michael, 117

Ultimate Fighting Championship (UFC), 185, 187, 192, 193, 195

Uniform Code of Military Justice, 224, 240

United Kingdom, 41, 58, 131; military's use of banned substances, 170, 230

United States Anti-Doping Agency (USADA), 188

Upper Darby, Pennsylvania, 139

USA Powerlifting, 90

US Army Public Health Command, 228

US Forces–Iraq Bodybuilding Championships, 170

Valenti, Kevin, 45

Valentine, Brady, 89–90

Vietnam War: and motorcycle gangs, 200; and psychotropic drug use, 220–221

Village Voice, 84, 144

violence. *See* domestic violence; police brutality; "roid rage"; sexual assault; steroids, anabolic: and violence correlation

Vo, David, 51

Volpe, Justin, 54, 60–61, 101